CHAOS
IN THE
COURTHOUSE

The Inner Workings
of the
Urban Criminal Courts
Paul B. Wice

PRAEGER

PRAEGER SPECIAL STUDIES • PRAEGER SCIENTIFIC

New York • Philadelphia • Eastbourne, UK
Toronto • Hong Kong • Tokyo • Sydney

Library of Congress Cataloging in Publication Data
Wice, Paul B.
    Chaos in the courthouse.

    Bibliography: p.
    Includes index.
    1. Criminal courts—United States. 2. Criminal
justice, Administration of—United States. 3.
Judges—United States. I. Title.
KF9223.W48 1985   345.73'01   84-15976
ISBN 0-03-001454-9 (alk. paper) 347.3051

Published in 1985 by Praeger Publishers
CBS Educational and Professional Publishing
a Division of CBS Inc.
521 Fifth Avenue, New York, NY 10175 USA

56789 052 987654321

Printed in the United States of America
on acid-free paper

THIS VOLUME IS DEDICATED TO MY WIFE
BERYLE, WITHOUT WHOSE LOVE AND SUPPORT
THIS PROJECT WOULD NEVER HAVE BEEN COMPLETED.

ACKNOWLEDGEMENTS

It should first be noted that every endeavor of this type is a collective venture, dependent upon the help and wisdom of many individuals. I am deeply indebted to the many judges, defense attorneys, prosecutors, and other concerned public officials and private citizens without whose cooperation this book would never have been possible. I sincerely regret that this debt can be repaid only through the meager medium of this acknowledgement.

I would also like to thank the National Institute of Justice of the United States Department of Justice for their continued support, both financially and spiritually, over the past 12 years. The views expressed in this book, however, are solely those of the author and represent neither the many individuals who aided him, nor the Justice Department whose generous aid was so important.

Finally, I would like to especially thank the following individuals to whom I owe a special debt of gratitude for their many kindnesses and support extended to me over the years: Richard Max Bockol, Fred Cohen, Stephen Franklin, William McDonald, David Neubauer, Stuart Nagel, Jim Alfini, Clemens Bartollas, Stuart Miller, Mark Greenberg, Judge Marvin Halbert, and especially to my son, Andy.

CONTENTS

PROLOGUE

> Barth reflects on the attention created by the power of his office. Court of-
> ficers open doors for him, lawyers thank him for doing the job that allows
> him to earn more than $35,000, defendants sometimes cry in gratitude, and
> strangers address him as Your Honor. Those fringe benefits are nice but
> they are not the real reasons that Barth is fascinated with his role as a judge.
> One of those reasons has to do with the uses of power and authority. How
> do you make someone do what you think ought to be done in a civilized
> society, short of beating him over the head? You try to do it with legal rules
> and with Judge Barth's authority to enforce those rules.[1]

Author James Simon chronicled Judge Barth's life as a criminal court
judge for a week as the judge attempted to enforce those rules which would
allow his city to remain a civilized community. Simon offers a fascinating
in-depth look at one man's attempt to wrestle with some of society's most
pressing and complex problems.

As a student of the criminal justice system, I have also observed judges
trying to resolve similar difficulties and have spent the last 12 years involved in a series of research projects which have allowed me to interview
and observe approximately 500 judges and other critical members of the
criminal court workgroup, including prosecutors, public defenders, private
criminal lawyers, and probation officers. My projects have resulted in my
traversing the country, devoting large amounts of time to studying the urban criminal courts in 15 major jurisdictions.[2]

This book, *Chaos in the Courthouse,* is the product of all of these
travels and experiences. It offers a comprehensive portrait of our nation's
urban criminal court systems. Clarifying the book's subject matter even further, its primary focus is upon the urban felony court system, with particular emphasis upon the role of the judge. The felony process was selected
because of the serious nature of its cases and heightened public concern over

its performance. (Since most cities begin to process their felony cases in the misdemeanor courts, frequently referred to as *Municipal Courts,* these lower courts will also be examined, although only tangentially.)

Two other clarifications involve the emphasis upon primarily urban court systems, and the extended time period under consideration. Big city courts were selected because this is where the problems seem to be the most severe. Additionally, by controlling for the size of cities (all jurisdictions studied had metropolitan populations in excess of a million), one is better able to offer a viable model for comparing their operations and evaluating their relative levels of performance.

Athough the data for this book are the product of interviews and observations conducted during the entire decade of the 1970s, the most critical information concerning the professional behavior of the judiciary was gathered during the past three years (1979–82).* Because this book is also the product of 12 years of observations and study, it is believed that this extended time frame offers a unique opportunity to observe trends, changes, reforms, and counter reforms within the urban criminal courts. These years were an exciting time to study the criminal courts because this period nearly brackets the existence of the United States Justice Department's efforts to improve the administration of justice through the actions of the now dormant Law Enforcement Assistance Administration (LEAA). I was fortunate enough to observe this agency at close range during my tenure as an LEAA Visiting Fellow in Washington from 1976–78. Despite the great potential for reform during the 1970s and continued public interest, it was disappointing to find the problems and level of performance of the criminal courts remain so static during this period.

Moving beyond the clarifications just discussed, let me now return to discuss briefly the three major reasons for bringing this book into existence. As already noted, the book's first objective is to accurately describe the operation of the urban criminal courts with special emphasis upon the role of the judge. The breadth and depth of my research experiences should present a far-ranging empirical portrait of our urban justice system.

A second objective is to construct a model for comparing the operations and performances of our nation's urban felony courts. Based upon the visits to the 15 jurisdictions, this model can serve as a vehicle for noting both similarities and differences between these felony courts. The model can also serve to identify those factors which may contribute to variations in both style and performance. This range of factors has been organized into four categories—legal, institutional, political, and social. Each category has then been subdivided into more specific variables affecting urban court behavior, each variable being viewed as a continuum upon which cities can

---

*During this period approximately 50 judges in New York, Philadelphia, and Washington were interviewed and observed.

be placed relative to one another. Since many of the variables do not lend themselves to clearly quantifiable terms, the parameters for each will be set by the two cities which merit placement at either of the extreme ends of the continuum.

The third objective is to offer an analysis of the urban felony court's major problems. After identifying these problems and reviewing past reform efforts, a limited number of recommendations will be offered.

REVIEW OF THE LITERATURE

Political and social scientists have only recently turned toward the criminal courts as a worthwhile and professionally acceptable focus for their research. Before the 1970s students of public law limited themselves almost entirely to the federal court system, rarely venturing outside of the hallowed confines of the United States Supreme Court. Given the significance of these federal decisions, and the ease with which their pronouncements could be comfortably studied in local law libraries, the criminal courts were clearly out of the mainstream of judicial research.

During the past decade, however, several political scientists began to examine the local criminal courts. (Cynics may ascribe this development to the availability of federal research monies from the LEAA.) Nevertheless, it was an inevitable outgrowth of the public law discipline, as traditional federal judicial topics were exhausted. Whatever the case, several noteworthy studies were produced in the past 10 years. Herbert Jacob and James Eisenstein's *Felony Justice* is one such important contribution to the field of study. Their exhaustive three-city investigation (Baltimore, Detroit, and Chicago), stressed the importance of the courtroom workgroup as an influence upon the style and quality of urban criminal justice. They viewed the courtroom as a series of organized workgroups which had the common goals of "doing justice," disposing of caseloads, maintaining group cohesion and reducing certainty (avoiding trials). Eisenstein and Jacob were careful to emphasize that although these workgroups dispose of many cases during a day, they are not assembly lines. Even routine decisions involve discretion. Workgroup members must interact with one another in order to reach a decision.[3]

Another important book is Martin Levin's *Urban Politics and the Criminal Courts* which explains the influence of political variables upon the operation of the criminal courts.[4] Levin compares a "traditional city" (Pittsburgh) with a "reform city" (Minneapolis). He focuses upon the varying selection processes, differential patterns of socialization, and recruitment, that in turn, influences the judge's views and decision-making propensities. Levin concludes that Pittsburgh has judges "who as former politicians, are highly particularistic and nonlegalistic in their decision-making. The Minneapolis judges, however, come from the upper middle-class with business backgrounds, generating legalistic and universalistic decisions with little sympathy for the lower-class who fill their courtrooms.[5]

Although Abraham Blumberg's study of the Kings County (Brooklyn, NY) criminal courts was conducted almost 20 years ago, it still maintains its reputation as a seminal work in the field.[6] Blumberg's description of the criminal justice system as an "assemblyline" which functioned as an inverted sieve is still the prevalent metaphor for describing the process. Additionally, his analysis of the defense attorney as an agent/mediator in a declining adversarial relationship, working with a prosecutor who was more colleague than protagonist, was a groundbreaking theory of how the system really works.

A recently completed study by John Paul Ryan and his associates at the American Judicature Society is the most comprehensive analysis yet made of the American trial judge.[7] Although the majority of their study was based upon questionnaires mailed to nearly every state trial judge in the nation, they also visited briefly (three to five days per judge), with 40 judges in 15 courts and made even more intensive studies of three of those jurisdictions (Chicago, Los Angeles and Philadelphia). These three major court systems allowed the researchers to discuss the social, political, and legal environments in each city and how such environments seemed to influence the judicial behavior of the local judge.

The previously noted group of authors is not meant to be an exhaustive list of the best work by political scientists studying the criminal court systems, but merely a series of works believed to be most representative of recent studies of high quality. Another select group of studies by social scientists which were very useful and are highly recommended, dealt with much narrower topics within the broad spectrum of criminal justice research and includes works by the following authors:

1. *Albert Alschuler's* excellect series of law review articles on plea bargaining. Each article concentrates on a particular actor (judge, prosecutor, and defense attorney) and was the result of extensive interviews conducted upon a broad national sample.[8]
2. *Lief Carter's* work on police/prosecutor relationships.[9]
3. *Joan Jacoby's* national study of prosecutors.[10]
4. *Milton Heumann's* careful case study of plea bargaining in Connecticut.[11]
5. *David Neubauer's* in-depth case study of the criminal justice system operating in a small Midwestern city.[12]
6. *Wayne Thomas'* national study of bail and its reform movement comparing pretrial release practices over a 10-year period.

RESEARCH EXPERIENCE

The length, breadth, and variety of my research experiences have provided me with a unique opportunity to investigate our confusing legal system. Although the Blumberg, Levin, and Jacob and Eisenstein books are good, they only deal with one, two, and three cities, respectively. The Ryan study does have a national scope through its mailed questionnaires, but the actual interviews and observations were conducted in 15 cities during a six-month time period, observing 40 judges on the basis of three to five days per courtroom.

By briefly recalling the chronology of my research endeavors, the reader can grasp the uniqueness of my background and the variety of perspectives from which I have viewed the criminal court system. My first project was as a graduate student at the University of Illinois, Champaign/Urbana. Working under my advisor, Professor Stuart Nagel, I had selected a national study of bail and its reform as the topic for my doctoral dissertation. The year was 1970 and the Law Enforcement Assistance Administration was anxious to support research in the administration of local justice. I was fortunate to receive a dissertation grant for my bail research, which allowed me to travel to 11 cities across the country—Washington, D.C., Philadelpia, Baltimore, Atlanta, St. Louis, Indianapolis, Detroit, Chicago, Los Angeles, San Francisco, and Oakland. At least one week was spent in each city. An even longer period of time was reserved for Washington, D.C., because of the opportunity to use federal agencies as well as Congressional committees as an important source of information. Also, the new preventive detention legislation scheduled for implementation by the District's court system in February of 1971 offered an in-depth look at an unusual and controversial approach to bail reform. All of the interviews (nearly 120), were conducted between August 1970 and March 1971.

A minimum of 10 interviews were conducted in each city. I spoke to anyone in the city who was identified as knowledgeable on bail issues in his community. Among those interviewed in each city were judges, court clerks, defense attorneys, prosecuting attorneys, public defenders, bail project directors, court administrators, law school professors, and newspaper reporters.

The end-result of these travels was a 500-page doctoral dissertation on bail and its reform. The research was also published by the Justice Department's National Institute of Law Enforcement and Criminal Justice, and eventually appeared, in slightly rewritten form, as a book entitled *Freedom for Sale* published by Lexington Books in 1974.

This first excursion into the criminal courts had a profound effect upon my professional life. Obviously, its impact was significant since more than a decade later I am still mired in the same depressing system. The initial confrontation with the criminal justice system in 1970 overwhelmed both my intellectual and emotional senses. Today, I am still impressed by my own morbid fascination at witnessing the defendants and their families undergoing their traumatic experiences. Being privy to courtroom drama in which lives of both the victim and defendant are likely to be scarred permanently, can be exhausting, especially after having observed its frighteningly repetitive pattern during a 12-year period. After witnessing the tragedies of these past years, I am convinced that the only safe place for a citizen is outside of the criminal justice system entirely, regardless of guilt or innocence, irrespective of whether a victim or a perpetrator.

The machinations of the judge and his staff, the maneuverings of the attorneys, however, have a powerful intellectual appeal. How can these intelligent individuals make sense out of apparent chaos? How can even the barest approximation of justice be reached in such an inhospitable climate? Yet, despite the harsh and often repugnant working conditions, most judges do remain compassionate, most lawyers do try to offer a decent defense for their clients, and most members of the courtroom workgroup do try to remember that they are dealing with a human being, not merely a number on the docket. Thus, these overworked and oft-criticized officials must continue to wrestle with the most complex and seemingly unsolvable dilemma of having to balance (on a case-by-case basis), the need to protect and guarantee a safe and secure society with the protection of the constitutional rights of the accused.

These intellectual and emotional reactions were present during my very first ventures into the imposing courthouses visited as part of my bail study. Their intensities have not diminished over the years. A scene firmly etched in my memory is being present in the Cook County Courthouse (Chicago) when an escaped prisoner was shot to death in his unsuccessful flight to freedom one floor below, while I tried to nonchalantly interview a bail project director. The accumulated visions and impressions experienced during my first visits into the dismal world of the urban courts are still vivid. They, and subsequent adventures to be recounted within this volume, have produced an almost hypnotic effect, drawing me back again, and again to the criminal courthouses.

My second venture into the criminal courts was in 1973 with a national study of public defenders for the *Criminal Law Bulletin* and its editor, Professor Fred Cohen. This project was aided by a research associate, Peter Suwak, and resulted in an article entitled "Current Realities of Public Defender Programs: A National Survey" published in 1974 by the *Bulletin*.[14] During a four-month period in the Spring and Summer of 1973, Mr. Suwak and I investigated the operation of public defender programs in eight cities (Washington, D.C., St. Louis, Philadelphia, San Francisco,

Chicago, Los Angeles, Baltimore, Detroit, and Oakland), spending approximately one week in each city, and interviewing 100 public defenders and other knowledgeable court officials. An attempt was made to identify and measure those institutional (operational and procedural), and social factors involved in the relative effectiveness of these public defender programs.

During the period 1976–78, I left teaching to become a Visiting Fellow at the Justice Department's National Institute of Criminal Justice in Washington and completed two more national studies. The first (1976–77) was an examination of the private practice of criminal law. This venture into the inner workings of a "dying profession" required nearly 200 interviews with private criminal lawyers in nine cities—Washington, D.C., Philadelphia, Miami, New Orleans, Houston, Chicago, Denver, Los Angeles, and San Francisco. Approximately 10-14 days were spent in each city, interviewing and observing local defense attorneys. The lawyers were selected from mailing lists of professional organizations, recommendations of colleagues, and recommendations by other members of the criminal justice community. The results of this six month tour included several articles, a book entitled *Criminal Lawyers: An Endangered Species,* and a place on the American Bar Association's Committee on the Economics of Criminal Law.

The major theme of the first study was to empirically test the hypothesis that the private practice of criminal law was in a state of serious decline. In addition to confirming this depressing hypothesis, an attempt was also made to describe the professional folkways of these practitioners, both in and out of the courtroom. The final objective of the study was to offer a relatively realistic alternative to the many stereotypes and myths which so often surround and distort the practice of criminal law. In order to achieve these objectives, I chose a rather eclectic style of analysis which combined elements of legal anthropology, sociological journalism, and political sociology.

The second study (completed in Washington for the Justice Department), was an investigation into the problems of the elderly victims of crime, devoting special attention to the response of public and private agencies to this issue. The project, which was sponsored by the National Council of Senior Citizens, and housed in their Washington offices, was a complex, multi-faceted undertaking. Although my research included a one-year study of how four major cities—New York, Milwaukee, New Orleans and Los Angeles—were attacking the problem of elderly crime victimization, it was actually a small part of a three-year, multimillion dollar project funded by several federal agencies—Health and Human Services Administration of Aging, Community Services Administration, Housing and Urban Development, as well as the Justice Department.

frequently (Washington, Los Angeles, San Francisco, Philadelphia, and Chicago), I spent well over one month in combined time in each locale. Time was most heavily devoted to conducting interviews, but at least one-quarter to one-third of each visit was devoted to courtroom observations.

METHODOLOGY

Personal interviews were the primary data-gathering techniques in all my research projects. Mailed questionnaires were utilized in the bail project to supplement the interviews and to extend the sampling to 72 cities. The most critical methodological issues associated with personal interviews are access and sampling. The problem of access was usually eased by my association with the United States Justice Department in most of my research projects. Local officials were willing to cooperate despite the inconvenience. One cannot be certain about the reason for local officials' cooperativeness, but the possibility of future federal funding from my sponsoring agency certainly did not lessen my opportunities. I have, in fact, noticed a serious decline in accessibility in recent years as the level of funding from the government has significantly declined.

In terms of sampling, I had to make certain important decisions with regard to which cities were to be studied as well as which officials were to be selected for interviews. The selection of interviewees also presented the related difficulty of locating individuals in the first place, since national directories rarely exist. The cities were typically selected in order to obtain broad regional representation, and of the 15 cities visited, especially the 11 visited twice, one finds every section of the country represented.

The second stage of sampling, the selection of interviewees, was usually a more complex problem. A few individuals would be identified prior to visiting a city, but the large majority of persons were located after I had arrived. I would first go to certain knowledgeable public officials in the criminal justice system, such as the deputy director of the public defender's office, or district attorney's office as well as the administrative judge of the criminal courts. Invariably, a sizable number of recommendations would be provided. During these interviews, I would ask interviewees whom else I should speak with, and a snowballing effect provided many additional names.

I realize that such sampling techniques are clearly below the rigorous standards of social scientific inquiry, but my research had to be accommodated to the realities of the criminal justic system. My projects have also taken on the eclectic blending of sociological journalism with a form of anthropological field work. The model for most of my work has been the classic study, *Wall Street Lawyers* by Erwin Smigel,[15] and has borrowed his methodological approach as indicated in the following quote: "When certain patterns become manifest, when certain values were uniformly expressed, when the content of the interviews and observations became similar, a point of diminishing returns was felt. When this point was reached we would move to another section of the agency. Forty people out of 100 employees were interviewed this way. The procedure is characteristic of anthropological field work."

In conducting the personal interviews, I also imitated Smigel's approach in choosing not to work with a rigidly fixed set of questions in which each person responded to identical inquires. I opted for a much more flexible set of questions which often permitted more open-ended responses and allowed me to probe into subtle and complex areas. This style of inquiry offered the advantage of taking into account the specialization, expertise, and candor of each interviewee, tailoring each interview accordingly. Lastly, this open-minded approach saved my sanity by not forcing me to ask the same questions hundreds of times. Whatever may have been lost in scientific rigor, I sincerely believe was more than regained in allowing the research to capture the interesting and elusive behavior patterns of our urban justice system.

Given the extremely busy and chaotic world of the urban criminal courts, the task of interviewing members of this harassed community offers a unique challenge to the inquisitive social scientist. Although the interviews lasted anywhere from one to four hours, they were seldom conducted without frequent interruptions. This forced me to be extremely flexible and patient. As an intruder in this busy world, I depended upon the charity of the interviewee. And yet, despite these frenetic conditions, and the obvious time pressures being exerted upon the public officials, I was continually pleasantly surprised at how receptive and helpful most of the interviewees were. Even the private criminal lawyers whose "time was money," were willing to take as much time as I needed for a project from which they would clearly receive no financial return. Nearly four-fifths of the officials contacted were willing to speak with me; only the New Jersey court system, and its Administrative Office of the Courts were unwilling to open their doors to my projects. (In that case, I believe the failings were due more to a blending of bureaucratic inertia and ineptitude than to malevolent design.)

The problems of attribution and confidentiality were of concern to most of the interviewees. Since I had not had previous contact with these individuals, they had to rely upon my promise that they would not be directly quoted and identified. The purpose of the projects was always explained as an attempt to demonstrate national patterns and trends rather than a presentation of anecdotal reminiscences and/or shocking exposés. If a quote was used, the attributed source would be a vague reference to a region or city. Since the promises of confidentiality were never broken, the subsequent visits to several of the cities produced even richer results as a closer and more trusting relationship developed.

Categorizing the defendants in terms of candor, fully one-third of the interviewees were totally frank and willing to answer any question as completely as possible. Another one-third were courteous and generally helpful, but careful to skirt potentially incriminating topics. The remaining third were skeptical about the research and remained cynical and cautious during the interview. Their answers were cursory and occasionally evasive.

In my book on private criminal lawyers, I commented on the necessity of looking and sounding like a lawyer myself, but being careful not to look too much like one for as Smigel noted in his conversations with Wall Street lawyers, one attorney warned: "We don't want you to look too much like ourselves—it takes some of the interest in the meeting away. We can see lawyers any day."[16]

A large portion of this book will be similar to my earlier work in which I served as a type of conduit or recorder for transcribing, synthesizing, and organizing the thoughts and impressions of the many criminal justice officials who had been interviewed. I will continue to adopt that role as a type of Studs Terkel of the criminal courts for most of the book. In the last chapter of the book, however, I will step from behind the protective mask of my respondents, and offer my personal conclusions and recommendations.

DEVELOPING A COMPARATIVE PERSPECTIVE

Students of the criminal justice system face the inevitable question before beginning research as to whether to conduct a case study, or a broader comparative approach. The case study appeals to most because of its logistical simplicity and opportunity for delving deeply into a specific topic. By limiting oneself to a single jurisdiction, the confusion of contradictory terminology is avoided. More significantly, one does not have to assess the impact of the potentially uncontrollable demographic variables, unique to each jurisdiction. Because the social and geographic factors are so difficult to measure in terms of their relative influence, the case study approach relieves the researcher of a virtually inherent weakness in his work.

The damning charge of "comparing apples and oranges" is heard frequently in comparative research. Anyone choosing to study a variety of cities realizes his or her vulnerability and is frustrated by the limitation to completely identify and assess those forces at play in the different court systems under examination. What difference does it make that San Francisco has a large gay community, or that New Orleans blacks are members of extremely stable family units of great longevity? How are the courts of the two cities affected, and do these differences eventually undermine the value of comparative research? Many researchers have answered this question in the affirmative and have concentrated on only one jurisdiction at a time.

Besides the drawbacks of comparative analysis, the case study approach possesses many positive attributes in its own right. By limiting the project to a single jurisdiction, the opportunities for a more intensive examination of the selected topic are greatly enhanced. Whether one chooses a single issue, such as bail reform or a survey of the city's entire criminal justice process, nearly every possible variable affecting the style and operation of the research subject can be explored. The confidence resulting from the greater likelihood of being able to control, understand, and explain the criminal justice functioning of a single court system is a compelling inducement favoring the case study approach. It is, therefore, not surprising that as one reviews the literature in criminal justice, the large majority of high quality work has been done by social scientists utilizing the case study approach. Blumberg's important landmark study, *Criminal Justice,* which is still the most frequently cited piece of urban justice research, was a case study of the Kings County, (New York) criminal courts.[17] Neubauer's complete analysis of criminal justice operating in the Midwest was a case study of Decatur, Illinois,[18] while Jerome Skolnick's study of police, *Justice Without Trial,* focused almost entirely on Oakland, California.[19] Even when researchers choose to study only one aspect of the criminal justice process, single jurisdictional analyses are the norm. Two of the most highly acclaimed treatises on plea-bargaining—Milton Heumann's, and Rosett and Cressey's—were also both case studies.[20]

Despite the persuasive reasons for selecting the case study approach over the comparative approach, I have always opted for the latter. The primary reason for my favoring the comparative perspective was a belief in the enhanced significance of such studies. By choosing to study approximately 10 cities in four of my five previous research efforts, it was hoped that other major urban centers with populations exceeding 1 million could gain useful insights through the experiences of my sample. Attempts were made on two occasions[21] to construct a conceptual scheme for aiding cities in evaluating their own efforts relative to the other jurisdictions being investigated.

Despite the noted pitfalls of comparative research, I believe they are outweighed by the personal and professional gains derived from multijurisdictional studies. On the personal level, the joy of traveling and learning the political, social, and legal cultures of a new city added significantly to the quality of my life both as a teacher and as a student. Even more important, however, are the professional rewards gained from these travels. The comparative perspective allows the cities under examination to see how they compare to each other as well as other jurisdictions. Moreover, their respective policy-makers can lean about the direction of national and regional trends.

The major drawback to the case studies is their narrowness which establishes barriers so that cities cannot profit from these experiences. It is very easy to dismiss the significant implications of Neubauer's Decatur study for other similar-sized locales. The Topeka or Omaha judicial officials may delude themselves into thinking that the problems of Decatur are unique to that locale and bear little relevance to their own criminal courts. By increasing the number of cities in one's sample as well as expanding their regional diversity, it is likely that the ensuing results will have greater scope and significance and therefore may be more difficult to ignore.

The limitations of comparative research are real and my preference for this approach has not been made blindly. Therefore, before examining the similarities and differences currently existing in our nation's criminal courts, as presented in the first chapter, a brief review of some of these difficulties will be offered.

The first dilemma encountered in comparative research is the variation in terminology. With an increase in the number of cities, one sees an exponential increase in the number of definitions and terms. This confusion is a natural outgrowth of our federal system which provides for the operation of 51 different judicial systems. Each of these state and federal judicial units has had its legislative branch create a unique criminal code and is governed through this code which offers a unique set of laws, rules, precedents, and other instructive devices. These formal prescriptions, plus the common law precedents of each jurisdiction are then shaped by the informal forces operating at the local level which create even greater diversity.

The resulting chaos poses major hardships for the researcher attempting to employ the comparative approach. When comparing the number of defendants being tried for felonies in a number of jurisdictions, how does one deal with the difficulties caused by several of the cities having different definitions of a felony? In one city, a felony may be defined as any crime involving the possible incarceration of a defendant, if convicted, of more than two years, while another city places the incarceration period at one or more years. One can, therefore, find certain crimes such as auto theft, manslaughter, possession of stolen property, or forgery to be felonies in one state and misdemeanors in another. The inclusion or exclusion of all of the auto theft cases can significantly affect the caseload problems facing felony court judges in different cities.

Adding confusion to the already muddied definitional waters, is the variation in terminology for the different stages of the criminal court process. As I traveled around the country examining the administration of bail, I learned that the stage at which a defendant made his initial appearance before a judge could be termed any of the following: pretrial arraignment, preliminary arraignment, initial arraignment, first appearance, and preliminary hearing. Given this definitional variation and resulting confusion, it is imperative that the researcher who chooses the comparative route, exercise great care to understand these terminological differences and clarify them for both himself and the reader. It requires an extra effort, but is not an impossible task.

The second difficulty facing the comparative perspective is even more serious and may be impossible to remedy. This problem relates to the presence of subtle and even unique external factors found within a specific city and which can exert meaningful influence upon the local criminal court system. For example, a city located in a warm climate (such as Miami), and which attracts large numbers of transients and elderly, can suddenly develop a reputation (and seemingly well-deserved) of being the "bunco capital" of the country. Its criminal justice system becomes flooded with elderly victims, bilked out of their life savings. One thousand miles to the west in Houston, Texas, the elderly residents are typically poor and commonly members of a racial minority, and do not have the money to become "bunco" victims. Houston, however, is a city in which more than half of the defendants cannot speak English, and 95 percent of all the judges, prosecutors, and attorneys speak only English. Fifteen hundred miles to the north is Minneapolis, where the court system has almost no black or Hispanic defendants, but seems overrun with poor whites from Appalachia and a disturbing number of native American Indians who are suffering from alcoholism or some antisocial result of their addiction. What is the significance of Minneapolis' drunken Indians, Miami's elderly bunco victims, and Houston's impoverished Hispanics upon the local court system? Is not each city's political, social or cultural situation causing a unique set of problems for their respective criminal justice systems?

The number of possible influences and the varying magnitude of their impact upon the local criminal courts presents a serious obstacle to researchers desiring to employ the comparative approach. Nonetheless, the knowledge gained from even moderate success can provide court systems with extremely valuable information; information which can help them learn of a new approach to an old problem, or possibly of identifying a developing problem before it becomes too serious to correct. By recognizing the presence of these outside factors, and appreciating their importance, social scientists through the development of typologies, paradigms, and testable hypotheses, can begin to make small and modest advances through the use of the comparative perspective.

The third weakness associated with the comparative approach is related to the idiographic nature of the legal process. The United States legal system focuses upon unique case situations and frowns upon the work of the social scientist who must rely upon trends, generalities, and statistical laws, all of which fall short of evidentiary requirements in a court of law. Relating these precepts to the study of criminal courts, lawyers and judges are disdainful of scientific generalities and insist that their criminal justice problems are the nearly exclusive concern of those judges and officers of the court who work together in the courthouse. Each case presents a unique problem to them, which they must carefully evaluate, considering society's best interests, the defendant's constitutionally guaranteed rights, and any other mitigating factors relevant to a particular case.

Although one can applaud the efforts of the judge and court officers as they evaluate each case in an individual and personal manner, there are, nevertheless, broader problems emanating from the operations of our judicial system which have repercussions far beyond the individual case. These broader policy concerns such as bail reform, plea bargaining, excessive delay, and abominable jail conditions, directly affect how the local courts and judges are able to mete out justice in the very same particular case with which they profess great concern. Armed with knowledge of how other court systems have dealt with similar problems and their relative degree of success, should provide help to criminal justice practitioners in their efforts to combat the serious problems crippling their legal systems. It is reassuring to note a discernible trend in recent years where judges and lawyers have become increasingly interested in expanding their horizons and learning about the experiences of other jurisdictions. There seems to be more national communication between all categories of criminal justice officials in which a vital exchange of information is provided. My travels during the past years have indicated a growing interest among all members of the criminal court workgroup concerning developments in other jurisdictions, and how they compare with their counterparts in other locales on a wide range of subjects.

I believe we are now ready to begin our journey into the complex and chaotic world of the urban felony court judicial system. Let us first develop the necessary comparative perspective and learn from the first chapter, some of the critical similarities and differences between our nation's felony court systems.

NOTES

1. James F. Simon. *The Judge*. (New York, David McKay, 1976), p. 7.
2. The cities studied by Eisenstein and Jacob were Baltimore, Chicago, and Detroit.
3. James Eisenstein and Herbert Jacob. *Felony Justice*. Boston, Little, Brown and Co., 1977, p. 36.
4. Martin Levin. *Urban Politics and the Criminal Courts*. Chicago, University of Chicago Press, 1977.
5. Ibid. p. 6.
6. Abraham Blumberg. *Criminal Justice*. New York, Quadrangle, 1967.
7. John Paul Ryan et al *American Trial Judges*. New York, Free Press, 1980.
8. Albert Alschuler. The Trial Judge's Role in Plea Bargaining, *Columbia Law Review*, 76 (November, 1976), 1059.

   Albert Alschuler. The Prosecutor's Role in Plea Bargaining, *University of Chicago Law Review* 36 (1968), 50.

   Albert Alschuler. The Defense Attorney's Role in Plea Bargaining, *Yale Law Journal* 84, 6 (May, 1975), 1179–1314.
9. Leif Carter. *Limits of Order*. Lexington, Mass: Lexington Books, 1972.
10. Joan Jacoby. *Prosecutors*. Beverly Hills, Sage Publications, 1980.
11. Milton Heumann. *Plea Bargaining: The Experience of Prosecutors, Judges and Defense Attorneys*. Chicago, University of Chicago Press, 1977.
12. David Neubauer. *Criminal Justice in Middle America*. Morristown, N.J.: General Learning Press, 1974.
13. Wayne Thomas. *Bail Reform*. Berkeley, University of California Press, 1978.
14. Peter Suwak and Paul Wice. Current Realities of Public Defender Programs: A National Survey, *Criminal Law Bulletin*. (March, 1974), p. 163.
15. Erwin Smigel. *The Wall Street Lawyer*. Bloomington, Indiana University Press, 1973, p. viii.
16. Ibid. p. 30.
17. Blumberg, op. cit.
18. Neubauer, op. cit.
19. Jerome Skolnick. *Justice Without Trial*. New York, Wiley, 1967.
20. Heumann, op. cit.
21. Suwak and Wice's study of public defenders as well as my study of bail and its reform, which resulted in a book and various articles and monographs, all utilizing a comparative methodological perspective.

1

A COMPARATIVE PERSPECTIVE

This is a book about big city criminal courts, focusing primarily upon the judges who are in the center of the action, and more importantly, who are responsible for their operation. This chapter, like most of the book, will compare the various judges and criminal court systems and how they perform their assigned tasks. Public opinion polls taken during the past decade indicate that the average citizen is highly critical of this criminal justice system, and has particular enmity toward the judiciary.[1] By combining all judges together, as well as all the criminal justice systems they dominate, the public has made serious errors in their simplistic and inaccurate generalizations. The intensity of their feelings is probably due more to their frustrations than to their knowledge of this complex and confusing system.

One of the most common mistakes made by the public in their attempt to find a scapegoat for rising crime (or at least perceived as rising), is the lumping together of all criminal court judges into a stereotypical portrait which stresses their incompetence, idealism, and unwarranted generosity (at society's expense), toward undeserving defendants. This portrait is far from the truth. My travels during the past decade, into countless courtrooms, have provided conclusive evidence of the great diversity of this group. Judges were found to be a complex body of disparate individuals, possessing a wide range of intellects, personalities, and capabilities. They performed their jobs with widely varying degrees of success, while imparting to their courtrooms equally divergent styles of performance. A lawyer who joins the bench and dons the black robe, does not shed all of the unique character traits which brought him into judicial service in the first place.

Before discussing the similarities and differences between our major urban criminal courts, I would like to offer four sketches of varying styles of judicial behavior witnessed during my travels. These brief descriptive passages will not only help to dispel the stereotypical myths discussed earlier but will also provide an opportunity for the reader to appreciate the rich diversity of judicial styles which are to be found within the criminal courts today.

THE ROUTINIZER

In a large midwestern city, the frigid weather and rising unemployment rate appear to be producing a staggering number of Skid Row alcoholics. This results in a steadily increasing number of arrests of downtrodden individuals charged with being "drunk and disorderly." In order to minimize the impact of this sizable group of defendants, the Court Administrator has designated one of the criminal court judges to conduct a morning "drunk court." With the accent on speed, the judge is able to dispose of 50 to 75 cases prior to his assuming his regular responsibilities 20 minutes later, at 10 o'clock. He is able to accomplish this speedy processing of defendants by handling all of the guilty pleas (which constitute well over 90 percent of the cases) by combining the defendants into small units for sentencing.

In sad groups of twos and threes, the inebriates try to listen attentively to the judge's litany which concerns the court's acceptance of the guilty pleas. Since most of the defendants are repeat offenders, they are well-versed in the entire procedure and patiently wait for the quickly revolving wheel of justice to spin them once more out into the chilly winter air. With vague promises of staying sober, finding a job or most commonly, leaving town (and thereby becoming a problem for some other city), these social outcasts are led out of the courtroom. The judge rarely lifts his head above the steep pile of casefolders, as he sips his morning coffee while accepting the guilty pleas, and noting each case disposition in the appropriate folder. His impatience with the rare defendant confused by the proceedings or unwilling to plead guilty, was readily apparent. This case would be rescheduled for later in the week, and the defendant would be led back hurriedly to the detention facility.

The judge seemed almost without personality, except for the isolated outbursts of displeasure with recalcitrant defendants. Otherwise, he appeared like an automaton or a foreman on an assembly-line, cranking out cases as if they were drive shafts. Peering up at the large clock to his right, working against the 10 o'clock deadline, he deftly shuffled through the paperwork and the defendants associated with it. The message was clear—do not tamper with the mechanized process. Those who failed to comprehend this message, could expect harsh words from the judge and face the maximum penalty of the law.

THE EDUCATOR

Believing in the necessity for educating the public, especially school-age children, this judge from a large eastern city invited school classes to sit in and observe his courtroom in action. Fortunately, he has been provided with an ample-sized facility in the city's historic courthouse, and the judge reserves large areas of the room for his "pupils." Despite the noble ends, the judge's educative endeavors did seem to generate some serious problems. The judge continually annoyed both prosecutor and defense counsel by pausing in the middle of proceedings to carefully explain a point of law to the class in attendance. Although the judge is restricted to non-jury cases, the attorneys appeared unnerved by the interruptions and delays.

On one occasion, the attorneys did seem justified in their consternation as the judge appeared to have carried his "courtroom classroom" too far. The case involved a man accused of assaulting his girlfriend. The outcome of the case was wholly dependent upon whether the version of the events in question given by the victim or defendant was to be believed. Following cross-examination of both parties, the judge turned to a class of sixth graders (about 30 in number) and asked for a hand vote of which party was to be believed. The majority of the class accepted the woman's version. The judge stated his agreement with their perceptions and found the defendant guilty. The defendant, who had watched the judge's behavior in wide-eyed disbelief, became irate at the court's decision and had to be restrained by his attorney and two bailiffs, while the judge calmly terminated his lecture to the class on how the judicial process works. It was just another class/case for this judicial educator.

THE HUMANIST

Although judges may appear to process cases in an assembly-line style as described earlier, sacrificing individual attention for speed and efficiency, many judges of the criminal courts make a conscious effort never to go so rapidly as to lose concern for the constitutional rights of the individual defendants appearing before them. One judge, observed in the far west, exhibited such care and unwillingness to allow his judicial decisions to be affected by heavy caseloads. Both the prosecutor and defense counsel were visibly frustrated by the judge's attention to detail and snail-like pace. Their eyeballs would frequently roll skyward as the judge dwelled for what seemed an eternity on a seemingly obvious point involving a blatantly guilty defendant.

Despite the judge's lack of popularity with other court officials, he continued his careful, and sometimes plodding ways. I observed him in the fall of 1981 when it appeared that this careful scrutiny may have saved an innocent man from accepting an unjustified guilty plea on the questionable advice of his seemingly unconcerned attorney. The defendant, who spoke only halting English, felt embarrassed to ask for an interpreter. He initially stepped before the judge, all too willing to accept the advice of his attorney to plead guilty to a lesser charge. It was only after the judge questioned the defendant as to the certainty of his plea did the language problems begin to become apparent. Once an interpreter was obtained, the judge spent the next hour questioning the defendant as to what had actually happened during the time of the original incident which led to his arrest. At the conclusion of the testimony, the judge was convinced of the defendant's innocence and moved for a new trial, rejecting the defendant's initial guilty plea, and instead accepting a new plea of not guilty with some advice to the prosecutor that he was contemplating dropping the charges entirely. This judge may be an exception, and this case may be remarkable and unique. However, it did happen, and there are many more judges who refuse to compromise their constitutional obligations to the pressures of caseloads and efficiency.

THE ADVOCATE

It seems ironic to most observers of the criminal courts to have the judiciary criticized by the public for being too liberal and too favorably disposed toward criminals. Most of the judges within the criminal courts have prosecutorial inclinations (and in many instances, prosecutorial experience as well). If they are to be accurately criticized, it should be on the grounds of being too "hard" rather than too "soft" on the defendants before them. Judges were found to vary greatly in the degree to which they adopted the prosecution bias, but one judge observed during a visit to a large western city, illustrated one of the most extreme prosecutorial orientations discovered in all of my travels.

The case involved one of the city's underground newspapers and its possible relationship to some terrorist activities that included the bombing of the local police station. The editor of the paper, a long-haired flower child who was clearly a throwback to the radicals of the Vietnam War protest movement, was being both evasive and somewhat belligerent toward the young prosecutor while he was attempting to cross-examine her. The judge, sensing the prosecutor's tentative approach, and also aware of his lack of experience in cases of this type, quickly became an active participant in the cross-examination, and soon took over the questioning of the defendant entirely. The antagonistic attitute of the judge toward the young editor, who refused to back down or show any deference toward the judge, was reflected in his acerbic and aggressive style of questioning. He went so far as to comment to the jury his conclusion that the defendant was not a very truthful individual. The frustrated defense counsel made countless objections, but could only insist that all the judge's antics be recorded by the stenographer and all of his objections preserved for the obvious appeal.

His only recourse was to try to build a record of the judge's prejudicial behavior for an appeal, for it soon became apparent that the defense had little chance of victory at the trial level.

These four judges and the highlighted incidents serve primarily as examples of the varied styles and personalities of the urban criminal court judiciary. They were purposefully selected to challenge the simplistic vision of judicial behavior held by most of the public. How much diversity does actually exist between, and even within, our criminal court systems? How great an influence can the broad range of judicial personalities, as well as the personalities of other important members of the courtroom workgroup (i.e., prosecutors, defenders, bailiffs, court clerks, etc.), have upon the operation of these courts? This chapter will attempt to provide at least partial answers to both of these inquires by analyzing the similarities as well as the differences that were found to exist in the 15 criminal court systems observed during the past 12 years.

SIMILARITIES

In reviewing the similarities discovered in nearly every big city criminal court system, the reader must realize that the problems may not be identical in terms of degree and complexity in all cities. *Similarity* will be used here to mean the presence of a specific problem area or institutional development which each city's criminal justice bureaucracy is cognizant of, and has been described to the author in concrete terms. Additionally, it is usually an undesirable trend that the local public officials are attempting to correct or modify.

Inadequate Staff

The first problem faced by all cities visited was inadequate staffing. Although particular agencies or institutions within each city's criminal justice system may have differing levels of understaffing, all were handicapped in some degree by personnel shortages. Probation officers, especially at the misdemeanor and juvenile courts were the groups most persistently plagued by the severest staffing deficiencies. These shortages were documented by federal commission studies in 1967 and 1973.[2] Continued fiscal reductions in city budgets have forced the cancellation of plans for the hiring of additional personnel during the 10-year period following the most recent federal study. It is most probable that with reduced governmental spending and increasing numbers of defendants passing through the criminal courts, the probation department's staffing problems have significantly worsened since these shortages were first described in the previously noted national studies.

The implications of these personnel shortages in probation services affect two of the agency's major responsibilities: preparation of pre-sentencing reports for the judges as well as monitoring, and hopefully improving, the behavior of the defendant during the probationary period. The criminal court judges are continually frustrated by the lengthy delays in waiting for completed reports. These delays often averaged between two to four weeks after a plea was accepted at arraignment. Additionally, many judges complained of the sloppy composition of these reports which were frequently replete with errors. Tension between the New York Criminal Court judiciary and the city's probation department will be discussed in future chapters and is only an exaggerated form of an institutional tension which was found in nearly every city visited. In New York, the head of the city's probation department cited severe understaffing as the primary cause of the problem, but stated that the judges wanted to use his agency as a scapegoat for the constant barrage of criticism directed toward the judiciary.[3]

The personnel shortages have also created impossible caseloads for each probation officer, negating any viable efforts at supervising the defendant's conduct. Having responsibility for nearly 100 defendants, the probation officer sees his clients so infrequently as to exert no control over their behavior during this period. It is a tragic situation because misdemeanant and juvenile probationers are most likely to be those defendants who are experiencing their initial contact with the courts and offer the greatest potential for being deterred from a life of crime. Instead, the defendant soon recognizes the ineffectiveness of the probation effort and its inadequate rehabilitative and supervisory activities. The deterrent effect of this experience with the probation department is so minimal that "street wise" young defendants soon believe that the court's revolving door will allow them to continue their criminal endeavors while suffering only minor inconveniences. As a pattern of recidivism develops, it is not until the defendant has escalated his antisocial behavior into a much more serious category that he or she realizes that the revolving door has stopped.

Judges, prosecutors, and public defenders have experienced staffing problems nearly equal to that of the probation staff. The judges appeared to be most understaffed at the earlier stages of the adjudicative process—initial appearance, preliminary hearing and arraignment. The arraignment court may also be responsible for deciding pretrial motions, scheduling trials, and conducting pre-sentencing hearings in addition to accepting guilty pleas. By the trial stage, the staffing shortages had generally abated to a tolerable level in most cities. The sharp contrast between the crowded and understaffed courtrooms used for these early stages, and the somber, more leisurely-paced trial courts, is a confusing paradox to the first-time visitor. It is quite puzzling to find some courtrooms spilling over with defendants and their

families while the harried judge and court staff work through their day's crammed calendar. Yet, on another floor, courtrooms are empty and judges are either in chambers or totally absent. Even if a trial is being conducted, only a handful of people will be in attendance. As with all of the criminal justice agencies, the personnel deficiencies are caused by increasing caseloads, shrinking budgets, and rising costs.

To give the reader a clearer sense of the type of caseload an under-staffed judge must face, I shall focus mainly upon those courtrooms responsible for pretrial functions. At the initial appearance, where judges must set bail, determine whether a counsel needs to be appointed, clarify charges, and set the date for the preliminary hearing, literally hundreds of cases are processed daily by an individual judge. A Chicago court-watching organization, hoping to reform the city's bail-setting practices, observed that judges in that city averaged less than one minute per case during this initial court appearance.[4] In arraignment court, where plea bargains are made, motions considered, and trial dates set, it is not uncommon to have a judge handle 40 to 50 cases per day.

Backlog of Cases

Closely related to the staffing problems, is the serious backlog of cases which has resulted in nearly all cities experiencing increased periods of delay from arrest until final disposition. Given the seemingly intractable nature of the urban fiscal crisis, and its negative effect upon staff size, nearly all cities have attempted to reduce backlog and delay by implementing a variety of programs designed to both rid the system of as many cases as quickly as possible, as well as streamlining the processing of those cases remaining within the system. Efforts to speed up the criminal process have ranged from speedy trial rules, pressuring attorneys to be ready to go to trial within a set period of time, or face the possibility of having the case dismissed, to utilization of computers to insure that witnesses, defendants, and lawyers will all receive ample notice of when to appear in court. Despite the great amount of time and money spent on these attempts to move cases more rapidly through the system, breakdowns continually occur. In every city visited, I witnessed similar incidents of frustrated judges waiting to begin some proceeding, but having to grant a postponement because either a witness, attorney, defendant, or some critical piece of paperwork was missing. At the subsequent court date, it was only a 50 percent chance that an additional postponement would not have to be granted.

Courts have experienced a modicum of success in diverting certain cases out of the traditional adjudicative process. These programs which include a variety of diversion and extra-legal mediation efforts have been successful in developing alternative forums for adjudication and treatment.

Unfortunately, they only scratch the surface, leaving the more serious cases, whose incidence appears to be increasing at an alarming rate, still in the system, with no perceptible reduction in the overall amount of time necessary for their disposition.

Plea Bargaining

The most common method criminal courts utilize in dealing with their caseload and delay problems is the practice of plea bargaining. Despite the negative connotations of this term, it describes a negotiating process which has been taking place within our nation's court systems (both civil and criminal) for many decades. A *plea bargain* is simply an agreement between the defendant (with the advice of his attorney) and the prosecutor, that in exchange for a plea of guilty, he will receive favorable consideration by the court. This consideration usually takes the form of being charged with a less serious crime, which will usually result in a lighter sentence, or receiving the minimum punishment allowable for the originally-charged offense. The rationale behind this exchange of favors is that the defendant is given the lesser sentence because of his cooperation with the court in choosing not to go to trial and thereby saving the city a great deal of time and expense.

Although the relative frequency of a city's use of plea bargaining may vary from city to city, its presence as a significant method by which cases are disposed is a national phenomenon. Its recent bad name is likely related to public concern over rising crime rates, and growing anger over the failure of police and the courts to solve the problem. Increasing public awareness of the operation of the criminal justice system has done little to develop empathy for the efforts of the courtroom workgroup, and instead has made the citizenry more cynical and less tolerant of the court's difficulties. Plea bargaining has seemingly become a symbol of the court's supposed leniency in dealing with defendants. It is a much more visible and comprehensible target for blame than the more complex social and psychological forces which are most likely contributing even more significantly to creating conditions which foster the growth of criminal behavior.

The high frequency of plea bargaining agreements has much to do with the public's negative attitude toward this procedure. Various studies have indicated that approximately 75 percent of all defendants indicted for felonies plead guilty.[5] It is assumed that nearly all of these guilty pleas can be technically described as plea bargains in that the defendant believes that he or she will receive a shorter sentence by pleading guilty at arraignment, than the sentence prescribed if he or she were found guilty after a trial.[6]

The criminal courts have generally been unresponsive to the public outcry against excessive plea bargaining. The mass media and local politicians, such as the mayor and city council members, are the groups most commonly applying pressure upon the judges to reduce plea negotiations in terms of both frequency and leniency. The criminal courts may attempt to ride out the present period of excitation by remaining silent, or by having an isolated court leader justify their actions as merely following the law. Occasionally when the criticism reaches a higher degree of intensity, the court may be pushed into lashing back at the local political leadership by accusing them of failing to provide the necessary resources which would permit the court to reduce the amount of plea bargaining and allow them the capability of handling a greater number of trials.

In a rare instance, a city may attempt to deal with the problem of plea bargaining by establishing a policy outlawing such negotiations. Two jurisdictions, the state of Alaska and the city of El Paso, Texas, have gone this route and have legislatively abolished its practice. The results of this reform effort have been described by James Cramer and William McDonald of Georgetown University's Institute of Criminal Law and Procedure. As part of their national study of plea bargaining for the United States Department of Justice, they concluded that more than a legislative decree is necessary to remove plea bargaining from the criminal justice system.[7]

Despite continued disappointments with the plea bargaining system as it now dominates the criminal justice process, there does not seem to be a growing national movement toward replicating the Alaskan and El Paso experiments.

Indigent Defendants

The fourth similarity found within urban criminal courts is the overwhelming number of indigent minority group members who constitute the court's clientele. Although the specific minority group may vary from city to city depending upon the relative percentage of black or Hispanic defendants, the combined totals were consistently high, usually in excess of 75 percent of the total number of defendants.[8] The purpose of this discussion is not to offer a possible explanation why these indigent minority group members are over-represented. It is simply to describe the presence of this statistical trend, and then to briefly discuss a few implications of this development. Roughly 25 percent of the court's clientele who were not indigents were typically charged with drug-related offenses if they were less than 25 years of age and with white collar crimes if they were over 25. Examples of white collar crimes at the state level are check forgers and an assortment of "bunco" schemes.

There are several significant ramifications to administering a criminal court system in which the large majority of defendants are indigent and/or a member of a minority group. Turning first to the impact of the indigency of the defendants, the local courts are under constitutional obligation (as a result of U.S. Supreme Court decisions in *Gideon* v. *Wainwright* and *Arger-singer* v. *Hamlin*),[9] to provide a competent legal defense at public expense. Whether represented by an assigned counsel or a public defender, the trial will be an extremely costly public expenditure.[10] Additional expenses related to indigent defendants involve their rights on appeal not to have to pay for reproduction of court transcripts and any other factors denying them equal protection of the law as a result of their economic status. On the negative side for the indigent defendant is the increased likelihood that if bail is set, he or she will not be able to raise it. Thus, the costs of pretrial detention, at approximately $15–20 per day per inmate, is yet another financial burden thrust upon the city.[11] The indigent defendant, as seen from this brief survey, creates major financial problems for state and local government.

A special problem for Spanish-speaking defendants is the failure of the criminal courts to hire adequate numbers of translators. Many Hispanic defendants were observed notifying the court that they thought they could comprehend the proceedings without an interpreter, but this often proved to be an unwise decision as the defendant's confusion quickly became evident. It was surprising to find a serious shortage of translators even in cities such as Houston and Los Angeles, where large numbers of Spanish-speaking defendants have been in the criminal courts for years. The appalling scarcity of Spanish-speaking judges, prosecutors and public defenders in these same cities was also a disappointment.

The language difficulty represents an extreme example of a larger communication problem which exists between court officials and most of the indigent defendants. Whether the product of inferior schooling, or suffering from a more contemporary cause emanating from a transient and often irresponsible lifestyle, indigent defendants did not appear to grasp what the court was telling them. This becomes even more tragic because these failures in communication can lead to criminal penalties as a result of a missed court appearance or a confused plea bargaining agreement.

In conversations with criminal lawyers, as well as bail administrators, it was continually noted that the typical defendant did not seem to possess the same concern for punctuality as the average middle-class citizen. Frequently unemployed, with time on his hands, the indigent defendant may also be without a watch or even the inclination to learn the time of day, or day of the month. Compounding the communication problems further, is the transient lifestyle of these defendants. With no fixed address, in constant movement, rarely having a permanent phone number where he or she can be reached, the court cannot rely on any of society's conventional means (i.e., telephone, telegram or mailed letter) for reaching its clientele, after they return to the streets.

The defendants inadvertently contribute to the communication problem because of their unwillingness to admit their confusion. Street-wise defendants were heard to utter the argot of the courts without really knowing what was happening, or about to happen to them. No one likes to appear ignorant, and many defendants may wish to impress the judge, their lawyer or friends in the courtroom with their supposed knowledge of the law. Judges and other members of the courtroom workgroup should recognize when this charade is occurring, and make a serious effort to ensure that the defendant is clearly apprised of his rights and obligations. Given the chaos and decibel level of most courtrooms, even an educated person, experienced in the law would have to pay extremely close attention, and occasionally request repeated instructions. The judge cannot allow the pressures of his caseload to serve as an excuse for ignoring his obligation to ensure that the defendant understands all that is happening to him.

The final implication of the defendant's indigent minority status relates to his difficulties at the time of sentencing. The judge is usually in sharp socioeconomic contrast to the indigent defendants clogging his or her courtrooms. He or she is most likely to be an upper middle-class white. Outside the courthouse, judges and defendants move in distant social circles. The sentencing decision was found by nearly every judge to be the most difficult and anxiety-producing part of his job. He or she has been given the almost impossible task of trying to do what is best for both society and the defendant. How can the judge reconcile these seemingly irreconcilable ends? By not being able to easily identify with the defendant, and understand what type of disposition will best deter him from future misconduct, most judges admitted to erring on the side of caution. White collar, middle-class defendants convicted of forgery, or swindling an elderly citizen, usually present backgrounds much more similar to the judge's who can then feel more comfortable knowing what punishment is most likely to deter himself or herself if he or she were to change places with the defendant. Engaging in this psychological role-playing can be effectively utilized with the middle-class white defendant, but unfortunately, the majority of defendants come from sharply divergent backgrounds with which the judge has had little personal experience. Given the present pressures on the courts to increase the severity of their sentencing, it is likely that judges will grow even less empathetic toward those indigent minority defendants convicted of serious crimes.

Juvenile Felons

A fifth problem faced in all cities visited, is the increasing number of juveniles committing felonies. A recent federal commission studying juvenile crime recommended that one way to curb this problem, and circumvent the supposed ineffective juvenile courts, would be to treat more juveniles as adults.[12] This solution carries the dual benefits of relieving the jammed juvenile courts of their most serious cases, as well as offering the court the chance to impose more severe sentences upon the juvenile defendant than were previously available.

Several cities studied did follow the commission's suggestions and began to legislatively expand the jurisdiction of the adult court into what was formerly the exclusive province of the juvenile process. This usually took the form of lowering the ages for several types of felonies, generally involving violence. New York City's experience with this type of legislation indicates the serious drawbacks to such an approach. Despite the opportunity to charge large numbers of juveniles as adults, the city's prosecutors declined the opportunity in 80 percent of the cases. With their current adult caseloads creating severe staffing problems, the prosecutors were unwilling to add several thousand more defendants to their responsibilities.[13]

Loss of Confidence

As a result of all of the problems previously described, both the defendant and the general public have begun to lose confidence in the criminal justice system's capacity to protect society, while also providing a fair trial for the defendant. In all of the cities visited, there was an especially strong public outcry against the criminal court's inability to safeguard the local citizens. The criticism of the court's failure to carry out its societal obligations has been so intense and so persistent as to challenge the very legitimacy of the institution itself. Although reasonable explanations of the court's limited role in combatting crime as well as their multitude of legal and constitutional restrictions may temporarily satisfy an enlightened segment of the society, the large majority of citizens are result-oriented and more than willing to shortchange the defendant of his constitutional protections. They are afraid of being victimized; they cannot understand that once a defendant is enmeshed in the criminal justice system, why he was allowed to slip out again, apparently with ease. Who else is there to blame but the judges?

The defendant and his family are also extremely angered and disillusioned by his treatment. The defendant's economic condition seems to impose serious obstacles in his fight to regain his freedom. Beginning with his probable inability to raise the necessary bail, and extending to the perceived (and often actual) disparities in sentences compared with others facing similar charges, the defendant is frustrated by the consequences of his lack of financial resources. The inability to choose one's own lawyer, and forced dependence upon the public defender's office with its tarnished reputation of advocacy, compounds the mistrust and disrespect which he directs toward the court. The result of the defendant's experience, almost regardless of outcome or severity of punishment, is to create a subclass of individuals who are contemptuous of our legal system. Believing themselves *victims* of an uncaring, biased institution, dominated by a white power structure that controls, and occasionally oppresses their existence, many defendants usually emerge from their confrontation with the law without remorse, rehabilitation or respect for society.

As cities attempt to resolve their local crime problems in terms of satisfying the public's demand for greater protection and the defendant's demand for fairer treatment, the local governments are faced with an extremely serious financial crisis. Even in the more compassionate, and sometimes generous years of the Carter administration, the urban economic problems were driving cities such as New York, Boston, Cleveland and Memphis to the edge of bankruptcy. Now with President Reagan's planned New Federalism, the local governments have been put on notice that Washington will no longer come to their aid, and must develop a new self-reliance.[14]

Thus, our nation's cities face hard times in the eighties, and the implications for the criminal courts are very serious as recent developments are already beginning to indicate. The elimination of the United States Justice Department's Law Enforcement Assistance Administration in April 1982, is a clear-cut example of the Reagan Administration's intention to severely curtail federal spending at the local level. Several states, such as Ohio, Missouri, and Alabama, have run out of money for assigned counsel cases and are now asking the state bar to provide legal representation without compensation. Local citizens are unwilling to see their tax dollars go toward improving the criminal justice system; voters in several states, including New York, have recently defeated numerous bond issues for building and improving criminal justice facilities.[15] Howard Eisenberg of the National Legal Aid and Defender Association summarized the situation as affecting the financing of attorneys for indigent defendants in the following pessimistic tones: "All over the country pressure is being brought on the bar and the judiciary to reduce the fees paid to counsel in order to conserve revenue for state or county. . . . There is a discernible trend toward cheap systems and toward elected officials placing political and media pressure on the bar to do work for less and less money."[16]

In closing this discussion on similarities between criminal court systems in our major cities, it is difficult not to be pessimistic regarding the ability of any city to possess *and* allocate the necessary funding to deal with the abundant problems just noted. To even hope to contain the problem at its current level seems an impossible task, given the fiscal realities of the forthcoming years and the inexorable rise in the crime rate.

DIFFERENCES

Despite the presence of so many similarities discovered between the numerous urban criminal courts visited, there were also several significant differences. Because nearly all of the similarities were general conditions or trends, the differences identified are best characterized as being perceptible variations in degree, rather than kind. This may, therefore, result in some confusion and possible overlapping, but an attempt has been made to only select those factors which represent significant variation, albeit in degree, between the 16 cities studied.

Sentencing

Whenever comparative research is attempted in the study of criminal courts, the variation in terminology has always ranged from being a persistent irritant to a major obstacle. These differences in terminology are most vividly seen in the variation in penalties attached to similar types of crimes. Studies of sentencing disparities have repeatedly documented how certain crimes, such as drug addiction, are treated much more seriously, and penalized much more severely in certain regions of the country than other sections. General trends show the southern and southwestern states to impose the most severe sentences while the middle atlantic and far west are the most lenient.[17] The implications of this variation between court systems is unclear since defendants do not usually stray from one jurisdiction to another in search of the most lenient penal code. Defendants are angered when hearing of persons receiving a lighter sentence from a judge in the same court system, but most defendants rarely have a chance to gather information on sentencing proclivities of other jurisdictions.

Discretionary Powers of Judges

Related to the sentencing issue is the question of how much discretionary power has been granted to the criminal court judge in making certain critical decisions affecting the final disposition. In order to minimize the possible abuses of lenient sentencing, several states have moved away from the broad grant of judicial decision-making power found in jurisdictions utilizing *indeterminant sentences*, toward a narrower range of options in what has been termed *determinant sentences*. This reform has limited the amount of choice available to a judge in sentencing a defendant for a particular type of crime and with a specific prior record. Additionally, the range of time between the minimum and maximum period of incarceration has been shortened. Finally, the elimination of certain sentencing alternatives such as probation or suspended sentences, has also been included for various categories of offenses.

The recent tendency to legislate decreasing judicial control over criminal proceedings has extended far beyond the publicized area of sentencing. Judges in different cities were found to possess significantly varying degrees of authority in the critical area of controlling the voir dire (jury selection), use of the contempt power, instructions to the jury, assigning counsel for indigent defendants, and controlling the calendar (including the granting of permission to attorneys to "Judge shop"). Considering the judge's control over jury selection as an example, some cities followed the federal government's guidelines, and allowed the judge to ask all of the questions, and if an attorney was not satisfied, he or she would have to submit specific questions to the judge for additional inquiries. Meanwhile, in certain southern cities, the attorneys were given free rein to ask potential jurors almost anything they desired, while the judge passively observed.

Other actors in the system were also found to have widely divergent grants of authority. Comparing the relative power of assistant district attorneys (prosecutors) to make binding plea bargains, at one extreme is the Philadelphia district attorney's office (observed during the Spector and Fitzpatrick years). Here, each assistant must return to the District Attorney's main office in order to receive approval before negotiating a plea. In most other cities, the assistant district attorney could work out a plea bargain with the judge and defense attorney, and finalize the agreement without having to receive permission from a superior in the department.

The Private Practice of Criminal Law

Although the private practice of criminal law is generally on the decline in nearly all of the cities surveyed, there were discernible differences between the relative prospects for survival. The criminal lawyers in Miami and Houston, for example, were doing fairly well. In Miami, there had been a recent explosion in major drug cases as well as a rapid rise in fraud and extortion arrests. These cases frequently involve affluent defendants who can afford a private criminal lawyer. In Houston, as in all Texas cities, there is no public defender system, so the defense bar receives assigned counsel fees, as well as paying customers. Criminal lawyers in these two cities are still struggling to earn a living, but their prospects are considerably brighter than in any of the other jurisdictions visited.[18]

At the other, more negative, end of the continuum, one finds Philadelphia and Los Angeles. The private criminal lawyers are visibly disappearing from the practice as interviewees estimated that there were only one-half to one-third of the total defense bar compared to 20 years ago. Blame for the decline was generally placed upon a competent public defender office which was believed to be handling nearly 80 percent of the felony cases in each city.[19]

Level of Adversariness

One interesting byproduct of the variation in legal procedures from jurisdiction to jurisdiction is a noticeable difference in the "level of adversariness" found in the criminal courtrooms. This term refers to the amount of competition existing between the competing attorneys. In Houston, for example, one finds a city in which it was common for judges to have to occasionally physically restrain the advocates from attacking each other in the courtroom. Outside, in the hallways, defense attorneys and prosecutors would often continue their heated arguments until a shoving match might develop or the tone of verbal abuse became vitriolic and the attorneys had to be separated. Most cities, however, had much less combative protagonists. Many defendants frequently complained that their attorneys seemed in league with the judge and prosecutor. The persistent air of cordiality, especially outside the courtroom, was a worrisome indicator to the defendant that his lawyer was not totally committed to his defense.

The primary legal procedures which seemed most closely related to the level of adversariness were the *rules of discovery. Discovery* is the procedure by which the opposing sides in a legal dispute learn the essential elements of the opponent's case. In criminal matters, this may relate to the list of witnesses and arrest report. The prosecutor, who usually has most of the information initially, may be required to turn over to the defense attorney the police report, the defendant's prior record, and any damaging comments he may have made during interrogation. In cities where both sides are compelled to turn over large amounts of information, the intensity of competition seems to wane. The converse also seems to be true, for when both sides have less knowledge of each other's case, they were more likely to adopt a more aggressive posture toward each other and be less likely to plea bargain.

A second group of legal procedures also relevant to the "level of adversariness" are the rules limiting the involvement of the attorneys in the voir dire. In cities such as Washington and Denver, where the judge, for reasons of expendiency, almost totally dominates the jury selection process, the attorneys seemed much less aggressive, even during the actual trial.

Reform Efforts

For some inexplicable reason, possibly grounded in the unique historical developments molding each city, there were recognizable differences in the willingness of the local criminal court system to engage in reform efforts designed to improve the operation of their courtrooms. In his excellent study of urban politics and criminal courts, Professor Martin Levin compared two court systems. One, (Pittsburgh), was designated as *"traditional"* while the other, (Minneapolis), was termed *"reformed."* The *reform* type of city was operationally defined as one which had a clear history of attempting to continually implement a series of programs designed to either make the court more efficient, or provide greater assistance to the defendant in his quest for fair treatment. Reform cities have readily turned to court administrators as well as attempting to computerize record keeping. Additional areas of reform have focused upon bail reform projects, diversion programs, and drug rehabilitation units.[20]

Cities vary as to their willingness to adopt these types of reform programs. Houston still does not have a public defender office, let alone a bail reform project. New York City, however, seems to be willing to experiment with every conceivable mode of reform suggested by criminal justice experts. Most of the other cities fall somewhere between these two extremes, although with the cessation of federal monies from the now deceased LEAA, most cities can be expected to reduce their reform efforts.

Level of Politicization

A final major difference between the numerous criminal justice systems was their relative degree of politicization. The politicization question may be examined from two sharply contrasting perspectives. The first is the viewpoint of the local politicians, and whether crime is perceived as a salient public issue affecting the quality of life of the electorate. As the perceived level of public concern mounts, so does the level of concern and involvement by the local politicians. The second perspective is that of the criminal court officials, especially the judiciary. As they analyze the intensity of feelings concerning crime and public safety, the judges look not only to the local political leaders, but also to concerned citizen groups, mass media interest, and bar association pressure as tangible measures of local concern.

The level of politicization of the criminal courts may be related to tangible factors, such as whether the judges are elected on a partisan basis or simply appointed by a blue ribbon commission charged with selecting the best nominees available, regardless of political affiliation. Politicization can also be affected by more subtle, and less direct factors, such as the interest of the mass media or the long-time presence of a respected civil service system.

The prosecutor's office may also offer clues as to the influence of politics upon the criminal justice system. Similar to the question of judges, it is of critical importance whether the prosecutor is elected or appointed. Additionally, the question of whether the prosecutor's assistants are patronage appointments or must qualify through civil service, is crucial. Since most prosecutors are elected, one must determine if they are the career type who are devoting their lives to fighting crime in the city, or are political opportunists who are using the prosecutor's office as a stepping stone to higher political positions.

The determination of how much, and in what way, politics appears to be influencing the operations of the criminal courts is a critical factor in better understanding why the courts are behaving in a particular manner. By understanding the amount and type of pressure being exerted upon the court system by the political power structure, one may better understand the responses of the judiciary and the courtroom workgroup.

Miscellaneous Differences

This list of differences between criminal court systems was not meant to be exclusively limited to the six just noted. They were selected as being the most prominent and relevant to the forthcoming presentation of an overall conceptual framework for comparing urban court systems. The following are a few of the relatively less important factors which were also found to vary between cities:

1. *Specialization of judges*—Were the judges restricted to only criminal cases or were they frequently rotated onto the civil side?
2. *Degree of centralization*—Were the criminal courts located in one central building or were they regionalized into a series of "neighborhood" courthouses as in Los Angeles?
3. *Degree of isolation*—Were the criminal courts joined in one building with the rest of the judicial system or isolated from them in a separate part of town as was done in New Orleans?

CITY SKETCHES

Beyond the narrow confines of the procedures and institutions of the criminal law, broader social and cultural factors may exert subtle, yet meaningful influence upon a city's criminal justice system. It may, therefore, be necessary to comprehend, or at least be sensitive to, the overall social and cultural milieu of each city in order to better understand the criminal courts. By offering the following series of sketches of eight of the cities visited, the reader may have a clearer sense of how the local sociocultural variables may affect the operation of the criminal courts. The following descriptions will stress those unique or unusual characteristics which may affect the operation of each city's criminal courts.

New Orleans

The "Crescent City," with tourism its major industry, likes to forget about its crime problem. Both major newspapers rarely have news stories describing violent crimes which might frighten away potential visitors. Demographically, New Orleans is one of the nation's most heterogenuous cities, and becoming even more so as large numbers of illegal aliens from the Caribbean islands and Central America migrate to the city.

What is unique about the city's black population is its longevity through deep family roots. Neighborhood stability for both blacks and whites was more apparent than in any other city visited. Since most of the families have known each other for several generations, a victim frequently can identify his or her assailant. Many families refuse to notify the police following an assault or robbery, preferring to gain revenge by harming some member of the offending family. The New Orleans version of the biblical "eye for an eye" morality may reduce police involvement in local crime problems, but has likely led to an escalation in violence which will eventually involve the police and courts.

The city has a legacy of fascinating political leaders who engage in bizarre escapades. The current mayor (Morial) seems only slightly less colorful than his predecessors. The judiciary has maintained a low profile, isolated from public scrutiny, although the office of district attorney, peaking with Jim Garrison, is a highly visible and politicized operation. Like most of the other southern cities visited (Miami, Houston, and St. Louis), New Orleans' judges mete out some of the harshest sentences in the nation. The state's prison and jail conditions are considered among the most decadent.

One final observation is that New Orleans seemed to offer its citizens the most primitive and depleted public services of any city studied. The social welfare agencies and public housing departments were barely existent. The only positive side to this depressing picture is that because of the strong family life, most individuals can turn to friends and relatives for support and this personalized welfare system does seem to work. The city has recently attempted to upgrade the quality of these social services but its historically depleted public treasury does not seem adequate to the task. Its police department, which is pathetically understaffed, is reputed to be the lowest paid force in the nation.

Philadelphia

Despite being four times larger, Philadelphia and its criminal court system present the same small town, highly personalized atmosphere found in New Orleans. Often described as almost an invisible or forgotten metropolis on the northeast axis, it is overshadowed by its neighboring cities of Washington, New York and Boston. Philadelphia was not always so isolated, for until the middle of the nineteenth century it shared with Boston the co-leadership of urban America in both population and economic growth. By the 1900s, however, the city's importance declined, and although it maintained a steady rate of growth, it began to retreat from its leadership position and turn inward.

The result of this stunted development has been a city with many unique features including the most inbred political and judicial system discovered in any of the cities surveyed, with the possible exception of Chicago. In interviewing nearly half of the city's private criminal lawyers, it was learned that every one of the 24 had either been born or educated in Philadelphia, and that nearly three-fourths had both experiences. The criminal courts are all located in City Hall, majestically placed in the center of the city. The offices of the legal community were all within two or three blocks of the courts. The informal comraderie existing between defense attorneys, prosecutors, and judges was at a level of intimacy and frequency unmatched in any other city. The abundance of commonality in the backgrounds of all members of the criminal courtroom workgroup appears to be an inevitable explanation for this condition.

Philadelphia, in terms of its highly politicized court system, which is still linked to a somewhat factionalized machine-style political organization, is very reminiscent of Chicago and its legacy of party bosses. Even the demographic foundation of the two cities is similar, with the population dominated by blacks, white ethnics, Jews, and a handful of patrician WASPs. The fact that both cities have recently elected black mayors makes the comparison even more fitting. The judges are elected on a partisan basis for 10-year terms. Intensifying the political tensions within the city are the local newspapers which have been extremely critical of the courts. *The Philadelphia Inquirer,* the city's major paper, has been especially aggressive in its critical posture toward the courts. The coverage was more complete and emotional than any other city visited.

Although the city's criminal courts have benefitted from its Quaker heritage of humanitarian ideals, and has been in the forefront of judicial reform, its growing racial tensions seem to overshadow these achievements. The city's police department gained national notoriety through its being charged by the United States Justice Department with violating the civil rights of its black population by its persistent acts of brutality. Although the suit was eventually dismissed, the racial tensions between police and the inner city have not disappeared.

Washington, D.C.

Adequately funded through the United States Congress, the criminal courts in the nation's capital are clearly the least political and most affluent of any of the systems surveyed. The result of its merit selection (by the President), and retention (by independent Commission) procedures, has been the establishment of an extremely competent group of judges, prosecutors (U.S. Attorneys), and public defenders. In addition, recent Presidents have attempted to make the District's criminal court system a model for the rest of the country. The results have been uneven, but reforms have been attempted, and the overall abilities of personnel have been raised to impressive levels.

Why then are there problems? The city still exists at the whim of the District of Columbia Committees of Congress. This reluctance to grant self-governance to the District is thought by many to be caused by the large black majority which could control elections (approximately 70 percent of the city's 630,000 residents are black). The white-dominated criminal courts handle a clientele almost exclusively black. This is merely another frustration for the local citizens when combined with their inability to achieve home rule, and has undermined the rather shaky racial compatibility which has existed in the city since the disturbances of 1968.

New York

Because of its great size and world class stature, New York has been often described as *"sui generis,"* a city so unique as to make it incomparable with other American urban centers. In my initial research experiences, I accepted this distinction and always chose to exclude New York from my sample. It has only been in the last five years that my timidity has been reduced (primarily as a result of living in its environs for nearly all of that time), so as to include it in my most recent research efforts. Because of my increasing courage, I have concentrated almost exclusively on the Manhattan (New York County) criminal court system to the exclusion of the other four boroughs.

The criminal courts, like the city as a whole, have an energy and vitality that can overwhelm even the most experienced researcher. In the four years in which I have been scrutinizing their activities, the New York County criminal courts have been engaged in a continual series of controversies, while experimenting with a never-ending succession of reforms. The crisis-management style of operation must be a draining experience for all participants. One of the most recent escapades involved a struggle between the Presiding Judge of the State Court system and the District Attorney for New York County (Manhattan).[21] At issue was the Presiding Judge's unilateral decision to alter the system by which certain qualified (at least according to an evaluation by the Chief Administrative Judge for the City), municipal court judges would be temporarily promoted to sit as Acting Supreme Court Judges (the felony trial courts) in order to aid their seriously short-handed brethren. The Presiding Judge declared that the merit selection process would be replaced by a simple rotational scheme in which all of the municipal court judges would have an equal opportunity for the elevated status (and pay). The District Attorney argued that judges unqualified for criminal court work would be promoted and would replace the competent acting judges currently sitting. The city's chief prosecutor successfully challenged the Presiding Judge in a court of law and had the Presiding Judge's own colleagues on the State Appellate Court decide against him, primarily because of the Chief Judge's failure to consult the rest of the bench while making the decision.[22]

Because New York is the media center for the nation, these incidents which may only be local news in other cities, can frequently be given nationwide exposure. Given this setting, and its prideful position as the Number One city in the country, if not the world, New York seems compelled to rush at its criminal court problems with a flurry of enthusiasm. Unfortunately, the city's near-empty public treasury and the complexity and depth of its criminal justice problems, leads to widespread frustration in both the community and the courthouse. Complicating the problem is the confusing borough system of governance with its five separate criminal justice operations. An additional complication, of even greater possible significance, is the sharply divergent socioeconomic and ethnic groups living in close proximity.

San Francisco

Another city heavily dependent upon the tourist trade, San Francisco has developed a reputation for civility and tolerance, probably unmatched elsewhere in the country. Its mild climate and attractive natural setting combined with the previously noted attributes, has made the city a haven for transients of all ages and persuasions. Unfortunately, these unsettled groups seem primed for interaction with the criminal courts both as victims and perpetrators. The city's reputation for a lively drug scene has also contributed to its growing crime problems.

To its credit, San Francisco ranks with New York and Philadelphia in its willingness to experiment with a wide range of social and criminal justice reforms. Partially due to the city's modest size, (when compared to New York or Los Angeles), the criminal courts appear to have been modestly successful in improving the quality of justice. Like other cities visited, however, San Francisco has been experiencing severe economic problems, and its black and brown populations have become increasingly aggressive and distrustful of the white power structure.

Los Angeles

Los Angeles, as the mythical capital of southern California, has the image of a laid-back society where the only major problem is navigating the freeways in order to find a better surfing beach. Hidden from this simplistic impression are the large sprawling neighborhoods where the blacks, browns, Orientals and elderly live. The communities in East Los Angeles, Watts, and North Hollywood are far removed from the youthful, surfer image popularly imagined. It is from these highly transient, economically deprived, and visibly decaying communities that the city's criminal courts receive most of its burgeoning business.

On a more positive note, the criminal courts appeared to be among the most efficient in the country. In a beautiful new complex of buildings in the City Hall area, as well as in smaller regionalized courthouses in five outlying regions, Los Angeles may have the best resources in the nation for dealing with its felony defendants. Large public defender and prosecutorial offices, combine with the most up-to-date computer facilities to make it a model for the rest of the nation. Despite its excellent resources and willingness to engage in reform efforts, the city's social problems may still be out-distancing its capabilities.

Miami

Miami had long been a city noted primarily as a resort town. Recently, it has gained national notoriety through several crime-related incidents. It has been the site of our nation's most recent serious racial disturbances. The disorders themselves developed from the reaction of blacks to the acquittal of white police officers charged in the murder of a black youth. Additionally, the city has emerged as the major entry point for drugs to be sold on the East Coast. Confiscations of millions of dollars worth of drugs are no longer isolated incidents guaranteed headline coverage, but repeated occurrences. Exacerbating the rising racial tensions has been a meteoric increase in emigrants from Cuba and other Caribbean and Central American locales. The result has been a seriously depressed local economy, a frighteningly high crime rate, and bitter tensions between all groups.

The court system has had a difficult time adapting to the increased workload. The large number of Hispanic defendants, many in need of translators, has also complicated the problems of the criminal courts. Several of the Cuban emigrés were lawyers in their original homeland but are frustrated by being unable to pass the Florida bar examination due to their inability to master English.

The white community in Miami also seems fragmented and at odds with each other. The original inhabitants of the area were WASPs (White Anglo-Saxon Protestants), and were not very different in racial and religious beliefs from their nearby southern brethren in Georgia, Mississippi, and Alabama. After the first World War, however, Florida was discovered by retiring "Yankees" who created a land boom. The major group coming to Miami during this period were retiring Jews from the East Coast. As the black community became larger and more vocal, and the various Hispanic groups competed with them for the few jobs available, racial tensions began to tear the city apart. The criminal court has done little thus far to convince any of the minority groups that they can be relied upon for fairness and compassion.

Houston

The city of Houston, through its great oil wealth and shiny new skyscrapers, likes to portray itself as the quintessential Texas metropolis, ready to blast into the twenty-first century. Despite its recent economic boom (which now seems to be slowing down as a result of an abundance of oil), the city has an underclass whose level of poverty and alienation is apparently equal to that of Miami. The lower class whites, blacks and Mexican-Americans are struggling against each other for the few jobs available. The city's police force with a national reputation for racial hostility equal only to Philadelphia's, has been involved in numerous incidents which threaten the very legitimacy of the criminal justice system.

Like Miami, Houston was so involved in its marvelous growth during the past 20 years, that it failed to notice that not everyone was sharing in the good times. Applying the concept of relative deprivation, one can appreciate the increased agitation of the blacks and Hispanics who observed so many others obtaining financial success while their own lives were mired in poverty and unhappiness.

The city does have a reputation as the home of some of the finest criminal lawyers in the nation. Standing in the shadow of Percy Foreman and Richard "Racehorse" Haynes, are at least a dozen high quality defense counsel who are more than willing to take on the local establishment, regardless of the defendant's race or ethnic background. Without a public defender system, this large group of able, committed defense attorneys are aggressively committed to serving as a forceful, independent advocate for their clients.

CONCEPTUAL FRAMEWORK

In order to provide a more organized framework to be used in comparing the nation's major urban criminal courts than the previous listing of similarities and differences, a typology of variables will be offered which appear to affect the quality and style of an urban felony court. These variables have been categorized into the following four groupings: legal, institutional, political, and social. Within each of these categories will be listed a number of sub-variables. Because so many of these sub-variables cannot be translated into quantifiable terms, they primarily serve the purpose of conceptual guidelines. Each variable should, therefore, be imagined as a continuum upon which the city under observation may be placed relative to its urban counterparts. Identifying cities who merit placement at one of the extremes of these concepts will serve as a guidepost for further comparison with additional jurisdictions.

This paradigm seems to possess heuristic value and can serve as a visual aid in comparing court systems. Nevertheless, its defects, in terms of the subjective nature of its utilization, are very real. Also, the temporal nature of such judgments also present problems. The courts are in constant flux and, therefore, evaluations may soon be outdated but the model will still be available as an organizing tool for the significant concepts. Each of the major categories and sub-variables will be examined briefly at this point since they will be more completely explained in the subsequent chapters, with specific illustrations of their significance. For now, they will be identified as part of the overall conceptual scheme.

Legal Procedures

As Max Weber sagely instructed sociologists, and a few attentive political scientists, the "rules" are rarely neutral, and this clearly applies to legal procedures as well. The following list of legal procedures were found to vary significantly from city to city and also seemed to be influential in affecting the behavior patterns of the criminal courts. These procedures related to (1) the amount of discovery permitted, (2) the importance of the preliminary hearing, (3) the formalization of plea bargaining, (4) the degree of judicial discretion permitted in sentencing, and (5) degree of judicial dominance during jury selection.

Institutional Variables

Beyond the formal rules, the criminal courts are also institutions which are strongly influenced by the various actors and subgroups whose performance can greatly affect the stability and effectiveness of the entire system. The strength and weaknesses of all the actors in the criminal courts will combine to affect the behavior of the system. The critical sub-variables falling within this category are: (1) the size and quality of the public defender program, (2) the size and quality of the private criminal lawyers, (3) competence of the judiciary, (4) size and quality of the prosecutor's office, (5) size and quality of the probation department, (6) size, quality, and responsibilities of the court staff, (7) the competence of the court administrator and his staff, (8) degree of court regionalism, and (9) relative isolation of criminal courts from the rest of the judicial system (civil courts).

Political Factors

The criminal courts, like the rest of the judicial branch of government, have been envisioned as being outside the political pressures controlling the executive and legislative branches. Recent research by journalists and political scientists has clearly refuted this idealized conception.[23] The amount of influence which politics exerts upon judicial behavior may be less than that found in the other two branches, but it can still be a critical factor in understanding the variation in style and quality between the criminal courts of our nation's cities. The following are the sub-variables relating to understanding this political influence: (1) degree of politicization of judiciary, (2) degree of politicization of prosecutor's office, (3) selection process for judges and prosecutors, (4) amount of media interest, (5) degree of partisanship in operation of city government (degree of professionalism, meritocracy), and (6) strong mayor vs. a weak mayor form of government.

Social and Demographic Variables

Beyond the three groups of internal factors just discussed which can assert influence over the behavior of an urban criminal court system, there are also a group of external factors which may also prove influential. This rather diverse group of variables has been lumped together under the rubric "social factors" and includes the following: (1) inbred nature of the court-room workgroup, (2) the degree to which the court system has been receptive to reform, (3) size of the city, (4) ethnic homogeneity, (5) degree of racial turmoil currently existing, (6) degree of poverty, (7) stability of neighborhoods, (8) number of transients, (9) salience of crime as a local issue, and (10) level of urban density (horizontal versus vertical housing development).

In the next chapter the institutional variables which relate to the criminal court judge's working environment will be carefully examined.

NOTES

1. *New York Times* Surveys which appeared in the *New York Times* December 22, 1981, p. A1, and on March 23, 1982, p. A14.
2. President's Commission on Law Enforcement and the Administration of Justice, *Task Force Report: The Courts.* (Washington, D.C.: Government Printing Office, 1967).

   National Advisory Commission on Criminal Justice Goals and Standards, *Courts.* (Washington, D.C.: Government Printing Office, 1973).
3. Barbara Basler, Justice Aides in Dispute Over Lag in Sentencing, *New York Times.* October 3, 1981, p. II, 1.
4. Alliance to End Repression, Cook County Special Bail Project Report, Chicago: February 10, 1970 (mimeographed).
5. Pasqual DeVito. An Experiment in the Use of Court Statistics, *Judicature.* 56 (August/September, 1972), p. 56.
6. Ibid.
7. Ibid.
8. Malcolm Feeley. *The Process is the Punishment.* New York, Russell Sage Foundation, 1978.

   United States Department of Justice, *Uniform Crime Reports,* Washington, D.C.: Government Printing Office, 1980.
9. *Gideon* v. *Wainwright* 372 U.S. 335 (1963).

   Argersinger v. *Hamlin* 407 U.S. 25 (1972).
10. Although some jurisdictions have now begun to reduce assigned counsel fees, the large majority of these defendants in major urban centers are defended by public defenders.
11. Paul B. Wice. *Freedom for Sale.* Lexington, Lexington Books, 1974, p. 96.

    Ronald Goldfarb. *Jails: The Ultimate Ghetto.* Garden City, N.Y.: Doubleday, 1975, p. 38.
12. "New York Fight on Youth Crime Called Ineffective," *New York Times.* March 3, 1982, p. A1.

    Marcia Chambers. "Family Court Assailed as Overprotective," *New York Times.* March 1, 1982, p. A1.
13. Philip M. Boffey. "Youth Crime Puzzle Defies a Solution," *New York Times.* March 5, 182, p. B1.
14. *New York Times.* January 16, 1981, p. A1; January 17, 1981, p. A1.
15. *New York Times.* March 10, 1982, p. A26; June 2, 1982, 1982, p. B4.
16. Paul Wice. The Private Criminal Defense Bar: A Re-Assessment of an Endangered Species, Willima F. McDonald. *The Defense Counsel.* Beverly Hills, Sage Publications, 1983.
17. Marvin Frankel. *Criminal Sentences.* New York, Hill and Wang, 1972; Twentieth Century Fund. *Fair and Certain Punishment.* New York, McGraw-Hill, 1976, p. 5.
18. Paul Wice. *Criminal Lawyers: An Endangered Species.* Beverly Hills, Sage Publications, 1978.
19. Ibid.
20. Martin Levin. *Urban Politics and Criminal Courts.* Chicago, University of Chicago Press, 1977.
21. E.R. Shipp. Temporaries in the Court. *New York Times.* September 29, 1981, p. B1.
22. Ibid.
23. Among the social scientists who have recently offered empirical proof of the inter-relationship between politics and judicial decision-making are Martin Levin, Herbert Jacob, Malcolm Feeley, James Eisenstein, David Neubauer, and George Cole.

2

THE WORKING ENVIRONMENT

This chapter will examine the working environment of the felony court judge. In addition to describing the physical, social and psychological dimensions of the criminal courthouse, this chapter will also study the judge's courtroom workgroup which includes prosecutors, public defenders, and court personnel. The only member of the criminal courtroom workgroup who will not be discussed in this chapter is the private defense counsel. In contrast to all of the previous actors who are either directly or indirectly controlled by the state and are dependent upon public monies, the private criminal lawyer is independent of these obligations. Because of the uniqueness of his independent status, he will be discussed separately in the forthcoming chapter. Finally, a select group of external influences will be analyzed in an attempt to better understand the total range of influences affecting both the judge's working conditions and patterns of behavior. These outside factors will include the media, local politicians, community groups, and appellate courts.

PHYSICAL DESCRIPTION

One of the first clues to the low status accorded the criminal courts (by both the general public as well as influential politicians), is their location. In at least half of the cities visited, the criminal courts were carefully tucked away from public view. The most common justification for these isolated and inconvenient locations was security. Since the pretrial detention facilities may be appended to the courthouse proper, it was necessary to place the entire structure out of the downtown business center. This was clearly the case in Chicago and New Orleans.

However, in San Francisco, which houses its pretrial detentioners many miles away in the county jail, the criminal courts are located in the shadow of a freeway, a significant distance from the rest of the city's governmental buildings located in the more respectable Civic Center area surrounding City Hall and the Opera House. The San Francisco situation is fairly typical as most of the criminal courts were located sizable distances from the downtown business district and could be found in decaying sections of town.

Although criminal court buildings may have been constructed in a variety of architectural styles, they nevertheless all seem to possess the same imposing facade. Regardless of age, they present an image of stolidity and unyielding strength. Entrance is usually gained by climbing an excessive number of steps. For security reasons, there may be only one door open to the inner sanctum, funneling in all visitors through a crowded, narrow entranceway. Once inside, most courthouses subject all visitors to a cursory security check. In San Francisco, where the courthouse has experienced a number of bombings and demonstrations, the police conduct a fairly thorough body frisk and careful perusal of all packages. With a seeming lessening of urban tensions in recent years, many courthouses have restricted their security precautions to specfic courtrooms in which potentially explosive trials are being conducted. Tight controls may also exist around particularly sensitive offices such as an unpopular prosecutor.

Another side effect of these security precautions which can prove extremely discomforting to the inexperienced visitor is the practice of locking all courthouse lavatories. Use is restricted to permanent personnel who are issued personal keys. This decision was explained as being the result of hostile protests conducted in the late sixties and early seventies in which radical groups released their frustrations against the supposed inequities of our criminal justice system by blowing up courthouse lavatories. Other reasons for their limited use was their reputation as homosexual hangouts as well as ideal locales for muggings. The irony of the situation is that when they are open to the public, the facilities are so abused that sinks and toilets rarely work and towels and toilet paper are nonexistent.

The interior of the courthouse is usually distinguished by a massive lobby, with an impressively high, arched ceiling. In the center of the lobby is the omnipresent information booth which is invariably unattended. A nearby bulletin board offers the only clue as to what cases are to be found in which courtrooms but the notices are usually outdated. In a distant corner is a small snack bar and a battery of telephones, a few of which are in service. It is rumored (and from my experience the rumors are frequently accurate), that these phones may be "bugged" either by the police or prosecutor's office. Once in the Detroit Wayne County Criminal Courthouse, I picked up the receiver of a public phone, and before I deposited my dime, I heard police radio calls coming from the other end.

Between nine to four o'clock each weekday, the cavernous lobby and most hallways are filled with animated conversations between lawyers, bail bondsmen, bailiffs, defendants, concerned family members, witnesses and a variety of other interested parties. For many bondsmen and private criminal lawyers these hallways are, in reality, their daytime offices. Although courthouses have attempted to reduce the cacophony in the hallways by providing for witness reception areas, lawyers' lounges, and other specialized and secluded hideaways, nearly everyone prefers to be near the action so as not to miss out on a business opportunity, or choice bit of gossip.

First-time visitors to the courthouse are frequently shocked by the amount of badinage which transpires between the various members of the courtroom workgroup. One wonders how so much conviviality can exist within an institution which has been charged with such serious responsibilities. Irving Goffman's theory of "role distance" may provide at least a partial explanation.[1] Goffman found an inordinate amount of joking around by surgeons, often during what seemed to be fairly serious occasions. Goffman reasoned that the lightheartedness was a way for the doctors to relieve the professional tensions by stepping outside of their professional role. Given the serious issues at stake in the criminal courtroom, it is also plausible that the officers of the court may also be attempting to create "role distance" between themselves and their somber legal duties.

Moving out of the hallways and into the courtroom, one notices a relative decrease in noise level, while the air quality improves appreciably. This is especially true in the spring and summer where most cities observe a policy of air-conditioning only the inside of the courtrooms, letting the hallways swelter without relief. The judge and bailiffs attempt to maintain an acceptable decibel level but disturbances are commonplace. It must be noted that the chaotic scenes depicted thus far pertain to only those courtrooms where pretrial proceedings are conducted such as initial arraignments, preliminary hearings, calendar, motions or arraignment. As one moves closer toward trial in a felony case, the courtroom scene becomes increasingly more tranquil. The end result is that the trial, which is a statistical rarity, is held in a quiet, sparsely-populated courtroom. The tedious and repetitive nature of most trials, in contrast to the public's misconception, serves to lull the most diligent observer into momentary lapses of daydreaming.

Since most of the criminal court action occurs at the pretrial proceedings with only about 5–10 percent of the cases actually going to trial,[2] a description of these earlier, less publicized proceedings seems warranted. The typical pretrial proceeding is conducted within a large courtroom. Entrance is gained through a double set of heavy doors. Once inside, the judge's elevated position becomes immediately apparent. Just below him is the court stenographer and the calendar clerk who attempts to control the scheduling of cases and keep the judge apprised of the relevant details of the case before him. Approximately 15 feet from the front of the bench are two tables reserved for the defense and prosecution, respectively. The prosecutor's table is piled high with manila folders representing those cases to be disposed of during the course of that day's business. This impressive pile of folders is invariably incomplete and results in last-minute scurrying by frantic assistant district attorneys trying to rectify the periodic lapses of the prosecutorial bureaucracy. If the other table is manned by a public defender, the mound of case folders nearly matches that of the prosecutor's. The private criminal lawyer maintains his own collection of case folders within the confines of his briefcase. Directly behind the defense and prosecution tables is a low railing or some other obstacle dividing the court officers (judges, lawyers, and clerks) from the general public who sit in several rows of benches. The first, and sometimes the second rows are reserved for police officers and lawyers who are waiting for their cases to be called. Sitting in the remaining rows are the defendants (those who have been free on bond or released on their own recognizance), family members, friends, and a variety of other observers. In the trial courts one finds large numbers of senior citizens who enjoy rooting for the prosecutor. They are often vocal in their thirst for severe sanctions against defendants whom they do not wish to have returned to their neighborhoods and continue to terrorize other elderly victims.

If a defendant did not obtain his pretrial release, he or she must enter the courtroom through a locked door behind and to the side of, the judge. Court bailiffs, who are responsible for maintaining order in the courtroom, control access through this door. On the other side of the door is a hallway which leads to a "lockup" area where the detained prisoners must wait until their cases are called. The bailiffs then escort the defendant out of the lockup cell and into the courtroom. Once in the courtroom, the bailiffs cautiously guard the prisoner, making sure he has no contact with anyone in the public gallery, unless permitted by the judge. Most courthouses were constructed with a concern for security both in and out of the courtroom. However, judges who work late and leave the building after dark, are faced with an unprotected path out to the parking lot. Security in each city usually improves after a judge or prosecutor is assaulted, but shortages of personnel in most cities limits the effectiveness of such protection.

The judge's chambers are located in the labyrinth of hallways found behind and alongside the courtrooms. Access to these offices and hallways is carefully protected by locked doorways and one can only gain entrance by pre-arranged appointments with the bailiffs or personal secretaries. The chambers vary greatly in age and quality but generally all contain an anteroom or reception area in which the judge's secretary works and serves as an additional obstacle in gaining access to the judge's actual office. Although the judge's office might be large, it is frequently crammed with law books, miscellaneous correspondence, legal memorabilia and overstuffed furniture. The walls are filled with photographs and diplomas. Given the age of the building and its poor upkeep due to fiscal cutbacks, the chambers are only modestly impressive.

Because the judges rarely work out of one specific courtroom, and are shifted around according to the court administrator's logistical demands, the judge's chambers are rarely located in close proximity to the courtroom in which the judge may be currently sitting. Adding to the judge's inconvenience is the problem caused by the recent additions to the bench which has necessitated the use of annexes to house the newly appointed judges. These buildings are usually located within a short walking distance of the main courthouse, but judges who reside in these "renovated" facilities often complain about their second-class status.

SOCIAL-PSYCHOLOGICAL DESCRIPTION

Beyond its physical characteristics, the criminal courthouse appears to be a living organism whose social and psychological dimensions are even more significant, and in many ways, more fascinating. Despite their locations in a hectic urban setting, the criminal courts which I visited seemed like traditional villages. The high level of intimacy and frequency of interaction between nearly all of the courtroom workgroup made many defendants and outsiders unfamiliar with the court's inner workings incredulous as to the possible existence of a viable adversary proceeding. Although the "kibbitzing" is curtailed during the time when court is in session, it is never completely absent. In the hallways, around the snackbars, in the courtrooms during recesses, and before and after the day's business, the friendly joshing never seems to end. Whether this exaggerated conviviality serves as a type of necessary social lubricant to disguise actual tensions, or is an accurate measure of their camaraderie, is difficult to discern. Whichever purpose it serves, it is still an omnipresent style of interaction that typified almost every city visited. There were, of course, variations in the general level of jocularity, with New York and Philadelphia topping the scale, and Denver and Los Angeles being the most somber, at the other extreme.

A second similarity between big city courthouses and traditional villages is their suspicion of outsiders. The legal community has always seemed to retreat into a defensive posture behind its stylized jargon and plethora of confusing procedures. The criminal courts appear to take an even more recalcitrant position toward anyone wishing to penetrate their inner sanctums. The paranoia is not based entirely on whimsy since the criminal courts have borne the brunt of the public's frustration over the rising crime rate. (Politicians have also used the courts as scapegoats for their own inability to deal with the problem of making our society a safer place.)

The result of this external criticism is for the courtroom workgroup to adopt a "siege mentality" and draw together within the courthouse walls, often hiding their hostility behind nervous laughter.

This negative picture does not mean that researchers and journalists will be effectively barred from entering the inner workings of the criminal courthouse. It has meant, however, that before one is allowed to penetrate the court's defenses, one must prove through responsible reporting and unbiased research that he merits the trust of the courthouse personnel. Once this trust has been established, court personnel can be as helpful and open as any public official. Again, using the village metaphor, the initial suspicion of outsiders must be worn away by tangible acts of good faith conclusively proving one to be both reliable and trustworthy.

The nearly complete control exercised by the judge over his courtroom creates a third similarity between the traditional village and the contemporary courthouse. Each judge resembles the patriarchal head of the village or ruling family, possessing virtually dictatorial powers over all who enter his domain. In the courthouse, anyone who disturbs or challenges the processes of justice will be summarily removed from the courtroom. Regardless of the status or prominence of any visitor to the courtroom, once within the judge's domain, unquestioned obedience is demanded. There is no appeal from his decision as he quickly dispatches his bailiffs to carry out his immediate dictates. Although each city has a presiding judge who oversees the operation of *all* the courtrooms and can theoretically control and discipline a judge who violates the professional norms, this is rarely done.

The occasional outlandish or demagogic antics of individual judges are common topics of courthouse gossip. I have never witnessed a direct confrontation between a judge and lawyer or clerk in which a successful challenge to judicial behavior was made. Lawyers (both prosecutors and defense counsel) seem to simply catalogue these judicial idiosyncrasies and store them away for future use. This type of information may be useful the next time an attorney appears before a judge with a reputation for some form of unusual behavior.

The judge is clearly the most imposing and intimidating figure in the courtroom, particularly in his relationship to the other members of his workgroup. The style of judicial interaction can take various forms from aloofness to extreme gregariousness, but the judge is clearly the one who sets the tone of the relationship. The only individual observed to be not consistently intimidated by the judge is the defendant. This is especially true if the accused has had several previous experiences with the law. His familiarity with the criminal courts appears to have lessened his fear and respect for all of the members of the court, including the judge.

It is amazing to see defendants who face the possibility of very long prison sentences behaving contemptuously in the judge's presence. Their attitudes are clearly reflected in both their demeanor and dress. The defendants seem, at times, to purposefully antagonize the judge by adopting a posture of defiance, staring unconcernedly into space or glaring toward the bench. Much of this posturing, particularly if the defendant is youthful, seems to be directed toward impressing friends and family in the courtroom. It is almost a symbolic assertion of independence, notwithstanding his imminent fate. Slovenly dressed, many young defendants appear to have inadvertently wandered into the courtroom after having finished a recent game of basketball at a nearby playground. Possibly because the judges face so many defendants striking these disrespectful poses, there is rarely little interest in correcting defendants' behavior. The judges may also reason that there is little need to react since his sentencing responsibilities give him the final say in every confrontation. Another possible explanation might be that after sitting on the bench for an extended period of time, a judge is no longer shocked by such conduct and almost expects it from repeat offenders.

Although the judge's control over his or her courtroom seems to establish a clearcut pecking order among the rest of the courtroom workgroup, there are frequent power struggles which even extend to challenging the authority of the judge. In a recent exchange of charges, the New York City Criminal Court Judicial Administrator and the city's probation department have publicly blamed each other for the related problems of error-filled probation reports and lengthy delays in their preparation.[3] In the subsequent sections of this chapter we will examine the other members of the courtroom workgroup and see how they fare in their continual power struggle with the judiciary and each other.

COURTROOM WORKGROUP

The Courtroom Staff

Aiding the judge in the day-to-day operations of his or her courtroom are a group of loyal associates. This team is headed by the calendar clerk who is responsible for moving the flow of cases and keeping track of important dates and decisions. Like many members of the judge's staff, a myth usually surrounds the power and influence which the clerk can exert over his boss. His imagined influence usually reaches its zenith during the first year or two following the judge's selection. The clerk is generally pictured as a critical socializing agent whose advice is eagerly sought by the novice judge. In a subsequent chapter, which describes this socializing process in greater detail, the myth about the clerk's inflated role will be punctured. A growing trend was discovered which revealed that many judges were better prepared for their criminal court positions, and were quickly adapting to their new professional responsibilities without the prolonged tutelage of their clerks.

Even though the calendar clerk may not be as influential a figure in molding the judge's behavior as once imagined, he frequently does enjoy a relatively close working relationship. Many judges have retained the same clerk for several years, although in recent years most cities assign a calendar clerk to a particular courtroom, and he will serve any judge who is sitting for the requisite period of time. When judges are able to select and retain their own calendar clerks, a warm relationship frequently develops. Because of the necessary case-by-case communication between judge and clerk in monitoring the docket, the two generally grow increasingly compatible.

Lawyers also appreciate the power of the calendar clerk, for he can decide, if he is so inclined, to manipulate the docket. As a result, a lawyer might have to wait two hours rather than two minutes before his case is called. Although some experienced lawyers with influence may go directly to the judge and request the favor of a speedy call, most attorneys restrict their efforts at obtaining favorable scheduling to lobbying the calendar clerk. In a few cities, private criminal lawyers admitted bestowing gifts upon calendar clerks in exchange for a favorable place on the docket. In most instances, the judge is either oblivious or turns his back on these low-level machinations. As a general rule, the calendar clerks attempt to strike a happy medium between being flexible enough to accommodate a justified request, and yet rigid enough to ensure a smooth flow of cases.

I was more impressed with the high level of performance by the calendar court clerks as a group than by any of the other courtroom personnel. Their accomplishments are even more noteworthy given the chaotic conditions in which they must keep track of an endless flow of complex paperwork. It was interesting to observe some mounting tension between the clerks in courtrooms responsible for pretrial proceedings which processed a never-ending flow of cases each day, and those who worked in the trial division who had relatively little to do, even during those rare occasions when a trial was in progress.

Nearly every judge also utilizes a law clerk whose responsibilities are much more varied and less clearly defined than those of the calendar clerk. The law clerk usually falls into one of two categories. One group of clerks are young, recent law school graduates who were selected because of either their political connections, law school accomplishments, or deep interest in criminal law. The other type was an older person who had been friendly with the judge for many years. The former group usually are given research and briefing responsibilities, aiding the judge in handing down decisions in motions court or during an actual trial. These young lawyers usually stay on for only a year or two before moving on to their own practices. The latter group, older law clerks, rarely engage in legal research, but perform a wide range of other duties ranging from that of messenger to representing the judge at social functions. In Philadelphia, with its many archaic customs, each judge is required to have a "tipstaff" who specializes in performing just the valet services, while young law graduates serve as law clerks.

Each judge is also furnished with a private secretary who performs all of the expected secretarial duties in addition to serving as a protector of the judge's privacy. Most secretaries feel it is their primary function to carefully screen all outsiders. The closeness of the relationship between the judge and his secretary depends heavily upon whether she had been with him for several years, often at his previous position or law firm, or is a civil service appointee of relatively short duration.

In order to maintain order in each courtroom, a judge is presented with a number of bailiffs. The size of this group varies greatly from city to city, although the typical courtroom has two or three. In New Orleans, where the bailiffs obtain their positions through political patronage, the courtrooms are filled with their less-than-imposing presence. Despite their colorful insignia-bedecked uniforms, their aged and misshapen bodies did not seem capable of dealing satisfactorily with crisis situations. In a few cities, budget cuts have reduced the number of bailiffs to the barest numbers and raised serious doubts as to their capability of providing adequate security.

Several court systems have recognized the importance of computers as an aid in dealing with their expanding caseloads. In addition to this mechanical marvel, some courts have also created the office of court administrator to help the judges battle their dockets and streamline their operations. Most judges are reluctant recipients of the technological expertise emanating from the court administrator's office, but are able to recognize the necessity for its utilization. The profession of court administrator flourished in the 1970s with several fine programs producing well-trained graduates. With current urban fiscal cutbacks and LEAA's demise, the newly-emerging profession may be struggling to sustain its existence.

The one judicial officer who is most likely to be interested in the court administrator's services is the presiding, or chief administrative judge of the local court system. His or her primary responsibilities are to keep the cases flowing in as efficient a manner as the administration of individual justice permits. The other functions of this chief judicial officer varies depending upon local tradition and preference but most perform the following tasks: (1) assign judges to various courts, (2) initiate disciplinary action against members of the bench, (3) act as spokespersons for bench to bar and general public, (4) preside over functions involving the bench, (5) serve as *ex officio* members of various committees within the court system, (6) decide administrative matters such as vacations and retirements of court members, and (7) plan and execute continuing education projects.[4]

This rather extensive list accurately implies that the presiding or chief administrative judge has a great amount of work. However, the criminal court judges are only occasionally bothered by his concerns, with the exception of his assignment responsibilities. Since some criminal proceedings are much more desirable than others, the individual judge's preferences and tempers frequently run high. If he or she is assigned to a court that is perceived as being either too boring or too fast-paced, the judge will soon desire a change. Because every judge has preferences for the types of proceedings he or she likes, the presiding judge, if he cares to promote harmony and reduce dissonance, will try as best he can to satisfy the varied tastes. Beyond annoyances over assignment problems, most judges only seem aware of the presiding judge when one of his decisions directly affects them. Although the title seems to infer added prestige, nearly all the judges appeared disinterested in being elevated to such lofty heights. Instead, they saw it as an escape from the real job of judges—dealing with criminal matters—into the world of administrative tedium.

Prosecutors

The prosecutor is considered by many analysts and observers of the criminal courts to be the key performer within the criminal justice system.[5] His powers are often in excess of the judges in terms of influencing both police and correctional officers. Adding confusion to the actual powers of this important member of the courtroom workgroup are the following idealistic expectations which the general public appears to hold: (1) that he will enforce all the laws without regard to political and personal considerations, (2) that he will be engaged in a spirited adversarial relationship with the defense attorney, (3) that any deals he makes with defendants during the plea bargaining process will be protective of the public's safety, (4) that he will follow the legal and professional requirements for discovery proceedings, and (5) that he and the police will work amicably in a coordinated effort to reduce crime. How accurately do these expectations reflect the reality of the prosecutor's job? The following series of observations can shed some light on how closely this idealized picture can be verified.

Most prosecutors are forced to be somewhat selective in their law enforcement activities because of political pressures and the pressures from a steadily increasing backlog of cases. The selection process involves deciding which cases are most serious and in need of prosecution, and which appear to present the least amount of potential danger to the community. Felonies, especially those involving physical injury or the loss of a sizable amount of personal property, are nearly always prosecuted. In deciding whether to prosecute less serious crimes, such as victimless crimes, prosecutors exercise their extensive discretionary powers.

Studies of the criminal justice system and my observations during the past 12 years seem to point toward a perceptible weakening of the adversary system.[5] Faced with the unrelenting pressures of an increasing backlog of cases, the prosecutor is placed in the position of desiring to negotiate the best possible deal with the defense attorney. Thus, instead of entering into an adversary relationship with the defense attorney in which the prosecutor seeks to protect the public's interest, he or she is willing to exchange a light sentence or a reduction of charges for a guilty plea.

From the local prosecutor to the United States Attorney General, there have been incidents involving abuses of prosecutorial powers because of political and personal considerations.[6] Among the more prominent examples of such misconduct are the dogged prosecution of Jimmy Hoffa by Attorney General Robert Kennedy, and FBI Director J. Edgar Hoover's harassment of Martin Luther King, Jr. Another example of the abuse of prosecutorial power is the growing tendency for prosecutors to manipulate the grand jury. Michael Tigar and Madeline Levy present a convincing picture of how some prosecutors are using grand juries "as the new inquisition."[7]

Finally, tension seems to be growing between the police and the prosecutors that is reducing the effectiveness of both groups as crimefighting institutions. The cause of the breakdown in this relationship may be related primarily to the police department's growing awareness that the central role in plea bargaining is played by the prosecutor, rather than the judge. Police also tend to feel that prosecutors are too politically oriented, and they will not take a case they might lose. The continual second guessing of police tactics by prosecutors and dismissals of what the police view as legal arrests have also contributed significantly to the erosion of the relationship. Many prosecutors believe that the police are poorly trained in gathering evidence that will stand up in court. The consequences of the hostility between police and prosecutor are difficult to evaluate because it is relatively recent; however, it will probably complicate the prosecutor's job in the future.

The discretionary power, central position and covert nature of the prosecutor's job provide him with a wide range of choices in the style in which he chooses to carry out his office. Wayne LaFave in his study of arrests, has classified these choices into four broad categories in which a prosecutor may act as (1) a trial counsel for the police, (2) house counsel for the police, (3) a representative of the court, or (4) a reflector of community opinion.[8] The choice among these approaches may, in turn, be affected by the role orientation the prosecutor brings to the position. He or she may have selected a representational role, emphasizing a concern for upholding community values and expressing an interest in maintaining positive community relations. The purposive role is based upon what the prosecutor construes to be the major goals of his office, such as restoring public confidence following a scandal, keeping the streets safe, protecting businesses, or curbing a serious community drug problem. Or the prosecutor's career orientation might determine his role behavior. If the office is his final career goal (as in the case of Frank Hogan of New York City), the prosecutor will seek to remain the city's chief crime fighter for the rest of his professional life. However, if the prosecutor looks upon the position as merely a stepping stone to higher political office, then his behavior will be focused toward achieving a high conviction rate and public acceptance of his policies.

Because the power of the prosecutor is enhanced by vaguely defined guidelines, lack of supervision, and strategic location, he probably has more choice in determining his behavior pattern than any other public official within the criminal justice system. His discretionary power is at its zenith during the pretrial stages of a case. Acting as a quasi-judicial officer, the prosecutor evaluates each case to decide whether to charge a defendant with a specific crime. Among the alternatives available are: dismissal of the charges, reduction of charges (possibly from a felony to a misdemeanor), reduction of the number of counts in the indictment (i.e., of the number of crimes of which the defendant is accused), referral of the case to other government agencies, either law enforcement or social (as in the case of defendants who are thought to be mentally unstable, alchoholics, or drug addicts), or simply proceeding with the prosecution of the original charge. After a charge has been made, the prosecutor may reduce it in exchange for a guilty plea.

In selecting among these alternatives, the prosecutor is acting not only under ambiguous guidelines, but also unilaterally—i.e., neither the judge, the police, nor any other public official has the authority to directly modify or reverse the prosecutor's choice. That the police are unable to affect these charging decisions is the major source of friction between them and the prosecutor's office. The police are directly affected by these decisions and are frustrated by their finality.

What are the factors that appear to influence the charging decision? George Cole, in an exhaustive study of prosecutors, concluded that there are three types of considerations that affect the decision to prosecute: evidential, pragmatic, and organizational.[9] The evidential element refers to whether there is sufficient evidence to arrest an individual for a specific crime. It is also related to the fact that the evidence must be of the type that can be successfully presented in a criminal trial. Pragmatic considerations, which stem from the prosecutor's joint responsibility both to the accused and to society, require the prosecutor to evaluate the factors such as the character of the defendants and complainants, the effect of the case upon the families of all the parties involved as well as on the community as a whole, and the mental and physical welfare of all parties. Organizational considerations refer to the internal pressures that the institutions of the criminal justice system exert upon the prosecutor. The most obvious example of an organizational consideration is the backlog of cases that are tying up nearly every urban court system. In attempting to deal with this logjam, the prosecutor is affected by the office's institutional resources, by pressures exerted by the police and judiciary as well as by political and community demands.

In view of the great discretionary power available to the prosecuting attorney, and the variety of considerations that may influence each charging decision, it is easy to see why so great a difference exists between the operation and disposition of various prosecutor's offices as they make charging decisions. A study by McIntyre and Lippman made for the American Bar Association illustrates the variation in the disposition of criminal cases.

Table 2 graphically summarizes the findings of this six-city survey (Chicago, Los Angeles, Brooklyn, Detroit, Baltimore, and Houston). Although a similarity exists among the six cities studied at the input (arrests) and output (sentences) stages, all systems have a considerable "dropout" of cases early in the criminal process. The manner of reaching the decisions varies greatly in terms of who makes them, the criteria that are used, and the time required.[10] These researchers also found that 50-80 percent of the felony cases initiated by police arrest went no further than the prosecutor's office and somehow vanished during the pretrial arraignment, preliminary hearing, or grand jury action.[11]

A recent addition to the prosecutor's arsenal of alternatives in connection with the charging decision is *pretraial diversion*. *Pretrial diversion* programs permit the prosecutor to select certain good-risk defendants (those whose youth or lack of previous involvement with the law may indicate they might be able to be rehabilitated) who, following their arrest, but prior to their preliminary hearings, will be temporarily removed from the criminal justice system. If they complete the diversion program without committing any further crimes, the charges are dropped and their criminal court records are destroyed. The prosecutor may attach certain conditions to the pretrial diversion program such as a return to school or an entrance into a vocational training program. Deferred prosecution programs, which now number 150 projects in 37 states are the most widely used means of pretrial diversion.[12]

The role of the prosecutor in the judge's bail-setting decision has been deemphasized and is rarely publicized, but I found in my research, that 70 percent of the public officials surveyed believed that the prosecutor played a significant role in determining the amount of the bond in their court system.[13]

The prosecutor can effectively use his charging decision to control the size of the defendant's bond. Because the amount of the bond is related to

TABLE 2 Major Dispositional Points in Felony Cases

	Cook County (Chicago) Population 5,500,000	Los Angeles County Population 7,200,000	Kings County (Brooklyn) Population 2,600,000	City of Detroit Population 1,700,000	City of Baltimore Population 980,000	Harris County (Houston) Population 1,800,000
Number of felony arrests	22,000	69,000	15,000	20,000	8,000	16,000
Police screening	In all jurisdictions studied there were no records kept on the number of releases or "dropped charges" at the police level. Unofficial estimates from police officials, however, indicate there is relatively little screening of felony cases after arrest; estimates ranged from 1% to 2% in Chicago to around 10% in Baltimore and New York.					
Prosecutor screening	Only in major cases, business frauds & white collar crimes.	Extensive screening; approx. 50% of cases are rejected.	Only in major cases or highly publicized ones.	All cases are reviewed; approx. 30% are rejected.	Only in major cases or highly publicized ones.	Review at examining trial (preliminary hearing) reduces caseloads 25%.
Preliminary hearing	Major dispositions point; approx. 80% of cases receive final disposition.	10% dropout; hearing is formal & designed to produce transcript for later trial.	Major dispositions point; approx. 65% of cases receive final disposition.	Majority of defendants waive preliminary hearing.	Little screening; no records available; prosecutor usually not present.	25% of cases screened out (see above).
Grand jury	Approves virtually all of prosecutor recommendations.	Less than 1% of cases are referred to G.J. (information used).	Rejects about 5% of cases, mostly on recommendation of D.A.	None (information used).	Approx. 3% of cases are rejected.	Approx. 10% of cases are rejected.
Indictments or informations	5,000	21,400	3,000	9,000	6,500	7,000
Guilty pleas	2,300 Conference with judge & prosecutor available on request.	9,400 Little judicial participation in bargaining.	2,500 Mandatorily referred to "conference & discussion" court before docketing.	4,800 Mandatory pretrial conference without judicial participation	900 No practice of encouraging plea.	5,500 Heavy emphasis on plea negotiations between prosecutor & defense.
Dismissals and nolles	1,300 Mostly superfluous charges.	1,500	200	3,500 Mostly superfluous charges.	1,300	400
Contested nonjury	600	9,500 Majority are adjudicated on transcript of preliminary hearing.	100	600	5,000 Juries are traditionally waived.	60
Contested jury	300	900	200	300	125	300

Source: Donald M. McIntyre and David Lippman, "Prosecutors and Early Disposition of Felony Cases," *ABA Journal*, 56 (1970), 1156.

the seriousness of the charge, the prosecutor can influence the judge's bail-setting decision by raising the charge against the defendant. The prosecutor also has the advantage of being in control of any data on the defendant that is supplied to the judge. Even more than the police, the prosecutor is able to indicate to the judge the strength of the state's case against the defendant. This information has a decided influence on the judge's evaluation of the defendant's probable guilt or innocence, because judges frequently believe that guilty defendants are more likely to attempt to avoid prosecution by fleeing. The prosecutor, too, plays an important role in the subsequent judicial hearings that review the amount of the bond, as his main function at these hearings is to counter the defense attorney's argument for lowering bond.

Fred Suffet, who observed nearly 1500 cases in the New York Criminal Court, produced the most complete examination of the relative degree of influence exerted by the prosecutor during bail setting. He found that the judge and the prosecutor were consistently found to carry a great deal of weight and to strongly influence the judge's final bail-setting decision.[14]

A 1972 national survey of bail practices which I completed for the U.S. Justice Department disclosed that the Philadelphia district attorney's office, then headed by Arlen Spector, was most influential in affecting the setting of bail. In Philadelphia, an assistant district attorney is always at the preliminary arraignment court where bail is initially determined. This attorney makes recommendations as to the amount of bail, and most judges were noted to follow this suggestion. For such serious offenses as burglary, robbery, arson, rape and murder the judge cannot set bail without the consent of the district attorney's office and cannot set bail lower than that recommended by the prosecutor's office.[15]

Prosecutors also have a number of bail-related functions. In Atlanta, the district attorney is in charge of supervising the city's bondsmen and is responsible for collecting all surety-bond forfeitures. Bail is used in many cities by the prosecutor as part of the arsenal of coercive devices designed to convince the defendant to plead guilty. In Indianapolis, a prosecutor can recommend to the judge that the period of pretrial incarceration be subtracted from the length of the sentence if the defendant is willing to plead guilty, and the judge usually follows this recommendation.[16]

The prosecutor must convince the judge, during a preliminary hearing, that there is sufficient evidence of probable cause against the defendant to bind him or her over for indictment. The indictment traditionally has been conducted by a grand jury, but in recent years, several jurisdictions have attempted to bypass this sometimes cumbersome procedure by simply having the judge alone review the case and then issue *an information*—the functional equivalent of a grand jury indictment. Whether a system uses a grand jury indictment or an information, it is the prosecutor who must convince the responsible decision-making body that sufficient evidence exists.

In most states, grand juries are initiators of the criminal justice process. Before there is any police action, the prosecutor appears before a grand jury and attempts to convince it that sufficient evidence exists to warrant the issuance of an indictment charging accused individuals with a crime and ordering their arrests. Cases based on grand jury indictments usually involve complex or highly charged offenses, such as organized or white-collar crime. Most prosecutors will only send controversial cases to the grand jury.

In addition to prosecutors' broad discretionary powers inherent in the charging decision, their role in plea bargaining negotiations offers them an equally important chance to affect the administration of justice. Since prosecutors are generally conceded to be the central figures in plea bargaining, they are able to maintain a considerable amount of maneuverability. For example, the prosecutor may "overcharge" defendants with a serious crime and thereby initiate the proceedings at a very high level—a crude form of blackmail. By charging the defendant with a number of counts related to the same offense, the prosecutor is able to negotiate not only for reduced charges but also for additional crimes the defendant may have committed. An indirect consequences of this control of the charging power is the leverage it provides the prosecutor; charges can be made that are serious enough to warrant bail that will exceed the defendant's fiscal capacity. Having caused the defendant to await trial in a detention facility, the prosecutor is then able to exert a great amount of pressure upon the offender who wants to extricate himself as quickly as possible from pretrial detention.

Albert Alschuler identified certain major prosecutorial roles associated with plea negotiation. He found that a prosecutor may be acting in any or all of these roles:

1. As an *administrator*, with the goal of disposing of each case in the quickest, most efficient manner;
2. As an *advocate* with the goal of maximizing both the number of convictions and the severity of the sentences that are imposed after conviction.
3. As a *judge* attempting to do the best he can for the defendant in view of the defendant's social circumstances, or the peculiar circumstance of the crime—with the qualification that the best will not be possible unless the defendant pleads guilty.
4. As a *legislator* granting concessions because he believes the law is too harsh when it is applied to all defendants.[17]

As a result of interviews with a broad sample of prosecutors, Alschuler concluded that most of them disavowed the legislative role and few thought the judicial role useful. Most agreed, however, that the first two roles, those concerned with administrative expediency, were basic.[18]

Some of the additional factors which influence the prosecutor's success in plea bargaining involve his relationship with the judge and defense attorney. If a prosecutor is owed favors because of leniency in prior cases, he has the advantage during the plea bargaining process. The willingness of the judge to engage in plea bargaining, and to accede to prosecution recommendations must also be considered. Past experience with both the defense attorney and the judge will usually offer the prosecutor some dependable clues for future negotiations. Political considerations, such as the amount of public exposure, the sensationalism surrounding a case, or the pressures exerted from the mayor's office or chief prosecutor's office can also influence plea bargaining.

However, the fact that many jurisdictions are now forcing prosecutors to share with the defense counsel increasing amounts of information about a case has decreased somewhat the prosecutor's power over the plea bargaining process. Allowing both defense and prosecution to understand the relative strengths of their respective arguments means both sides will have access to more complete data, and the defendant's decision on whether to go to trial can be made more intelligently.

If a defendant does not choose to plead guilty and decides to go to trial, the prosecutor is responsible for arguing the state's case and attempting to convince the judge and/or jury of the defendant's guilt "beyond a reasonable doubt." A prosecutor must make extensive pretrial preparation when forced to try a case. This usually includes an intelligent voir dire examination of jurors, careful examination of witnesses, and the acquisition of thorough familiarity with the strengths and weaknesses of his adversary's case. During the trial itself, the prosecutor is called upon to offer a strong and persuasive opening statement, a skillful presentation of his witnesses, effective cross-examination of defense witnesses, and forceful closing argument. National figures place the prosecutor's conviction rate at about 60 percent in trials. This is not disappointing, considering that most defendants will risk a jury trial only if their attorneys believe they have a very good chance of being acquitted. Most prosecutors' offices reserve the trial role for the experienced members of the staff who have been involved in prior litigation.[19]

Because of the prosecutor's dominant role in settlements arrived at through plea bargaining, it is not surprising to find him or her a major figure in the sentencing decision.[20] Prosecutors justify their involvement with the sentencing decision by virtue of their role as representatives of the victim and of society. In a survey of district attorney offices throughout the nation, William Teiterbaum found that most prosecutors take an active part in sentencing, and they firmly believe that their participation is beneficial to the effectiveness of the criminal justice system. Three-quarters of the prosecutors surveyed stated they participated in the sentencing decision, either by presenting arguments concerning the crime and the defendant's criminal history, or by expressing a position on the desirability of probation or recommending a specific sentence. Teiterbaum found a degree of collaboration between the prosecutors and the probation officers, as they usually endorse each others' recommendations. This was found to mean that the judge usually follows the prosecutor's recommendation all the time (48 percent of the respondents), or most of the time (42 percent of the respondents).[21]

Prosecutors, especially those who come to the job with specific personal motives or political aspirations, are dependent upon public opinion. Public opinion is usually interpreted first by the local politicians, who in turn, transmit their responses to the court system, and the prosecutor's office. Since most prosecutors are elected, they receive periodic feedback on how effectively they have been interpreting messages from the community. With crime in the streets continuing to be an issue of considerable public concern, prosecutors necessarily will remain attuned to public sentiment. Despite the central role played by the prosecutor in the administration of justice, this actor's reputation and performance appear to be hampered by two interrelated problems—politics and professionalism.

When examining the relationship between politics and prosecutorial behavior, one must first realize that in nearly every state in the nation, the district attorney is a locally elected official. George Cole has analyzed the role of political partisanship in prosecutorial behavior, and carefully studied the various ways in which politics can enhance the district attorney's status, especially if personal advancement can be linked with political expedience. He writes:

> The appointment and utilization of deputies may serve the party's desire for new blood and the prosecutor's need for young lawyers. Also, the prosecutor may press charges in ways that enhance his own and his party's objectives. Of greater significance is the fact that certain groups and persons may not receive equal justice because of the prosecutor's determination.[22]

As previously mentioned, there is great variation among prosecutors' offices as to the degree of influence exerted by politics upon job performance. Studies in New Orleans and other cities have shown that the political potential of a prosecutor's office may depend upon the community's willingness to tolerate politics in its criminal justice system.[23] In a comprehensive review of prosecutorial behavior, McIntyre and Lippman also found great regional variations. They believe that the nature of the office differs for as many reasons as cities themselves differ—growth rates, minority problems, economic conditions, and the presence of obtrusive political influence.[24]

When politics affects the selection and operation of prosecutorial offices, there are both advantages and disadvantages. The major advantages are that (1) election often means that public officials are responsive to citizen demands (unlike the insulated civil servant who is statutorally protected from public pressure), and (2) given the regularity of elections, there is a chance for new blood and an opportunity for reforming a stagnant and lethargic operation.

On the negative side, the President's 1967 Task Force Report on the Courts offered these comments:

1. The high political orientation was found to be related to problems of low pay and part-time service as well as rather transient status (high turnover rates).
2. With assistant prosecutors also being selected primarily on the basis of party affiliation, many highly qualified practitioners and recent law school graduates would be discouraged from or unwilling to obtain the requisite political backing.
3. Political considerations may potentially force some prosecutors into basing their decisions on political expediencies and personal ambition rather than on the public's best interest.[25]

The Task Force Report suggested several reforms for correcting the problems that result from political influence, such as using civil service procedures for the hiring of assistant prosecutors, thereby freeing them from all political obligations, and urging political leaders to raise their sights in selecting candidates—that is, to choose professional, competent and long-term candidates for the job.[26] More than a decade has passed since the task force issued its report, and few noticeable changes have resulted.

In addressing the issue of the lack of professionalism for the office of the prosecutor, the National Advisory Commission on Criminal Justice Standards and Goals stated:

> The personnel, policies, size, and organization of many prosecutors' offices do not promote an effective response to the complex demands of the criminal justice system. It is believed that the office of the prosecutor should be on the same level of professionalism as private law firms of comparable size.[27]

The rapid turnover of assistant prosecutors resulting from lack of professionalism is a serious problem. Recruits are typically hired fresh out of law school and leave within two to three years after acquiring some trial experience, seeking higher pay, prestige, and security. A case study by R.H. Kuh of the New York City prosecutor's office in 1961 illustrates this typical turnover rate in one of the nation's most respected offices. Of 85 assistants, 23 had been there more than 10 years, but 56 had been there for less than five years, and 12–15 departed annually. Kuh concluded that the public is the real loser since it is faced with an inexperienced prosecutor's office operating as an internship program. As soon as the assistants learn how to conduct investigations and trials competently, they are off to better jobs.[28]

Fortunately, new developments in the prosecutor's offices have resulted in a decline in this transiency. Better pay as well as a scarcity of opportunity "on the outside" have contributed to stabilizing and improving the operation of prosecutors' offices, thereby creating an increasing pool of competent and experienced attorneys. Although there are many examples of successful former prosecutors moving into the political spotlight (Henry Jackson, Sam Ervin, Earl Warren to name just a handful), there are also many local prosecutors who decide to make a professional career of the office.

Prosecutors, like other members of the courtroom workgroup, are receiving more entry-level and in-house training than in the past, and this may also improve their levels of performance. New employees in prosecutors' offices usually need systematic training in office policies and procedures, on relationships with the courts and police, and on such issues as the exercise of discretion in screening or charging of defendants. The agency itself, or a state prosecutor-training program, typically conducts the training.

Public Defenders

Since nearly two-thirds of all defendants accused of committing a felony are indigent, the state is constitutionally obligated to provide the overwhelming majority of defendants with assistance of counsel. In nearly every city visited, the local courts decided to establish a public defender program in order to meet this mandate. For the remaining defendants, they will select a private criminal lawyer of their choice. This unique professional dilemma will be examined in detail in the next chapter.

The two alternatives to the public defender plan, for indigent defendants, are either to rely entirely upon an assigned counsel system—privately-appointed members of the bar who are typically paid on a per hour basis—or a mixed system in which the courts have decided to limit the percentage of cases which the local public defender can handle, and reserve the sizable remainder for private attorneys through an assigned counsel system. Large cities rarely find the assigned counsel system cost-effective (although it is most popular in small cities and rural areas). Houston, Texas was the only city I visited which relied completely upon its usage. Washington, D.C. and Detroit, Michigan were the only cities visited which used the mixed system in which both offices were limited to approximately 20 percent of the indigent caseload.[29]

In most cities, the defendant first notifies the judge of his indigent status and desire to have a court-appointed lawyer at his initial appearance. It is at this brief hearing that bail will be fixed and the date for a preliminary hearing set. The judge rarely inquires into the financial capabilities of the defendant in an effort to determine if he satisfies the court's definition of indigency. Most judges seem to feel that if a defendant is willing to settle for a public defender, then he is not likely to be in possession of the funds necessary to hire a private attorney. Rarely is a representative from the public defender's office present at this initial appearance, except in an administrative capacity to commence the paperwork.

Shortly after the defendant's initial appearance, and prior to his preliminary hearing (which is usually set in one week to 10 days), the defendant will meet with a representative from the public defender's office. If the defendant is released on bail (which is unlikely in a felony case if the defendant is actually indigent), he must travel to the public defender's office to speak with the representative from that office reviewing the case. When the defendant is unable to post bail and is detained in jail, the public defender's office will send someone to interview him at the jail.

Two of the major frustrations facing the indigent defendant who is being represented by a public defender are apparent very early in the process. The first, and for many defendants, the most disheartening, is the absence of choice of attorney. From his initial contact with the publc defender's office, the defendant is forced to deal with whomever the office has selected. In only the most unusual instances, when a severe personality clash appears so blatant as to impair the defense effort, will the public defender's office be willing to assign a new attorney.

The second frustration, exacerbating the already noted absence of choice, is the assembly-line system of defense in which the indigent defendant may be assisted by a different attorney at nearly every stage of the proceedings up to the arraignment. This means that the indigent will briefly meet with three or four different public defenders for a few minutes before each of his pretrial proceedings. It is also likely that interviews and meetings outside of court may be with an assortment of different public defenders. The feeling of being passed along like a sausage link through the criminal court system, has much to do with the indigent defendant's lack of confidence in the quality of his own defense, as well as his bitter feelings toward the system's seemingly insensitive treatment of his case.

For many defendants, the assembly-line style of operation is another indication that the public defender's office is simply an uncaring bureaucracy which is both financially and emotionally subservient to the criminal court judiciary. I found most defendants believing that public defendant offices were not viable adversaries in comparison with the private criminal lawyers. As Jonathan Casper discovered in his research on the perceptions of the criminal courts held by defendants, the public defender and prosecutor were both thought to be bureaucratic organizations under the thumb of the judiciary, and easily manipulated by public opinion and political pressure.[30] Given the high percentage of defendants found guilty, the public defenders prove ready scapegoats for the unhappy conclusion to their criminal court experience. It seems only natural that public defenders would receive blame; however, the degree of bitterness and frustration directed toward this institution by their indigent clientele exceeds even reasonable expectations.

Does the bureaucratic style of the public defender office seriously undermine the quality of their services? Although I am sure that their clientele would vociferously disagree, I do not believe that the quality of public defender services has suffered. After conducting national studies of both public defender programs and private criminal lawyers, I am in agreement with the findings of nearly all of the empirical research which concluded that the ultimate case dispositions are not significantly affected by the type of defense.[31] I still concur with personal conclusions reached in 1978 that "although the middle 50 percent of public defenders and private attorneys were operating at similar levels of ability and achieving nearly identical results, there were marked differences at the extremes. Thus it was generally agreed by the criminal lawyers that the top 25 percent of private attorneys were clearly superior to the best public defenders, while the bottom 25 percent of the public defenders were believed to be significantly better than the bottom group of private attorneys."[32]

It must be remembered, however, that perceived legal expertise is only one component of the defendant's evaluation formula. He is also greatly concerned with the loss of his freedom of choice as well as the absence of a direct and sustained personal relationship with his attorney. Despite the absence of these "psychological benefits" the public defender office may even offer some distinct advantages unavailable to certain private practitioners. Most public defenders have access to their own law libraries, as well as limited use of investigators. Additionally, the public defender is clearly a criminal law specialist. Finally, because of his continual involvement with the prosecutors and judiciary, the public defender can frequently develop a positive working relationship in which the exchange of favors, so necessary to greasing the squeaky wheel of justice, can directly benefit the indigent defendant.

On the negative side, it does appear that the public defender's office is plagued by a serious morale problem. Often described as a "burn-out" factor—young attorneys may lose their zeal for justice after a short period of time. Forever dealing with bitter, ungrateful clients, rarely experiencing a courtroom victory, seeing their professional colleagues on the outside earning more money, the public defenders soon become dispirited and eager to abandon the program. In the past, the trial experience gained by the young public defender made him or her easily marketable and permitted an assured transition into private practice. Unfortunately, the past few years have seen the legal marketplace become overcrowded with unemployed attorneys. This has meant that the public defender may become trapped in his job, unable to find a new position; few private firms are able, or willing to match the public defender's salary. The result of this freeze on mobility appears to be an increasing number of public defenders who are stuck in their positions with little prospect for the immediate future. The detrimental effect of such a development upon the spirit of the public defender's program is obvious, and its implications for the quality of legal services potentially disastrous.

The Defendants

One of the troublesome aspects of visiting a criminal courthouse is that it soon becomes apparent that it is impossible to detect the appearance of a typical defendant. As the various defendants appear before the judge, they are indistinguishable from most other city inhabitants from the same community. It is true that the court's clientele is disproportionately young and poor, but beyond these broad clues, there are no physical indicators distinguishing the victims from the defendants.

Aside from being young and poor, the typical defendant appearing before a felony court is likely to have prior experience with the criminal law. It is continually amazing to me how defendants so young have compiled so exhaustive a record of anti-social behavior in so short a period of time. With so many diversion programs designed to help the first offender, and the caseload pressures facing the courts, only first-time offenders accused of a very serious crime are likely to reach the felony courtroom. The average felon can be best categorized as falling into one of three groups: (1) violent sociopaths who present a serious threat to society, (2) recidivists who cannot seem to fit into society, but do not present a threat in terms of physical violence, and (3) the isolated case of an individual acting out of a unique set of circumstances which has triggered his criminal behavior.

The first group seems in need of psychological aid in order to curb sociopathic tendencies, while the latter group needs career counseling and other forms of vocational and educational rehabilitation. The second group does seem to have the potential for being capable of rehabilitation, but this category also contains a high percentage of professional criminals who believe that arrest and incarceration are simply occupational hazards.[33] These include professional safecrackers, burglars, and receivers of stolen property. They have selected criminal activity because of its perceived lucrative returns and are not generally very good candidates for rehabilitation.

The third category is a highly diverse group. It contains a large number of middle class, white-collar criminals who occasionally fall within the jurisdiction of the urban courts but are nuch more likely to be found in the federal district court. These defendants are commonly involved in major drug cases or complex economic crimes such as fraud, bribery, or extortion.

EXTERNAL FACTORS

The various personnel comprising the courtroom workgroup combine to produce a combination of internal factors exerting a tremendous influence upon the style and quality of urban justice. Nevertheless, there are several external factors which can also have a significant impact upon the operations of the criminal courts. Among these external factors to be briefly considered are the mass media, politicians, community groups and the appellate courts.

The local newspapers and television stations can play an important role in determining the level of isolation felt by the local court system. In cities like Philadelphia or New York, the criminal courts are constantly aware that their miscues and unpopular decisions may soon be tomorrow's headlines. Given such coverage, combined with the likelihood that the judges are popularly elected, it is not unexpected that the court may act cautiously. The direct effect of such apprehension, in this period of heightened civic concern over rising crime, may be severe sentences and closer control over plea negotiations. In other cities where the media is less interested in the criminal courts, (such as Miami and New Orleans), the judges can confidently make their critical decisions without constantly looking over their shoulders.

Closely related to concerns over media exposure is the amount of interest and pressure generated by local politicians toward the criminal courts. Again, this can affect the sense of remoteness and independence the criminal courts find desirable. This issue will be discussed in greater detail in the next chapter under the topic of *judicial selection*. For now, it need only be pointed out that certain cities such as Chicago and Philadelphia consider the criminal courts an integral part of the local political scene and therefore subject to the same scrutiny and obligations as any other facet of their political power struggle. Occasionally, a member of the local judiciary will be identified with a particular faction of one of the city's political parties such as former Chief Judge Boyle with Richard Daley's Democratic machine in Chicago. Most judges, however, shy away from such identification, realizing the negative effect that it is likely to have upon the independence and legitimacy of the local criminal courts.

As crime remains an increasingly salient issue for the big cities during the 1980s, citizen concern with the criminal courts is expected to be sustained.

This heightened interest has manifested itself in the growth of citizen groups attempting to draw attention to the unique problems of some specific group of victims, or the more general concerns of a particular neighborhood. Included in the former group are national, state, and local groups interested in the problems of elderly crime victims, victims of child abuse, victims of drunk drivers, victims of spouse beatings, and victims of rapists. All of these groups are constantly lobbying the courts and legislatures for preferential treatment. This often means having the local courts and law enforcement officers elevate their particular problem to a higher level of priority, or some form of special treatment. Some groups have even gone so far as to hire public relation firms to better publicize the seriousness of their plights.

Community groups have always been able to exert electoral pressure on ward and city-wide leaders but recently they have been effective in forming "neighborhood watch" programs designed to monitor their local areas for suspicious characters. On occasion, when a community group has become especially outraged by an apparent threat to their neighborhood's safety, they mount a frontal attack upon the city's judiciary. This frequently means organized court-watching groups which sit in on cases involving community victims. These groups hope to serve as visible reminders to the sitting judge that the community is very concerned with the disposition of particular cases. Their desire for swift, certain, and severe treatment of the offender are easily noted by both the judge and any attending media personnel.

Professionally, some felony court judges are most concerned with how the state and federal appellate courts are going to view their decisions. Several judges interviewed were cavalier in their disregard for how the appellate division might react to their initial rulings, but the majority of judges viewed these higher courts as a necessary limiting factor on their behavior. Although the trial judges did not have to fear appellate decisions, they nevertheless realized that they had to be aware of recent higher court decisions and had to accede to current constitutional directives.

NOTES

1. Erving Goffman. *Encounters: Two Studies in the Sociology of Interaction.* Indianapolis, Bobbs Merrill, 1961.
2. Pasqual DeVito. An Experiment in the Use of Court Statistics, *Judicature.* 56 (August/September 1972), 56.
3. Barbara Basler. "Justice Aides in Dispute Over Lag in Sentencing," *New York Times.* October 10, 1981, p. II, 1.
4. H. Ted Rubin. *The Courts.* Pacific Palisades, Goodyear Publishing Co., 1976, pp. 187–198.
5. Among those respected social scientists whose work on prosecutors has supported this conclusion have been George Cole, Abraham Blumberg, and Joan Jacoby.

6. Prosecutorial Vindictiveness, *Vanderbilt Law Review* 34 (March, 1981), 431–60.
7. Michael Tigar and Madeline Levy. The Grand Jury as the New Inquisition, *Michigan State Bar Journal.* (November, 1971).
8. Wayne LaFave. *Arrest.* Boston, Little Brown and Co., 1965, p. 215.
9. George Cole. *The American System of Criminal Justice.* North Scituate, Mass.: Duxbury Press, 1979, pp. 272–74.
10. Donald McIntyre and David Lippman. Prosecutors and Early Dispositions in Felony Cases, *American Bar Association Journal* 56 (1970) 1154.
11. Ibid. p. 1156.
12. Clemens Bartollas. *Introduction to Corrections.* New York, Harper & Row, 1981, p. 137.
13. Paul B. Wice. Bail Reform in American Cities, *Criminal Law Bulletin* 9 (November, 1973), p. 770.
14. Frederic Suffet. Bail Setting: A Study of Interaction, *Crime and Delinquency* 12: (October, 1966) 318.
15. Paul Wice. *Freedom for Sale.* Lexington, Mass.: Lexington Books, 1974, p. 47.
16. Ibid. p. 48.
17. Adapted from Albert Alschuler. The Prosecutor's Role in Plea Bargaining, *University of Chicago Law Review* 36:50 (1968).
18. Ibid.
19. For a more detailed account of the prosecutor's trial role, see James Mills. *The Prosecutor* New York, Farrar, Straus, and Giroux, 1969.
20. George Freeman, Jr. and Anthony F. Earley, Jr. *U.S.* v. *Di Francesca*: Government Appeal of Sentences, *American Criminal Law Review* 18 (Summer, 1980), p. 81.
21. William J. Teiterbaum. Prosecutor's Role in the Sentencing Process: A National Survey, *American Journal of Criminal Law* 1 (February, 1972), p. 75.
22. George Cole, op. cit. pp. 245–46.
23. The Herbert Jacob study of New Orleans, which appeared in the Tulane Studies Series, presents the most credible empirical statement verifying this theme. Roberson's *Rough Justice*, and Klonoski and Mendelsohn's *Politics of Local Justice* also deals with this issue.
24. Donald McIntrye and David Lippman. Prosecutors and Early Disposition of Felony Cases. *American Bar Association Journal* 56 (1970), p. 1156.
25. President's Commission on Law Enforcement and the Administration of Justice. *Task Force Report: The Courts.* Washington, D.C.: Government Printing Office, 1967, p. 73.
26. Ibid. p. 74.
27. The National Advisory Commission on Criminal Justice Standards and Goals. *Courts.* Washington, D.C.: Government Printing Office, 1973, p. 222.
28. R.H. Kuh. Careers in Prosecution Offices, *Journal of Legal Education* 14 (December, 1961), p. 175.
29. The public defender for the District of Columbia, which also has responsibility for selecting the assigned counsel, has been accused of keeping the most interesting cases for their own attorneys.
30. Jonathan Casper. *American Criminal Justice: From the Defendant's Perspective.* Englewood Cliffs, N.J.: Prentice-Hall Spectrum Books, 1972.
31. Jean Taylor et al. An Analysis of Defense Counsel in the Processing of Felony Defendants in San Diego, *Denver Law Journal* (1972), p. 233.
32. Paul Wice. *Criminal Lawyers: An Endangered Species.* Beverly Hills, Sage Publications, 1978, p. 201.
33. A West Coast criminal lawyer recognizing the two main groups thought that the principal job of the criminal courts was to separate these two groups and treat them accordingly. He used the rather crass terminology in referring to them as "bad asses and fuck-ups."

3

THE PRIVATE CRIMINAL LAWYER

Although the private criminal lawyer can be an integral part of the courtroom workgroup, his independent status warrants separate treatment in this volume. In contrast to judges, public defenders, prosecutors and miscellaneous courtroom personnel, the private criminal defense counsel is not paid from public funds nor housed in public facilities. He is in business for himself, commonly a solo practitioner, or a member of a small two or three person association. His offices are located distinctly apart from the criminal courthouse, typically in an office building where he shares the legal facilities with other attorneys. It should also be noted that most private criminal lawyers think of themselves first as trial lawyers who happen to be willing to accept criminal cases. In my national survey of criminal lawyers, it was found that these private practitioners usually devoted between 25–40 percent of their practice to criminal matters, reserving the majority of their time for civil matters such as negligence and divorce litigation. These are areas of the law which were described by the criminal lawyers as being less interesting but more lucrative than criminal work.[1]

Because private criminal lawyers cannot rely upon a regular salary from the public coffers, they are forced to compete against each other for the dwindling number of available clients who are able to afford their services. The major theme of my book, *Criminal Lawyers,* reflects the consequences of this intense competition for a rapidly declining market referring to them as an "endangered species." In most cities visited, there are presently half the number of private criminal lawyers as compared to 1960. Clearly the *Gideon* and *Argersinger*[2] decisions, which provide counsel to indigents in all misdemeanor and felony cases, have had a momentous impact upon their profession.

A final rationale for treating private criminal lawyers separately is related to the great amount of information collected on these beleaguered practitioners during my years as a U.S. Justice Department Visiting Fellow (1976–77), as well as my continued interest in their plight during the past five years. Through my position as a member of the American Bar Association's Committee on the Economics of Criminal Law since 1979, I have been able to maintain a close association with their struggle for survival. It will be the major focus of this chapter to examine what has transpired during the past five years to affect the professional life of this important member of the courtroom workgroup. Special attention will also be paid to the unique relationship between criminal court judges and private defense counsel. Let us now examine this "endangered species" in January of 1982 as they are about to hear a news item that will depress their spirits even more.

On Tuesday, January 12, 1982, attorney Donald Wolff of St. Louis heard disappointing news. The United States Supreme Court had denied his appeal in a case challenging the right of the State of Missouri to compel him to defend a criminal suspect without pay.[3] The decision seems to mark a low point for the private criminal lawyer.

THEIR IMPORTANCE

Before proceeding to an examination of what has occurred during the past five years, I would like to address an important issue that was omitted from the original study of private criminal lawyers, and upon reconsideration, needs to be presented. I refer to the basic question of why it is important to maintain the existence of the private criminal lawyer. If he is an "endangered species" as was indicated in the book, of what significance is his continued existence? In order to assess the correctness of the assumption that the private criminal lawyer's extinction is an undesirable development, let us examine the impact which his or her decline may have upon the criminal justice system, the entire legal profession, and ultimately the general public.

Turning first to the criminal justice system, what difference does it really make whether a defendant has a public or private counsel? Recent studies indicate that little variation in ultimate case disposition can be associated with the type of defense.[4] Nevertheless, it is the private attorney's independence from the state which places him in sharp contrast to all other actors in the system, *including* the public defender, and makes his continued existence essential to the viability of this nation's criminal justice system. The judiciary, the prosecutors, and the public defenders all receive salaries from the same public treasury. Although there have been only rare instances where this joint funding has caused certain coercive measures against any of the actors, the potential is still present, and very real. Considering that the defendant's future freedom is placed in the hands of these public figures, it is rather frightening to realize that the very same institution which is attempting to convict the defendant is also paying the salaries of the men who are theoretically doing their utmost to refute these charges and win an acquittal. The obvious question in the minds of many disillusioned individuals convicted of crimes after being defended by a public defender is how far his or her lawyer was willing to go in pursuing his client's case if such an aggressive posture jeopardizes the lawyer's future employment by angering other criminal justice actors.[5]

By being totally independent of the public treasury and the fiscal resources of the criminal justice system, the private criminal lawyer is dependent upon his client for his subsistence. As was shown in Chapter Three of *Criminal Lawyers: An Endangered Species*,[6] a criminal lawyer has a difficult time collecting fees, and it is only through the development of a reputation as a successful advocate, that his or her economic condition may improve. The public defender will receive his or her salary regardless of the outcome of the case, but the private attorney knows that his economic worth is directly related to how well he satisfies the client.

Thus, the criminal lawyer can offer several benefits, usually unavailable at the public defender's office. Although these advantages may not be related to the ultimate disposition of the case, they nevertheless do heighten the prestige of the private criminal lawyer in the eyes of his clientele. The major advantage offered by private versus public defense is the guarantee of personalized attention, often cynically referred to by attorneys as "handholding." Because of the massive caseloads facing public defender programs, they are often forced to adopt an assembly-line type of system where the client may be handled by a battery of lawyers. The defendant rarely has a lawyer he can call his own, and quickly senses that he cannot drop in on his public attorney during the day for a leisurely chat in a secluded office. The private criminal lawyer, however, affords the client the advantage of being imminently reachable. Having such a lawyer is almost a status symbol among defendants who may be heard describing their good fortune in possessive and laudatory terms to their less fortunate (and usually less affluent) peers. Many live vicariously through their distorted visions of their attorney's glamorous lifestyle. The lawyers themselves often contribute to this glossy image through their expensive clothes and lavish surroundings.

A third advantage, which is probably the most realistically related to the quality of the private attorney's performance, is his or her willingness to take an aggressive stance toward both the judge and prosecutor on his client's behalf. Private criminal lawyers were found to be much more willing to risk contempt citations and other forms of judicial anger than public defenders, many of whom were assigned to a specific judge for a length of time, and would be making their own lives miserable by creating such confrontations.

At the risk of sounding sanctimonious, the private criminal lawyer can be described as the last bastion against the oppressive powers of the state. He stands between the accusatorial powers and the individual rights of the defendant. No matter how high the quality of a public defender program, it is still tainted by its relationship to the state. The private criminal lawyer is, therefore, the sole vestige of an independent adversary to the state's ability to indict and convict.

A second group of individuals especially affected by the private criminal lawyer's diminishing role is the entire legal profession. His importance to this group is both symbolic and pragmatic in nature. The symbolic value of his healthy existence is evident because it is through the publicized exploits of such men as F. Lee Bailey, Percy Foreman, and Richard "Racehorse" Haynes, that the public receives its most positive and compassionate image of the legal profession. Without the image of these courtroom advocates, the public would probably consider corporate law firms and public bureaucracies as models for a contemporary portrait of the modern lawyer. It is difficult to imagine such a portrait appealing nearly as much to the public as that engendered by the traditional criminal lawyer, eloquently and doggedly battling for the rights of his client. Neither tax issues, nor labor arbitration, nor real estate transactions could capture the public's imagination as much as would a murder case.

The decline of the private criminal lawyer may also affect the legal profession in a more pragmatic way. The field of private criminal law has always been an accessible stratum of the legal profession with few barriers to entry other than the rigors of the practice and the dedication of the individual. For decades, criminal practice has been a haven for those lawyers unable to break into the more prestigious and lucrative firms. Even today, this study discovered that a disproportionate number of private criminal lawyers had come from religious and racial minority groups, those very groups which have been historically excluded from the mainstream of the legal profession. Although such discrimination has recently abated, its legacy still permeates the thinking of most private criminal lawyers.

With the ever-increasing surplus of lawyers being turned out by our nation's law schools, elimination of the private criminal law field further drains an already depleted job market. In the past, young lawyers have always depended upon the acquisition of an occasional, or even regular, criminal case to keep them from starvation while moving toward a more secure professional position. As public defender offices become overrun with applicants and private criminal lawyers fade from the scene, the underemployed young lawyer will find one more avenue closed.

The third group of individuals who would suffer as a result of the extinction of private criminal lawyers is the general public, particularly those members of society in search of legal defense. We have touched indirectly on this issue in the previous discussion comparing public and private lawyers, but there are additional considerations which have not yet been addressed. First is the critical question of freedom of choice. The public should have an opportunity to select the best lawyer it can for its legal defense. Although the client's financial resources obviously limit his choice, he can still decide how much he wishes to spend on legal counsel and who specifically will defend him. The public defender program is probably disliked by defendants because of the impersonal way in which a lawyer is shoved in the defendant's direction. The loss of freedom to choose is clearly one of the major complaints of indigent defendants, and conversely, one of the most attractive features of private criminal lawyers who are hired as the personal choice of the client. The power to hire and fire his own attorney may be one of the last ego-saving devices left to a defendant whose probable conviction looms in the immediate future. The nine-to-five nature of the public defender's office, its bureaucratic setting, and long-term. stable tenure all seem to undermine traditional consumer values. The American public has always believed that "you get what you pay for," and if you get something for nothing (a public defender, for example), it is inherently inferior to that for which you pay much (your private attorney).

WHAT HAS *NOT* CHANGED

By referring to those lawyers who engage in the private practice of criminal law as an "endangered species," the original study was not implying that they would soon vanish entirely as did the dinosaur. The metaphor was selected in order to dramatize the plight of this struggling group of professionals. With almost no new blood coming into the profession, and a shortened professional life span, frequently distinguished by a "burn-out" effect, the absolute number of criminal lawyers has been visibly declining. This decline has continued, and although the pace has not accelerated, neither has it abated. The economic struggle and its related frustrations have not lessened during the past five years and recent evidence warrants continued pessimism for the future.

The creation by the American Bar Association in 1980 of its Committee on the Economics of Criminal Law signifies that the seriousness of this problem has been recognized. Although it may be construed as a positive sign that the mainstream of the bar has finally become aware of the need to confront the financial problems of private criminal lawyers, the Committee's investigations have revealed an extremely depressing picture. Additionally, such a committee appears ineffective in developing successful means to ameliorate the situation. The two major issues with which the Committee has chosen to deal are first the pricing of services substantially below their fair market value and second, the continued failure of public agencies to pay private counsel a reasonable fee for work in assigned counsel cases. These fees were often considered inadequate when established more than a decade ago, and have not been increased despite the spiralling rise in inflation during this time period.

Services may be underpriced for two reasons: either the lawyer is unaware that he can command higher fees, or he is attempting to attract clients away from more experienced lawyers whose services will probably be more costly. The competition for clients has reached the point where private lawyers in several jurisdictions have joined together to underbid the entire public defender program and offer their services at reduced rates. This new strategy is entitled the *"contract system,"* and although it will be discussed in greater detail in subsequent sections, it needs to be briefly identified and explained at this point.

The *contract system* is attractive to public officials responsible for the administration of justice because it is designed to save the local government significant amounts of money. A law firm or group of lawyers will offer to provide wholesale representation to all indigent defendants for a fixed, as well as modest fee. Howard Eisenberg, Executive Director of the National Legal Aid and Defender Association, in a recent report to the American Bar Association General Practices Committee explains that a "jurisdiction will sell all or some of its cases to one lawyer of a law firm for a set fee per case, perhaps $50 or $75 per misdemeanor, or $100 or $200 per felony. The initial evaluation of these systems has indicated that while they save the county money initially, very quickly the vendors realize that the level of compensation is inadequate in order to perform effective representation, and thus the costs rise much more dramatically than they would have under either traditional assigned counsel or public defender systems."[7]

There seems to be little that the private criminal lawyer can do to prevent the intentional underpricing of services by his competitors. If, however, the reduced pricing is unintentional and simply the product of ignorance as to not knowing what fees the market will bear, then, according to the Committee of Economics, lawyers can learn the true value of their efforts and price them accordingly. The Committee has recently held a roundtable workshop on this topic. That this initial educative effort will eventually benefit the beginning practitioner is unlikely, but at least it is a step in the right direction.

The second issue of inadequate funding by public agencies for assigned counsel fees has also been documented in the Eisenberg report for out-of-court representation in this country for assigned counsel was slightly more than $23 per hour while the in-court fee was just in excess of $29 per hour. These amounts have remained virtually unchanged for the past 10 years according to his comprehensive survey.

Compared to the average hourly rate charged by most attorneys (the rate has been estimated as being between $50 and $75 per hour), as well as the amount paid by the court for civil matters, such as probate work, assigned criminal lawyers are receiving one-half to one-third of what they would normally expect to receive for handling unassigned cases. The problem is further exacerbated by the fact that in most jurisdictions, the trial court must approve the attorney's request for the fees and the sitting judge has the power to reduce the amount requested if he believes that the attorney exaggerated the amount of time spent on the case. This reduced fee may also represent the judge's evaluation of the attorney's efforts and reflect the judge's low opinion of a lawyer's performance. This has been a continuing problem and was recently noted in a 1975 report on the District of Columbia's assigned counsel system which concluded that the Court failed to adopt any overall policies or guidelines to inform the bench and bar of relevant standards for reviewing, cutting, and approving pay vouchers. Attorneys were rarely told why cuts had been made and no grievance procedure was available to protest what might have been an unwarranted reduction. A final frustration is caused by the lengthy time during which lawyers have to wait for the awarding of their fees. Attorneys reported delays of up to six months following the conclusion of a case.[8]

Why has this fee-cutting persisted despite its deleterious effect upon the morale of the private criminal law bar and their willingness to accept unassigned cases? The answer seems to stem from the low esteem in which many members of the criminal defense bar are held by members of the bench. In the author's recent examination of the world of the criminal judge, the subject of the defense attorney's competence was a frequent topic. The judges interviewed were nearly unanimous in their low estimation of most members of the private bar.

Howard Eisenberg adds another noteworthy factor which has prompted these reductions by judges of assigned counsel vouchers. He believes that judges are frequently pressured by the funding source to reduce compensation whenever possible. Eisenberg concludes: "It is not at all unusual, for example, for county boards to order an across-the-board cut in all court costs. It is not particularly relevant to the elected officials in county government that the attorney's fees are already well below that which is required for an attorney to adequately run a law office."[9]

Three additional issues which were noted in the original research on criminal lawyers were all found to continue unchanged throughout the past five years. First is the capability of a few cities to still offer a profitable and expanding professional life for the private criminal lawyer. These cities are typically located in the Sunbelt and are exemplified by Miami, Florida which has been experiencing a rapidly rising crime wave, especially in the areas of drug trafficking and crimes of violence. The drug cases seem to provide a growing number of potential clients who are facing serious charges, and most significantly usually possess ample means to afford private counsel. Since many of these cases involve federal crimes, the applicable speedy trial act has forced defense lawyers to handle fewer cases simultaneously since they must be prepared to go to trial in a short period of time. This has resulted in drug cases being diffused among a broader base of attorneys than has traditionally handled this type of case.

The second ongoing issue is the declining prestige of the legal profession in general, and the private defense bar in particular. Although it has been nearly a decade since Watergate, John Dean's frustrated inquiry as to how so many lawyers could have become involved in such a mess still seems to saturate the public's consciousness. Recent scandals such as ABSCAM and a host of local incidents of public corruption, have helped to perpetuate a low level of public confidence in the legal profession. Private criminal lawyers still appear to be outsiders, rarely influencing bar association policies and concerns.

The third issue is the continued harassment of defense attorneys by some federal attorneys and judges. This problem appeared to reach its zenith during the Carter administration and seems to have diminished during the initial year of the Reagan presidency. Such harassment was given recent national exposure by reporter Bobbie Moran of the *Atlanta Constitution* in early 1980. Her article, which was released by a national wire service, was inspired by a local situation in which a continuing number of Atlanta private criminal lawyers were facing federal indictments based on incriminating evidence supplied by former clients. Charges included suborning perjury, sharing in the fruits of the crime, and a variety of additional derelictions of professional and legal responsibilities. Despite the fact that nearly all of the indictments have since been dismissed, this harassment nevertheless had a chilling effect on many members of the defense bar.

WHAT *HAS* CHANGED

Although it appears that the plight of the private criminal lawyer has not significantly changed during the past five years, his professional life has nevertheless been affected by changes in the political and social environment. The major political shift during this five-year period has been the election of Ronald Reagan. His administration, along with a Republican-dominated Senate introduced policies of fiscal restraint and plans to shift responsibility for many domestic programs from the federal government to the states.[10] These cutbacks and shifts in responsibility have already begun to have an impact upon private practitioners.

Beginning with the elimination of the Justice Department's Law Enforcement Assistance Administration in April of 1982, the Reagan Administration has continued to severely curtail federal funding for state and local criminal justice agencies. This budget tightening has forced reductions in, or elimination of, diversion and rehabilitation programs as well as the funding of public defender and assigned counsel systems. Several jurisdictions such as Ohio, Missouri, and Alabama have run out of money for assigned counsel cases and are now asking the bar to provide representation without compensation. The state of Wisconsin, which has long been noted as a leader in compensation for legal services, has a bill before its state legislature requesting a *reduction* in hourly assigned counsel fees due to the state's fiscal crisis. Howard Eisenberg summarized the national situation in the following manner:

> "All over the country pressure is being brought on the bar and the judiciary to reduce the fees paid to counsel in order to conserve revenue for the state or county. At the same time, systems are being developed which raise grave questions regarding the adequacy of representation, but which are cheap—even if not cost-effective. There is a discernible trend towards cheap systems and toward elected officials placing political and media pressure on the bar to do work for less and less money."[11]

Norman Lefstein, a law professor from the Universtiy of North Carolina, has recently completed an important study entitled *Criminal Defense Services for the Poor: Methods and Programs for Providing Legal Representation and the Need for Adequate Financing* for the ABA Committee on Legal and Indigent Defendants. This study documents budgetary cutbacks and carefully assesses their impact upon the quality of defense services offered to the poor. He presents empirical evidence of the diminishing federal commitment to indigent defense. The federal contribution now constitutes less than 1 percent of expenditures for indigents nationwide and Lefstein believes that even this small amount may be reduced once LEAA closes its doors on April 1, 1982.[12] Lefstein was concerned about these reductions which would make it substantially more difficult for any defendant to receive the essential Sixth Amendment guarantees espoused in the *Argersinger* decision. Quoting a study by Boston University's Center for Criminal Justice, Lefstein found that misdemeanor defendants were "often not informed of their rights to counsel, or after long periods in custody without counsel and delayed trial, they were asked to waive their right to an attorney."[13] Inadequate financing of defense services and lack of sufficient qualified attorneys to handle the indigent caseloads were cited as prime causes of these practices.

The following is a list of a few selected jurisdictions identified by Lefstein as having serious funding problems in defense services as of June, 1981. (The implications of the entire report is that these are not isolated instances but rather are indicative of a growing national trend.)

a. In *Arkansas,* the legislature in March of 1981 refused to appropriate $400,000 to continue the LEAA-funded statewide Appellate Defender program. When the State Supreme Court requested $120,000 to supplement its budget to pay for appeals, the legislature again refused. As a result, the Court will be limited to the remainder of its last biennial budget to pay for private counsel for the next two years. This amounts to a total of approximately $40,000, or less than $100 per appeal.

b. In *Georgia,* the Indigent Defense Act of 1979 established a statewide system with a local option. All counties willing to meet the statewide guidelines for criminal defense services received 50 percent matching funds from the state. Approximately 40 of Georgia's 159 counties participated in the program last year. In March of this year, the state legislature refused to appropriate $905,000 for the continuation of the program. This amounts to 30 percent of all the money expended throughout the state for indigent criminal defense services.

c. In *Indiana,* the state legislature refused to give even committee consideration to a bill to create a mixed statewide defender system. They also refused to enact enabling legislation sponsored by the Marin County (Indianapolis) Bar Association to create a county-wide mixed defender system, despite the fact that the program would not have been funded by the state.

d. In *Maine,* the state legislature failed to appropriate funds to continue an LEAA-funded coordinated assigned counsel program in a four-county region which received a generally favorable evaluation from Abt Associates, Inc.

e. In *Mississippi,* the state legislature refused to authorize an interim study commission to review extensive findings made by Ernest H. Short and Associates on behalf of the Mississippi Judicial Council. The report was somewhat critical of the present *ad hoc* assigned counsel system in all but five of Mississippi's 82 counties.

f. In *Montana,* the state legislature refused to appropriate the $75,000 needed to create a Public Defender Coordinator (PDC) office. The PDC, consisting of one attorney and one secretary, would have collected defense data for all 56 counties, and provided a brief bank, limited appellate support and some trial representation in the rural counties.[14]

In a subsequent section of this chapter, the failure to pay attorneys in assigned counsel cases will be examined as one of the current controversies facing the private practitioner.

Evaluating these budgetary reductions for public defender, diversion, and rehabilitative programs from a realistic (and possibly cynical) perspective, one may, indeed, conclude that they can be advantageous for the private criminal lawyer. With fewer public defenders available, a defendant who is on the edge of being able to afford a private attorney, may opt to do so rather than take his chances with a decaying public defender system. Additionally, without the availability of diversion programs to extricate him from the criminal justice system, a defendant may be more eager to seek a quality lawyer to work for his freedom—a quality lawyer which he believes is rarely found in a public defender office. One Philadelphia lawyer interviewed in the original study foresaw this development, and only half-facetiously applauded its appearance as a boon to his economic survival. The fact that these potential clients are probably not in a financial position to utilize private counsel is a weakness in his argument, but a select few may be wooed away from the public defender's door.

In addition to the deleterious effect which these program reductions have on the defendant's chances for free legal defense, or lenient treatment by the courts, there has been a revived interest at both the federal and state levels in taking a tougher stance in the fight against crime. This "tough stance" has manifested itself legislatively in politician's attempts to lengthen prison sentences and reduce the judge's discretionary powers. Judges, often blamed for the inability of criminal justice system to reduce the increasing crime rate, are thought to be too lenient in their sentencing policies. Current legislative trends indicate that more and more states are adopting determinant sentencing provisions which combine longer sentences with decreased judicial discretion. With the rehabilitative ideal clearly out of fashion as a viable objective for the criminal justice system, the punitive and "warehousing" concepts have been accepted by many public officials as the only realistic strategy. They feel safe in the knowledge that an incarcerated defendant cannot commit additional crimes while he is behind bars. This tough posture and the resultant lengthening of prison sentences may also convince indigents to scrape up the necesasary funds to hire a private attorney rather than trust their fates to the public defender.

If the executive branch is doing some things which might ultimately prove beneficial to the private defense counsel, the judicial branch —specifically the United States Supreme Court—has recently been making the defense attorney's life difficult. Decisions from the Burger Court have continued to undermine the significant advances made during the Warren Court years in rights guaranteed to persons accused of crimes. The *Miranda* and *Mapp* decisions in particular seem to have been eroded in recent years, although neither has been directly overruled. The following is a series of cases from the most recent term of the Supreme Court which indicates this trend:

Jenkins v. *Anderson*[15]—The Court held that the Fifth Amendment's prohibition against self-incrimination is not violated by the use of prearrest silence to impeach a criminal defendant's credibility. Defendant was not apprehended until he turned himself in two weeks after the incident (stabbing). At the trial he pleaded self-defense. He took the stand and twice during cross-examination the prosecution called attention to the length of time between the stabbing and the surrender.

New York v. *Belton*[16]—Decision held that the Fourth Amendment permits the police to search the passenger compartment of an auto without a warrant as an incident to a lawful arrest of its passenger.

U.S. v. *Mendenhall*[17]—Court held that there had been no illegal search and seizure in the case of a young woman who was stopped and then strip-searched by federal narcotics agents because her behavior fit a pattern believed to be typical of narcotic smugglers.

U.S. v. *Havens*[18]—Court held that illegally-obtained evidence may be used to impeach a defendant's false trial testimony given in cross examination. Havens and a co-defendant were arrested in Miami airport after a customs officer found cocaine sewed into makeshift pockets on a T-shirt that co-defendant was wearing under his shirt. Co-defendant pleaded quilty and testified against Havens. Havens took the stand in his own defense and denied any knowledge of the T-shirt. The T-shirt was admitted into evidence solely for the purpose of impeaching Havens' credibility.

Most of the attorneys interviewed in 1976–77 for the author's initial study stated that recent Supreme Court decisions by the Burger Court have made their job of defending clients appreciably more difficult. It, therefore, seems logical to conclude that this trend has only worsened in recent years since the court's membership has become increasingly conservative and prosecution-oriented. The 1981 appointment of Justice O'Connor to replace former Justice Stewart is a definite step in this direction. Even more indicative is the imminent retirement of Justices Brennan and Marshall whose replacements will probably be selected by President Reagan.

Two final developments which were noted as originating in the mid-1970s, and may hasten the decline of the private criminal lawyer, have increased in magnitude and significance during the past five years. The first is a product of the increased competition among lawyers. This increased competition has led to the use of advertising and the formation of law clinics or "legal supermarkets" which offer reasonably priced legal services. These new operations frequently advertise on television and may be exemplified by the national firm of Jacoby and Myers. Their use of paralegals as well as assembly-line processing techniques, has allowed these firms to handle large numbers of cases in short periods of time. Their efficiency in handling cases is then passed on to the consumer in the form of significantly reduced legal fees for ordinary legal problems. Their impact upon the private criminal lawyer, who is usually a solo practitioner or is an associate of a few other lawyers, is obvious.

The second development also has its roots in the struggle for economic survival, and involves the growing reluctance of the larger and medium-sized civil law firms to refer cases to criminal law specialists outside the firm. If one of these civil law firms has a client with a criminal law problem, they will attempt to deal with it internally. Despite the fact that there are a few private criminal lawyers in some of the large firms, often one or a group of the firm's members develop specialties in areas of the criminal law, such as tax fraud or white collar crime. The reason for this change may be an increased competition among law firms for new clients, as well as a fear of losing those clients they already have. A few criminal lawyers proudly commented that on more than one occasion, a client who had been referred to them with a criminal problem never returned to the referring firm, and was content to allow his new attorney to handle all of his legal problems.

CURRENT CONTROVERSIES

As the previous sections have indicated, there have been some important political and social changes affecting the private practice of criminal law during the past five years. These changes have occurred within the context of persisting economic troubles plaguing defense attorneys. As a result of these trends, there has emerged a group of serious issues which currently confront the private criminal lawyer. These current controversies (Spring 1982) can be categorized as follows: (1) charges of incompetence and malpractice; (2) financial collapse of the assigned counsel system; (3) the newly-developing "contract system" and (4) specialization and the limits of advertising.

The first problem area grows out of a criminal lawyer's constitutional obligation to offer a competent defense as guaranteed by the Sixth Amendment of the federal constitution. Defining what is meant by a "competent defense" has been a difficult task. Before the 1970s the performance of a defendant's lawyer was thought by appellate courts to violate the Sixth Amendment guarantee only if the trial could be described as a "farce and mockery." In the past 10 years, however, most jurisdictions have replaced this standard with a seemingly higher professional level of effectiveness generally defined as "reasonably competent assistance of counsel" or "within range of competence demanded by attorneys in criminal cases." William Erickson, a Colorado judge and authority on the subject, believes that this heightened level of responsibility has grown out of the *McMann* and *Gideon* decisions.[19]

The case of *U.S.* v. *DeCoster*, which was decided in the United States Court of Appeals, represents the most recent clarification of the competency standard.[20] This court found that a defendant was entitled to the reasonably competent assistance of an attorney who would act as his diligent conscientious advocate. The decision also listed several specific obligations which an attorney owes the client, such as conferring with him as early and as often as possible, advising him of his rights and taking all necessary steps to preserve them, as well as conducting the factual and legal investigations necessary to develop all appropriate defenses.[21] The implications of the DeCoster case appear to be that the appellate courts are now willing to examine a much broader range of attorney activities in order to see if the new standard of competence has been achieved. This probably means that the judiciary intends to examine the lawyer's trial preparation, investigation, interviews, quality and completeness of legal research, and finally, trial strategy.[22]

In order to provide the legal profession with even more concrete advisory guidelines as to what must be done to satisfy the constitutional requirements of competence of counsel, Judge Bazelon of the U.S. Court of Appeals for the District of Columbia, recently suggested that the ABA standards for defense should be used to designate the minimum standards required in *DeCoster*. He believed that by asking the following questions, the court could satisfactorily apply these advisory guidelines: (1) Did counsel violate one of the articulated duties noted in the ABA Standards? (2) Was the violation substantial? and (3) Has the government established that no prejudice resulted?[23]

Despite the slight step forward in clarification provided by the *DeCoster* case, most lawyers still believe that there are no meaningful guideposts for measuring attorney conduct against constitutional requirements. Recent interviews with both criminal lawyers and trial judges indicated a continued belief that the most satisfactory way of dealing with the problem of incompetence is not through the traditional remedies of appellate reviews or malpractice suits, but rather through direct action by the trial judge during the proceedings. In his authoritative article on the subject, William Schwarzer found that critical institutional limitations prevent appellate review from being an effective means by which to deal with the competence question. He writes that "The structural limitations arise because an appellate court is bound by the record of the trial court; it lacks the benefit of observing counsel in action. As a result, most of the trial lawyer's preparation and performance will be difficult to evaluate."[24] Schwarzer also believes that the process by which a trial judge determines the level of competence should be a type of comprehensive monitoring system which begins with the appointment of counsel, extends through trial preparation and finally reaches the pre-sentencing hearing. He concludes that "If at any time during the proceeding, the defendant makes a seemingly substantial complaint about the adequacy of counsel, the judge should conduct an inquiry and make findings on whether bona fide grounds exist for a change of counsel."[25]

The consensus among trial judges interviewed by the author during the past two years concerning their roles in dealing with incompetent attorneys, was a willingness to intervene only in the most extreme cases where it appeared obvious that the lawyer's level of performance was denying his client the opportunity for a fair trial. The judges also conjectured as to the likelihood that the appellate court would find the attorney's efforts below the current standards of competence. In order to avoid the time-consuming and frustrating experience of having to appoint a new counsel, or experience an appellate reversal requiring a re-trial, most of the trial judges would call the defense attorney to their chambers or conduct a side-bar conference in which the attorney would be notified of his sub-par performance and be strongly urged to raise his level of effectiveness. It was interesting to note what a low opinion most judges had of the attorneys appearing before them. Given such a negative estimation of lawyers' abilities, it was surprising to find the judges so reluctant to deal with the competence problem. With the meteoric rise in the number of defendants bringing up the competence question on appeal, trial judges may soon be forced to take a more active role in dealing with the problem.[26]

In addition to a defendant challenging his attorney's competence by appealing his conviction under the Sixth Amendment's protection, he may also use the rarer tactic of initiating a malpractice suit. Although this is an infrequently used civil proceeding, its utilization is increasing at a significantly rapid rate. Lawyers who already feel besieged by the crippling expense of malpractice insurance cannot help but feel nervous as a result of the more frequent usage of these suits by disappointed clients. Most criminal lawyers interviewed are in strong agreement with attorney Ned Nakles who argues that criminal defense lawyers should be entitled to the same absolute immunity from civil liability as are the judge and prosecutor. Nakles writes that the criminal lawyer "must be free to manage the defense. The defendant is not left without a remedy since he can overturn his conviction by a *habeas corpus* petition on the grounds of an ineffective assistance of counsel."[27]

Although criminal lawyers are acutely concerned with the possibility of their being involved in a malpractice suit, their actual chances of such involvement are quite slim. This is due primarily to a long-standing series of threshold barriers facing any defendant hoping to recover against a supposedly negligent attorney. The following list of obstacles which must be overcome by the plaintiff indicates why there are so few suits of this type: (1) plaintiff must be innocent—that is, he must prove his actual innocence of the underlying charge, (2) collateral estoppel relating to any earlier claim of ineffective assistance of counsel in the underlying case, (3) potential immunity of public defender or court appointed counsel, and (4) immunity granted from malpractice liability of the attorney.[28]

The second controversy which recently merited a full day of discussion at the 1982 ABA midyear meetings in Chicago, is the seemingly imminent collapse of the assigned counsel system. The system, which complements public defender programs in larger cities (such as assisting the multiple defendant cases) and constitutes the major source of indigent defense in most other communities (2100 out of 2300 counties nationally according to the President's 1967 Task Force Report on the Courts), has become the victim of the fiscal crisis affecting many public services. Since persons accused of crimes neither comprise a very large nor influential constituency, these programs have been among the first victims of economic retrenchment. As was noted in prior sections, assigned counsel fees lag far behind what lawyers would normally expect to earn and have remained frozen for a decade. In more and more jurisdictions the situation has deteriorated to the point where compensation has actually been reduced or eliminated altogether.

Norman Lefstein's report on the current state of indigent defense has carefully noted this growing financial crisis, as evidenced by the following examples:

In Massachusetts over $3 million is owed to the private bar for work performed during the past three years.

In February the Missouri Public Defender Commission announced that it had spent its entire appointed counsel budget for the fiscal year ending June 30th and could no longer pay attorney fees and expenses.

In West Virginia private lawyers are owed fees totalling $170,000 for work performed in 1978–79.

In one Louisiana county, the private bar fees of more than $240,000 have not been paid and there is no apparent carryover to the next year.

In Greenville, S.C., the County Commissioners voted to discontinue the $240,000 spent by the county for a mixed-defender system and replace it with a $90,000 contract for five part-time private lawyers. Similar proposals are presently pending in Oregon, Oklahoma, and Pennsylvania.

Cases in Florida, California, Georgia, Massachusetts, Montana, Oklahoma, Missouri, Oregon, Nebraska, Iowa, Alabama, and Tennessee are raising questions of adequate compensation, improper reduction of fees, involuntary servitude, and the denial of due process for their clients.[29]

What happens when the public monies in a jurisdiction run out for assigned counsel and yet the defendants must be provided with their constitutionally guaranteed right to assistance of counsel? Missouri recently answered this question when its Supreme Court in the case of *Wolff* v. *Ruddy* held that the members of the Missouri bar could be compelled to provide representation without compensation. The court added that failure to respond to an appointment order without just cause opens an attorney to the possibility of disciplinary action. On January 12th the Missouri decision was given even greater significance when the United States Supreme Court refused to grant a writ of *certiorari* on attorney Wolff's appeal.[30]

However, the judicial response to the plight of private defense attorneys assigned to indigent defendants has not been uniformly unsympathetic. In the case of *Hulse* v. *Wifirat*[31] an Iowa appellate court held that a court-appointed attorney is entitled to full compensation for his reasonably necessary services as gauged by ordinary and customary charges for like services in the community, and that no discount is required based on attorney's duty to represent the poor. Similarly, in an Illinois decision, the standard of "reasonableness" used for the assessment of fees for appointed counsel was abused by the court when it awarded fees of less than $8 per hour.[32] These cases, however, represent a minority viewpoint. Therefore, if state and county governments become either more unwilling or unable to appropriate monies in the months and years ahead, then most criminal lawyers can expect the courts to follow the Missouri case of *Wolff* v. *Ruddy* rather than those which took place in Illinois and Iowa.

Lawyers contend that funding is directly related to the quality of representation which the indigent defendant receives. The more time they can devote to a case, the better the defense. The ABA's General Practice Section has agreed with these sentiments, and in the summer of 1981 it passed Resolution 117 which expresses dissatisfaction with instances of insufficient funding for indigent defense and urges the individual states, in discharge of their constitutional obligations, to provide effective assistance of counsel to indigents accused of crime. The ABA and individual criminal lawyers interviewed were aware of the public viewpoint that *pro bono* or nearly free representation was a professional service owed to society. They did not dispute their general obligations to occasionally provide free legal representation, but were greatly upset by the coercive nature of the Missouri solution, where state compulsion robbed them of the opportunity to choose when they intended to offer their services. The bar argued that this not only unfairly discriminates against certain members of the legal profession—i.e., those competent to do criminal work, but also severely undermines the quality of representation received by indigent defendants.

This national crisis in legal representation for indigent defendants has also affected the public defender programs which operate in larger cities. As a money-saving alternative to public defender operations, some private lawyers have entered into contracts with jurisdictions to represent indigents. This controversial "contract system" has been experimented with in 22 states including, most notably, California. The contract system seems to have developed out of dissatisfaction with the expense of public defender programs and the possible fiscal savings offered by this new alternative. Instead of paying for the many indirect expenses inherent in operating a public defender office, the court system can contract with one or more law firms, or groups of attorneys, to provide defense for the indigent in their jurisdiction.

How well do these systems actually work? Since they have been in existence for only a few years, there are few evaluations of them presently available. The only current analysis was recently completed by Robert Spangenberg of Abt Associates, a Cambridge, Massachusetts consulting firm, who stated that "although contract defense systems owe their popularity to lower initial costs, after the first year the costs tended to rise dramatically. Traditional public defender office budgets are increasing at an average of 10 percent per year."[33] The report concluded that despite its uncertain longterm savings, the contract concept is the fastest growing form of indigent defense in the country.

The attorneys or firms who group together to offer these modestly priced services are, as one might expect, staffed primarily by young lawyers trying to devise a way to compete with their more experienced colleagues. Given the surplus of young lawyers available and their difficulty in achieving financial security, the contract system offers one possible means of economic survival. Perhaps because of their inexperience in fee-setting or failure to anticipate rising costs, the contract proponents have seriously underestimated their operating expenses. Richard Wilson of the National Legal Aid and Defender Association, does not believe this erroneous calculation is done intentionally but rather is simply the result of inexperience and poor judgment.[34] Given the frustration of public officials with the rapidly rising costs of these contract systems, and the bar association's opposition to them, a decline in their use seems both inevitable and imminent.

The fourth and final current topic to be discussed is closely related to the contract alternative and concerns the issues of specialization, certification, and advertising; especially as they affect the private criminal lawyer. In the initial investigation of private criminal lawyers by the author, little support was found for specialization and certification programs. Advertising was not thought to be a major concern since most clients were obtained on the basis of reputation or through referral, rather than through perusal of the yellow pages. It has only been through the recent development of the marginally professional activities by younger criminal lawyers that these issues have begun to affect the entire private criminal law bar. By being certified as a specialist in criminal law, and then being able to advertise this specialization, a young lawyer may attempt to challenge the established members of the defense bar.

A few criminal lawyers, generally younger and less experienced, argue that advertising is extremely useful to the consumer of legal services, and that it is no longer reasonable to expect clients to venture into the legal marketplace with only word-of-mouth knowledge. Despite the recent increase in the use of advertising by lawyers, a lengthy examination of the subject by the Marquette Law Review has concluded that "private conscience and peer pressure still constitute very significant constraints upon individual lawyers seeking to advertise."[35]

In addition to aiding the consumer of legal services, certification as a specialist in criminal law is also a mechanism for dealing with incompetence and raising the level of performance. By forcing criminal lawyers to exhibit a certain degree of knowledge, the incompetent lawyer would either be driven out of business or forced to improve himself to meet the minimum standards. Judge Bazelon of the United States Court of Appeals was recently quoted as stating that "if his court were to reverse every case in which there was inadequate counsel, they would have to send back half the convictions in his jurisdiction." He went on to point an accusatory finger at assigned counsel performance in criminal cases and to cite frightening examples of sloth, dishonesty, and indifference.[36]

The entire issue of performance evaluation as related to a certification program evoked the ire of most private criminal lawyers who were first questioned on this topic five years ago, and still evokes a visible degree of hostility when mentioned today. They especially dislike the testing portions of the plan which they feel are being unfairly directed at them by civil attorneys whose general practice allows them to escape from the possibility of such embarrassing examinations. Several private criminal lawyers cynically commented that such attempts at improving the "quality of the profession" were ill-disguised efforts to make the private defense lawyer a scapegoat for overall public disenchantment with the entire legal profession.

JUDGES AND LAWYERS

The major research endeavor of the author during the past five years has been an investigation of the urban criminal trial judge and his working environment. Although this work has only indirectly touched the private criminal lawyer, he is nevertheless a prominent actor in the judge's workgroup. Among the most important issues raised thus far which relate to the judge-defense attorney relationship are the following: (1) the judge's attitude toward attorney competence, (2) the handling of incompetent attorneys, (3) the role of the defense attorney during sentencing, and (4) the role of the defense attorney during plea bargaining.

The judges were generally very negative in their evaluation of the competence of private criminal lawyers. Most echoed sentiments similar to Judge Bazelon's critical comments noted in the previous section. They responded in a manner reminiscent of the 700 judges surveyed by Dorothy Maddi for the ABA Research Journal. Her study placed blame for this negative perception by judges on the judiciary's belief that law schools were not teaching the practical information required to produce competent litigators. Additionally, the judges in the Maddi study believed that there was a general lack of preparation for trial—usually thought to be too many cases at the same time. Their solution to the declining competence rested upon increased legal education through internships or apprenticeships with experienced lawyers.[37]

It might be worthwhile to note that I found the judges to be critical of nearly all members of the criminal justice system, frequently reserving some of their harshest criticism for many of their colleagues on the bench. Given the low public esteem of the criminal justice system generally, and the judiciary in particular, it is really not unexpected to have the criminal court judge to blame or at least partly blame the private criminal lawyer for the system's acknowledged malfunctioning.

Aware of the feelings of the judges toward themselves, and also chafing under the public's antagonism toward their role as defenders of criminals, defense attorneys commonly return the charges of incompetence back to the judiciary. Many criminal lawyers were angered by what they perceived as the judge's use of them as scapegoats when, in fact, the judiciary had an obligation to educate the public as to the nature of the adversary system and the dimensions of the criminal lawyers' professional obligations under the constitution. In other words, the public should know that a defense attorney is merely present to guarantee a defendant's constitutional right to a fair trial under due process of law. Therefore, it is unprofessional and extremely frustrating for a judge to be accusing members of the private criminal law bar with delaying justice, finding minor loopholes, or preying upon the emotions of ignorant members of the jury when these lawyers are merely staging an aggressive fight in their client's best interests.

When faced with a case in which the defense attorney appeared to be failing to offer his client a "reasonable defense," most judges tried to deal with the situation by speaking to the lawyer either in chambers or at a sidebar conference. Judges were divided over how much of a role they should play in aiding the errant attorney. Usually the judge would warn the lawyer that he was not doing an acceptable job and must come to court better prepared. Many judges would go so far as to indicate to the attorney, where in particular, his defense was inadequate and even suggest specific strategies or directions to pursue. Those judges with prior experience as litigators were most likely to adopt the interventionist policy in dealing with floundering defense attorneys. A sizable minority of judges chose to remain completely neutral and purposefully avoided intervening on behalf of either adversary.

The judges were troubled by the rising number of suits by defendants charging their attorneys with incompetence or malpractice. They nevertheless insisted that they must continue to maintain a vigilant eye over attorney performance because of their responsibilities for ensuring a fair trial. Several judges stated a clear preference for coming to the aid of a defense attorney before helping a prosecutor because they felt that they had a greater responsibility for protecting defendant rights than merely having a prosecutor lose a case.

The major opportunities for interaction between judge and defense attorney occur during plea bargaining and pre-sentence hearings. As a result of recent interviews and courtroom observations, each of these interactions appear to be increasingly dominated by the judge. In plea bargaining, the judge placed himself in the center of the negotiations. Although the defense attorney was generally allowed the opportunity to consult with his client, most judges made evident their feelings as to what was acceptable, as well as what might occur if a plea was not accepted and the case went to trial.

A shift toward greater specificity in the ultimate sentence was also observed. During the past 15 years there seemed to be more charge bargaining and less sentence bargaining. In the last few years, however, as judges have been criticized for being overly lenient, there has been a movement in state legislatures to enact bills limiting judicial discretion in sentencing by requiring determinant sentences for specific crimes. This has narrowed the range of sentences available to a judge for a particular charge. Thus, when a judge indicates acceptance of a plea for a crime, the defense attorney has a fairly good idea of what the eventual sentence will be. Armed with this knowledge, the defense attorney (as well as the prosecutor), appears to defer much more to the judge during plea negotiations than was previously observed five years ago when the judge frequently simply ratified a prior agreement between defense and prosecution.

The second opportunity for interaction between judge and defense attorney is the pre-sentence hearing which, similar to plea bargaining, seems to be characterized by increasing judicial dominance. This trend would seem to be a logical outgrowth of the increased use of determinant sentences which was noted previously. In the original study of private criminal lawyers conducted in 1977, most of the attorneys interviewed emphasized the importance of their contribution to the pre-sentence report. Since so few cases actually went to trial, the attorneys often directed their energies toward the preparation of comprehensive and persuasive pre-sentence reports. Although most attorneys would prepare their own background studies of their clients, they would also attempt to influence or monitor the report coming from the probation departments.

My recent study of judges has indicated that the judge is placing increased reliance on the probation department's report. This has caused a shift in the role of the private defense attorney toward adopting a more passive posture during the pre-sentence proceedings. He often limits himself to merely vocalizing his belief in the defendant's positive attributes and strong potential for rehabilitation. The attorney can also take this time to comment upon any mitigating factors lessening his client's culpability. As a concluding note, the defense attorney almost always notifies the judge of his client's heartfelt remorse over his past transgression(s).

CONCLUSIONS

It may be true that private criminal lawyers have not become extinct and a few may be enjoying prosperous times, however, overall they are in no better financial shape than they were when first examined by this author in 1977. Additionally, several recent trends seem to be making their present and future professional lives more tenuous.

The most obvious of these trends is the financial crisis facing the assigned counsel system of indigent defense. Since many private criminal lawyers depend upon such assignment for their economic survival, this development can have catastrophic implications. In several states, the private criminal lawyer is simply not being paid for the work assigned and completed. Even more threatening is the situation in Missouri where the state's Supreme Court has decided that lawyers must accept assigned counsel cases without pay, or face disciplinary action.

The intensity of competition for the few cases available to private defense attorneys seems to have increased during the past five years, despite the reductions and irregularities in assigned counsel fees. As noted in this chapter, legal clinics and national law firms have challenged the private criminal lawyer by offering defense services at reduced prices. Contract systems are recent phenomena which offer strong competition for the private defense bar. These contractors can vary from *ad hoc* groups of lawyers to an entire law firm, legal clinic, or even a nonprofit organization.

Unfortunately, as its economic plight continues to worsen, the private defense bar continues to be criticized. Public chastisement has taken many forms, including the pronouncements of esteemed jurists such as Judges Bazelon, Burger and Frankel decrying the incompetence of the criminal lawyer. It has also been manifested by the significant rise in the number of defendants bringing malpractice suits, or charging their lawyers with incompetence in violation of Sixth Amendment guarantees.

To end this chapter on a positive note, it does appear that the recent Missouri case of *Wolff* v. *Ruddy* has finally alerted the entire legal profession as to the financial crisis facing the assigned counsel system. At the January 1982 midyear meeting of the ABA, the General Trial Section has joined with a committee of the Criminal Justice Section to attempt to rectify the situation. The passage of previously mentioned Resolution 117 by the Association's House of Delegates is another indication of this growing concern and initial rise to action. Whether such activity by the ABA is caused by altruistic concern for the plight of the private criminal lawyer, or a more pragmatic fear that the entire bar may soon be directly affected by the problem if it is not resolved, is not important. For the first time in memory, the private criminal lawyer and his declining economic condition have gained the interest of the rest of the legal profession, and a coordinated effort is beginning to be made for its improvement. It will, therefore, be very interesting to view what the next five years will bring.

NOTES

1. Paul Wice. *Criminal Lawyers: An Endangered Species*. Beverly Hills, Sage Publications, 1978, p. 95.
2. *Gideon* v. *Wainwright* 372 U.S. 335 (1963) and *Argersinger* v. *Hamlin* 407 U.S. 25 (1972).
3. *Wolff* v. *Ruddy* 617 SW 2d. 64 (1981).
4. Jean Taylor et. al. Analysis of Defense Counsel in the Processing of Felony Defendants in San Diego, *Denver Law Journal* (1972) 233; An Analysis of Defense Counsel in the Processing of Felony Defendants in Denver, Colorado, *Denver Law Journal* (1973) 9. Joint Committee of the Judicial Conference of the D.C. Circuit and the D.C. Unified Bar. Report on Criminal Defense Service in the District of Columbia, (April, 1975), mimeographed.
5. Jonathan Casper. Did You Have a Lawyer When You Went to Court? No, I Had a Public Defender, *Yale Review of Law and Social Action* (Spring, 1971), pp. 4–9.
6. Wice, op. cit., pp. 108–13.
7. Howard Eisenberg. Compensation to Private Attorneys in Indigent Criminal Cases, *Report to the American Bar Association General Practices Section*, (1981), mimeographed.
8. Joint Committee of the Judicial Conference of the D.C. Circuit op. cit.
9. Eisenberg, op. cit., p. 5.
10. Reagan Reported Ready to Transfer Federal Programs, *New York Times*. January 19, 1982, p. I 1.
11. Eisenberg, op. cit., p. 6.
12. Norman Lefstein. Criminal Defense Services for the Poor: Methods and Programs for Providing Legal Representation and the Need for Adequate Financing, *Report to the American Bar Association Committee on Legal Aid and Indigent Defendants*. (August, 1981), p. 1.
13. Ibid. p. 2.
14. Ibid. p. G-1.
15. *Jenkins* v. *Anderson* 447 U.S. 231 (1981).
16. *New York* v. *Belton* 101 S.Ct. 2841 (1981).
17. *U.S.* v. *Mendenhall* 446 U.S. 620 (1979).
18. *U.S.* v. *Havens* 446 U.S. 544 (1979).
19. William Erickson. Standards of Competency for Defense Counsel in a Criminal Case, *American Criminal Law Review* 17 (Fall, 1979) p. 233.
20. *U.S.* v. *DeCoster* 624 F 2d. 196 (1976).
21. Geoffrey Alpert. Inadequate Defense Counsel: An Empirical Analysis of Prisoners' Perceptions, *American Journal of Criminal Law* 7 (March, 1979), 1.
22. Lefstein, op. cit., p. 5.
23. Erickson, op. cit., p. 241.
24. William Schwarzer. Dealing With Incompetent Counsel: The Trial Judge's Role, *Harvard Law Review* 93 (February, 1980), 633.
25. Ibid. p. 634.

26. Ned Nakles. Criminal Defense Lawyer: The Case for Absolute Liability, *Dickinson Law Review* 81 (Winter, 1977) p. 229.
27. Ibid. p. 230.
28. Criminal Malpractice: Threshold Barriers to Recovery Against Negligent Criminal Counsel, *Duke Law Journal* (June 1981) p. 542.
29. Lefstein, op. cit., p. G-2.
30. 617 SW 2d. 64 (1981) (Missouri).
31. 306 NW 2d. 707 (1981) (Iowa).
32. *People* v. *Johnson* 417 NE 2d. 1062 (1981) (Illinois App.).
33. David Ranii. Elbowing Out Public Defenders, *The National Law Journal* (December 14, 1981), p. 28.
34. Ibid. p. 29.
35. Lawyers Advertising: Of Shibboleths, Sense and Changing Tradition, *Marquette Law Review* 61 (Summer, 1978), p. 644.
36. Marvin Frankel. Curing Lawyers' Incompetence, *Creighton Law Review* 10 (June, 1977), p. 616.
37. Dorothy Maddi. Judge's Views of Lawyers in Their Courts, *ABA Research Journal* (1979), p. 689.

4

JUDGES: WHO THEY ARE AND HOW THEY WERE SELECTED

Who are the criminal court judiciary and how did they reach the bench? This chapter attempts to answer these questions by beginning with a group portrait of the judges, based upon first an overview of their backgrounds, followed by an examination of their idealized personality traits which will be contrasted with their observed personal styles. The judges who were observed over the past 12 years appear to fall into a four-part typology; each division of the typology being a reflection of the judge's attitude toward his major professional responsibilities.

The second half of the chapter will concentrate upon the socialization of the criminal court judiciary, focusing first upon the various methods of judicial recruitment and the diverse paths chosen by the judges as they moved toward eventual selection. The final section of the chapter will analyze the socialization process once the judge has been selected and is adjusting to his new position. A case study of the socialization experiences of the Philadelphia, Pennsylvania criminal court judiciary will conclude the chapter.

GROUP PORTRAIT

Who is the criminal court judge and from what type of background has he emerged? Based on national surveys[1] and from my own observations, the typical criminal court judge is a man in his late fifties, white, upper middle-class who had a fairly successful law practice before reaching his current position on the bench, which he has held for approximately eight years. My sample of judges is considerably more urban than other national surveys of the profession, so I was not surprised to find slightly higher percentages of representatives from racial, religious, and ethnic minorities, especially in the eastern and midwestern cities. In Philadelphia, for example, nearly every judge interviewed was either Jewish, Irish, or Italian.

Although the typical judge was in his mid-to late-fifties, there was a fairly wide age range. It was surprising to discover so many judges in their early-to mid-forties. Concurrently there appeared to be a noticeable reduction in the number of elderly judges more than 65 years old. Several cities had instituted a compulsory retirement age, but from conversations with the judges, it seems that increasing numbers of their colleagues are limiting their tenure on the bench to a single term. In Chapter Six, which describes the strains and hardships of the judge, the reader can better conprehend the reasons for the shortened professional lifespan. Nearly half of the judges interviewed were unwilling to commit themselves to the posibility of a second term of office.

The underrepresentation of judges from racial minorities—primarily black and Hispanic—has been a problem for many years, although several cities are attempting to make amends for past omissions. A recent study by the "Coalition of Concerned Black Americans" found that only 1 percent of the nation's judges are black, although it appears that those serving in the criminal courts might be a few percentage points higher. Nearly 50 percent of the nation's black judges are located in the following six large cities—New York, Chicago, Washington, Detroit, Los Angeles, and Philadelphia.[2] The number of Hispanic judges is even smaller and concentrated in a few western and southwestern cities in addition to New York. The percentage of minority judges lags far behind the racial breakdown of each city's population. The figure is even more disappointing when one discovers the racial composition of the court's clientele. In New York, which has made a conscious effort to select minority judges, only 10 percent of the bench is black compared to more than 30 percent of the city's population and 60 percent of the defendants.[3] The Hispanics are more grievously underrepresented.

What are the consequences, if any, of this significant underrepresentation of racial and ethnic minorities on the criminal court bench? There has been no creditable empirical research conducted to provide an answer to this critical question. Most defendants observed seemed to have more important matters on their mind than the racial background of the judge. Given the likelihood of defendant and judge coming from sharply divergent socioeconomic backgrounds, the mere fact of racial similarity would not be a significant factor drawing the two parties together. Also complicating the analysis, is the high percentage of defendants pleading guilty and the minuscule number remaining who eventually go to trial. For the overwhelming majority of defendants, this means they will experience only fleeting contact with a judge. The issue of race, or other characteristics of the judge, therefore, fails to have much opportunity to make a deep impression on the defendant.

Other members of the community, however, beside the defendant, are more concerned with the underrepresentation of racial minorities within their city's judiciary. It is this symbolic oversight by the white power structure that has proven so distasteful to sensitive members of these minority groups. It may likely be a part of a larger feeling of powerlessness, but since the judicial system has played such an important role in the lives of so many inner city families, it is certainly a critical institution. Without an opportunity to place increasing numbers of minority group members into criminal court judgeships, these groups will continue to grow more distrustful of the quality of justice dispensed. This can ultimately result in a loss of legitimacy for the city's courts, and the entire social fabric of the community can be threatened.

A recent study by the American Judicature Society has shown that black judges are slightly more likely to be appointed to the bench rather than to gain office through election. The reason for this weakened electoral position is likely due to the problems blacks and Hispanics face in any at-large election where their traditionally low voter turnout undermines the efficacy of their power. This phenomenon is present in New York City with appointed Municipal Court judges who may eventually become Acting Supreme Court (Trial Court) judges. Once reaching the court, studies have indicated that there was no discrimination against minority judges in their assignments or general level of treatment.[4]

Most of the judges surveyed by John Paul Ryan and the Institute of Judicial Administration, as well as the ones which I interviewed, had middle-class parents who were typically either white collar workers or skilled laborers. Only a very small percentage of judges had a parent who was a lawyer, and in my sample of approximately 100 judges, only two had a parent who was a judge. The ethnic and religious breakdown for white judges closely followed their respective city's demographic characteristics.

Although all of the judges were law school graduates, frequently from good to excellent schools, they had a broad variety of occupational experiences prior to joining the bench. The most common legal experience among the judges, aside from the general category of working in a law firm (75 percent), was a former position with the local district attorney's office. Nearly one-third had had at least one year's training as a prosecutor, while one-quarter of this select group had been career prosecutors and had entered the bench directly from the district attorney's office. The effect of this experience upon the judge's ability to maintain a neutral position between the adversaries without favoring the prosecution is a constant concern to private criminal lawyers. Approximately one-third of the judges observed in my travels visibly favored the prosecution, but the remaining group were responsibly neutral. Several were observed to make a noticeable effort to ensure that the defendant received a fair trial. A perceptible number of judges who had prior prosecutorial experience appeared to favor the defense. When queried about this seemingly paradoxical position, the judges usually replied that their prior experience had hardened them to many prosecutorial maneuvers which they found distasteful. Their reasoning sounded vaguely reminiscent of the adage that "familiarity breeds contempt."

The usual period of law practice by the judges prior to joining the bench was 15–20 years. Approximately one-third of the judges came from very small practices of two or three associates, 25 percent had worked in large law firms (more than 10 members), and the remainder in medium to small practices between three and 10 partners. A large number of judges (nearly two-thirds), specialized in the area of litigation and although only a few had more than a smattering of criminal cases, the percentage seems to be increasing, particularly in cities using the appointive style of judicial selection.

Besides their legal work, nearly half of the judges interviewed held some type of public office before reaching their present judicial positions. A large percentage were former state legislators or city council members (20 percent). Another 20 percent held some type of law-related governmental position. Only about 15 percent had any type of prior judicial experience, and this was typically at the misdemeanor court level. Many of the judges who were formerly committed to public service, or active in politics held several of the different types of public law positions as well as brief experiences in the private sector. Nearly every judge appeared to be moderately wealthy as a result of his past working experience. A disturbing number commented that they had taken significant salary cuts to join the bench and did not believe they could remain for an additional term due to the financial strain. For those coming directly from public service, the money problem was rarely noted. The salaries on the felony criminal court bench ranged from $35,000–$40,000 in the southern cities to $55,000–$75,000 in the western and eastern cities. A return to private practice was generally estimated to bring between a 50–100 percent increase in salary.

JUDICIAL PERSONALITY

The renowned professor of sociological jurisprudence, Eugene Ehrlich, has been quoted frequently as stating that "there is no guarantee of justice except the personality of the judge."[5] Very recently, the eminent legal scholar Maurice Rosenberg further clarified the important connection between a judge's personality and his decision-making propensities when he wrote: "The reason the judge makes or breaks the system of justice is that rules are not self-deciding or self-applying. Even in a government of laws, men make the decisions."[6] The import of both of these respected judgments is that a judge's personality is a key ingredient in the quality and style of justice which is dispensed in his or her courtroom.

In my earlier research on criminal lawyers, I was able to describe a persistent modal personality type. This type of attorney was driven by a strong ego which was combined with an aggressive or combative nature. The judges, however, seemed to possess such a wide range of personality traits and behavior patterns, that it is almost impossible to generalize about a modal judicial personality. The only persistent characteristic that did emerge was that like the criminal lawyer, the felony court judge also possessed a strong ego which was typically manifested in a high degree of self-confidence. Their experience as lawyers, and even more importantly as litigators, as well as the heavy responsibilities inherent in the sentencing of defendants, require a strong ego and self-confident attitude as occupational necessities. It almost becomes a self-fulfilling prophecy that such types of individuals are attracted to, and eventually reach, the bench.

Much has been written about the character traits considered desirable in the judiciary. The most frequently quoted list is offered by Bernard Shientag in an address to the Association of the Bar of the City of New York in 1944 when he presented the "Eight Cardinal Virtues of Being a Judge." The eight ideal character traits or "virtues" include the following: independence, courtesy and patience, dignity, open-mindedness, impartiality, thoroughness and decisiveness, compassion and social consciousness."[7]

One would be hard-pressed to find fault with this set of attributes in a judge. Actually, anyone who possesses a few of these laudatory characteristics would be a welcome addition to the bench. Shientag's list, as well as several other recommended collections of attributes, provide useful guidelines for describing the type of judge we would like to have sitting in our criminal courts. The difficult question posed in this chapter is: "what type of individuals do we have presently deciding our serious criminal cases?"

In order to deal with this complex issue, I have selected four critical areas of concern to criminal court judges and will use their response to these issues as a means of determining their feelings concerning their professional obligations. These attitudes will not only reflect the judge's feelings about his or her job but will also indicate the style of performance he or she has chosen to carry out his or her judicial responsibilities.

The following are the four problem areas which will help us define these judicial attitudes: (1) the degree of career orientation (perceived length of service), (2) the degree of importance placed upon case management (perceived need to reduce or dispose of the caseload), (3) the degree of commitment to playing an active role in proceedings (perceived necessity for controlling courtroom activities and procedures), and (4) degree of commitment toward neutrality (as opposed to favoring prosecution or defense). Each of these concepts can be stretched out as a continuum along which a judge can be placed. Clearly discernible extreme positions on the continuum offer an excellent vehicle for further clarifying a judge's approach to each of these four critical issues.

It might have been possible to simply compose a list of personality types which encompass the variety of judges interviewed. This was done by Blumberg and Smith as they focused upon the judge's role performance. They discovered that in Kings County, Brooklyn, New York, the criminal court judges fell into one of the following categories: intellectual scholar, routineer, hack, political adverturer, careerist judicial pensioner, hatchet man, and tyrant-showboat.[8] In order to provide greater flexibility and less strained pigeon-holing in the categorization of judges, the Smith-Blumberg model was rejected in favor of the author's typology presented in this chapter. It is hoped that this categorization scheme will offer the broader and more flexible framework lacking in the Smith-Blumberg model. It will eliminate the necessity for making all-or-nothing choices with regard to which personality type is designated most applicable. Judges are complex individuals, and it should not be surprising to find them at varying points of the continuum for each of the four attitudinal areas. Thus, a judge may be prosecution-oriented in his attitude toward defendants, and also be reluctant to speed cases along, or be interested in playing an active role in court proceedings. Let us now examine each of these concepts in greater detail with special emphasis on the extreme positions.

The first attitudinal area relates to the judge's future aspirations. Ryan's national study of trial judges concluded that "the age at which a judge is initially selected to the bench can indicate the *career meaning* of his judgeship from capstone to steppingstone".[9] Although my observations generally replicated Ryan's conclusions, so many exceptions were discovered during my later research travels as to seriously undermine the validity of the supposed relationship between age and career aspirations. The differences in type of jurisdictions investigated may have accounted for some of the variance in our findings, but I discovered a vocal minority of younger judges complaining about a perceived decline in prestige and working conditions which would necessitate their premature retirement from the bench after just one term. The traditional view, espoused by Ryan and others, is that judges either seem to be young and ambitious, seeking higher political office, or older and resigned to using the position as the capstone of their career. The Ryan generalization seems most valid when applied to electoral (particularly partisan), systems of judicial selection. However, in a city such as Washington, D.C. where judges are appointed by the President, the relationship between age and motivation toward higher political office is non-existent.

The judge's future career aspirations can logically be expected to have some impact upon his professional behavior. Judges who intend to seek higher office, such as an appellate position, should be expected to be aware of the political implications of critical judicial decisions. Thus, the aspiring judge is more likely to be looking over his shoulder at press coverage and expected public reaction. He or she may be careful to impress, or at least, not disappoint, those wielders of political influence who could affect his or her chances for future advancement. Given the public's increased concern over public safety and fear of judicial leniency, it is possible to find certain judges "playing to this audience" by adopting a severe sentencing policy. Of course, one can also argue that those responsible public figures who can influence judicial selection policies may also be looking for judges who do not pander to the public's thirst for vengeance and can remain compassionate, fair-minded jurists, despite public pressure for retribution.

Most of the judges interviewed did not seem to have a higher political office in mind when they were initially selected to the bench. After serving a brief period, approximately 20 percent of the judges did indicate an interest in an appellate position or some other higher political office (i.e., Mayor or Congressman). Nearly half were noncommittal about future plans, with the remaining portion of judges desiring to step down from the bench after concluding their terms of office.

The second issue area is the judge's interest in moving cases expeditiously. This is also closely related to the judge's desire to reduce the backlog of pending cases. In evaluating a judge's position on this variable, I had to be careful not to equate an interest in expediting cases, with a lack of concern for the individual defendant. Although such a relationship may seem natural and did, in fact, exist with several judges committed to efficient movement of cases, there were so many exceptions to this generalization that the correlation between both factors was almost nil. At one extreme are the judges committed to an efficient system of justice. They often view themselves as reformers, intent on ridding the courts of its burdensome backlog. Several judges interviewed stated that the challenge of clearing a large number of cases each day was the major task of their position, and their ability to successfully dispose of this steadily increasing workload was their proudest achievement. They wanted to be remembered at the end of each term for leaving with no backlog of cases and the fewest number of pending cases from the preceding term. The recent speeches of Chief Justice Warren Burger of the United States Supreme Court clearly lend support to the efforts of these efficient judicial bureaucrats.[10]

At the opposite end of the continuum is another group of judges, (estimated roughly to be equal in number to their colleagues at the other extreme), who believe that they must carefully evaluate each case on its own merits regardless of how much time it takes. These judges may euphemistically call themselves "humanitarians," but their relatively slow work habits draw the ire of the "expediting" judges who often refer to them by the less flattering rubric of "knee-jerk liberals" or "soft-minded do-gooders."

This issue appears to divide the criminal court more sharply and emotionally than any of the other four issues. The reason for this is probably related to a belief (which is occasionally well-founded), held by the expediters that when their slower counterparts fail to make a dent in the caseload, they (the expediters) are likely to be the ones eventually saddled with the remaining cases. This creates an hostility, bordering on a strong sense of persecution, as the more efficient judges believe that instead of being rewarded for their speedy efforts, they are being punished by being given the extra cases from their slower colleagues.

Many of the "slower" judges are not acting out of any ideological conviction, but simply are more methodical in their work habits. Nevertheless, a disproportionate percentage of their membership is defense-oriented and is extremely careful to preserve all of the defendant's constitutional rights, regardless of the time element. They typically defend their position by citing the adage that "it is better to see 10 guilty men go free, than one innocent person convicted." They also espouse a firm belief that given the chaos of the criminal courts and the caseload pressures, it requires a conscious effort to provide personalized, careful, attention to each case. The "expediters" rebuttal to this tedious style of judging was offered by an East Coast judge who cited statistics to show that nine out of every 10 persons who passed through his courtroom were guilty, and it was most common for the prosecutor to eventually dismiss charges against the tenth. Therefore, one need not tie down the entire operation in search of that rarest of commodities, the innocent defendant. Additionally, he thought the judiciary could rely upon the prosecutor's office to be responsibly selective in weeding out those cases in which the defendant's guilt was less than certain.

The third problem area concerns the degree to which the judge believes he or she should become involved in the adversary proceedings. Idealistically, the criminal justice system in this country is an adversarial struggle between the defense and prosecution, with the judge sitting as a neutral arbiter. The judge's primary function is to guarantee the constitutional rights of the defendant while ensuring that proper legal procedures are followed. Judges varied a great deal in their interpretation of how active a role they should play in guaranteeing a fair legal battle between defense and prosecution. At one extreme, a small percentage of judges, roughly estimated at about 10 percent of the sample, interpreted their role as "neutral arbiter" quite literally, and conscientiously attempted to remain aloof from the proceedings transpiring before them. This often resulted in exciting confrontations between aggressive adversaries, although it was unclear whether prosecution or defense benefitted from such emotional struggles. A New York City judge who adopted this style was observed to physically remove himself from the legal battle by swiveling around in his high-backed chair, so that his back was to the audience, and with half-closed eyes, gazed lazily toward the ceiling. Judges who adopt this noninterventionist posture were impossible to categorize ideologically as favoring either prosecution or defense.

The majority of judges interviewed tended toward a more activist posture. Their interventionist inclinations were not linked toward favoritism, but simply a personal desire to control the judicial proceedings occurring in their courtrooms. These judges did, however, seem to share rather aggressive, extroverted personalities. They were frequently described by courthouse regulars as "playing to the jury or gallery" at every opportunity. They rationalized their "active" style of judging as being necessary to control erring attorneys as well as the judge's responsibility to educate the jury. Both justifications grew out of the broader demands placed upon the judge to ensure that each defendant received a fair trial. Defense attorneys were frequently critical of judges who adopted this activist style since it was most commonly used to aid the prosecution. Such judges were referred to as "showboats" or "tyrants," depending upon the style and motivations of their intrusions.

The final problem area also relates to the judge's biases. It focuses upon whether the judge appears to favor either the prosecution or defense, as a consistent pattern of behavior. Many judges are keenly aware of how such biases conflict and undermine their legal responsibilities toward neutrality, but find it nearly impossible to stifle their natural instincts. Approximately 25 percent of the judges appeared successful in maintaining strict neutrality, but on the whole most judges seemed to favor the prosecution. The percentage of judges favoring the prosecution did seem to be declining during the 1970s, but given the current "law and order" backlash and public demand for more severe sentences, the current crop of criminal court judges (1983) appear to be returning to the prosecution orientation. An extremely rough estimate would place 40–50 percent of the criminal court judges favoring the prosecution, while the remaining 25–35 percent appear to be inclined toward the defense. A more detailed analysis of how biases affect judicial behavior will be presented in the next chapter.

The defense-oriented judges were commonly criticized for being too lenient and altruistic. It was impossible to find a persistent set of background characteristics identifying this group, although they were disproportionally associated with the Democratic party and a member of a racial or religious minority. Because the trial judges in most cities were likely to have a reputation as being harsh sentencers and prosecution-oriented, the judges handling arraignments (guilty pleas) and non-jury trials were often more likely to be defense-oriented and more moderate in their sentencing policies. This is not unexpected, given the common practice of trying to coerce defendants into plea bargains by threats of a heavier sentence if he was convicted after a trial. Thus, the judges placed in these jury trial courts often developed reputations as "hanging Judges." It was interesting to discover that judges who had prior work experience as prosecutors appeared to be no less likely to favor either the defense or prosecution.

Familiarity also seemed to breed contempt on the opposite extreme as former defense attorneys occasionally became "hard-nosed" law and order jurists. It seemed that they had suffered through so many unpleasant experiences at the hands of their former clients, especially in terms of their veracity, that they had become antagonistic and sometimes callous toward the defense position.

JUDICIAL RECRUITMENT

The two basic methods of selecting judges is either by appointment or election. Most states have opted for some form of the appointment process. Thirty-one states use commission plans of appointment to aid governors in selecting judges. Twenty of these states use the commissions for the initial selection, while the remaining 11 use this appointment style just to fill vacancies. It should also be noted that four states have the governor appoint judges without using a nominating commission.[11] These commissions are typically appointed by the governor and are composed of legislators, judges, and respected members of the bar, with the rare inclusion of a layman. They may offer the governor just one nominee, but usually provide him with the choice of at least three. This selection method, first gaining notoriety under the Missouri Plan nearly 40 years ago, has been closely associated with an effort to make judicial selection based more upon merit and less upon political favoritism. Although students of the judicial process have concluded that these nominating commissions have not totally eliminated political influence, they have sharply reduced its importance.[12]

A 1973 federal task force entitled *The National Advisory Commission on Criminal Justice Standards and Goals* has strongly advocated the appointment mode of selection by stating under Standard 7.1 that "The selection of judges should be based on merit qualifications for judicial office . . . The judges should be selected by a judicial nominating commission. Representatives from the judiciary, the general public, and the legal profession should organize into a seven-member judicial nominating commission for the sole purpose of nominating a slate of qualified candidates eligible to fill judicial vacancies from this list."[13]

Approximately 30 states choose most of their judges by some form of election. Partisan elections for all judgeships are used in 13 states, while eight states will employ elections in a limited number of positions, usually in the lower courts. Nonpartisan elections for most or all judgeships are held in 17 states.[14] It is difficult to assess the significance of the partisan versus the nonpartisan method of judicial elections, although most judges interviewed failed to see any noticeable difference in the degree of politics found in either. Both involved nominating processes controlled by the dominant political party. It usually meant that for a lawyer to gain nomination, he had to prove himself or herself acceptable to the party leadership.

How does a lawyer seeking a criminal court judgeship make himself acceptable to the party leadership? Most of the judges interviewed said that it was either through loyal party service or public notoriety. It also helped to have a clear association with the nominating party. Loyal party service could mean that a person had worked faithfully in a number of party jobs for a long period of time or had been a reliable contributor to the party's treasury. Notoriety might have been achieved through public service as a prosecutor or as a state legislator. Association with one of the city's top law firms or a leadership role in the local bar association could also serve as a means of keeping one's name before the public's attention.

A minority of cities visited employed a relatively less politicized appointment process. Nevertheless, the judgeship-seeking lawyer generally had to be of the same political party as the nominating governor and/or legislature. Although proof of party loyalty was not very evident, the notoriety requirement could be a critical obstacle. State and local professional reputations were enhanced through public service at the state and local level, leadership positions with the bar association, or association with a prominent law firm, or prestigious law school.

In terms of comparing criminal court judges who were appointed with those elected, only slight differences in background were evident. The appointed judges were more likely to come from public service jobs at the state and local level. Many were lower court or municipal court judges. There was also a high likelihood they were from a large, prestigious law firm. Given the tendency for the elective systems to be found in older, more traditional cities which are Democratically dominated, it was not surprising to find these judges coming from very small firms. The appointment process was most likely to be found in the more progressive cities of the far west and Rocky Mountain regions.

JUDICIAL SOCIALIZATION

Students of judicial behavior are thought to be offered an excellent opportunity to observe the process of adult socialization. In contrast to judges from most other countries, the United States has failed to create a career judiciary.[15] Instead, United States judges who rarely receive any training or education prior to assuming office, learn their craft through a form of "on-the-job training." The beginning judge in the United States must, therefore, be "socialized" into his new position, and be dependent upon his colleagues on the bench and other socializing agents for the necessary information and informal training.

It is true that nearly all United States judges have shared the common experience of a legal education. However, once completing law school, lawyers then specialize in divergent areas of the law and many almost never venture inside a courtroom. In contrast to most European countries, the United States has not chosen to develop a body of career judges in which one enters the profession at an early age and works his or her way up the judicial hierarchy. Instead, we have opted for what Professor David Neubauer has described as "essentially judicial amateurs . . . who have no practical experience or systematic exposure to the judicial world."[16]

As a result of the absence of any viable orientation or training program, the newly selected judge is thrust into a rather alien environment. It is at this point that the "judicial socialization" process goes to work to teach the beginning judge the accepted modes of behavior of his new profession. Daniel Feldman, an eminent social psychologist, has offered an excellent model for this process of "individual socialization into a new organization" and has identified three distinct stages leading to four possible outcome variables. Although Professor Feldman's study was conducted at a hospital rather than a courthouse, its applicability to the judicial scene will be readily apparent.[17]

The first stage is defined as *anticipatory socialization* which occurs before the recruit enters the organization and begins to form expectations about his job and starts to receive some preliminary information from his prospective employer. At the next stage entitled *accommodation*, the individual sees what the organization is actually like and attempts to become a member of it. The final stage which is termed *role management* finds the recruit having resolved some of his newly-emerging problems in his workgroup and now beginning to mediate conflicts within the organization.

The Feldman model soon proved to be a workable paradigm for the study of judicial socialization and was recently utilized by Lenore Alpert, Burton Atkins, and Robert Ziller in their 1979 study entitled "Becoming a Judge: The Transition from Advocate to Arbiter."[18] Although they modified the Feldman model, its influence is obvious. These authors developed a four-stage process which carries the judge completely through his or her judicial career. It begins first with *Professional Socialization* before he or she becomes a judge, when he or she is primarily a product of early legal experiences, including law school. The second stage, *Initiation and Resolution*, includes the judge's first five years on the bench, when he or she typically has an altruistic or legalist role orientation and begins to learn the reality of his or her newly accepted profession. The third stage is the *Establishment Period* which lasts from the sixth through the fifteenth year and has the judge adopting the role orientation of "guardian of the law." There follows a long term process of coping and possible role re-definition. The final period is the *Commitment Period* after the judge has served 15 years. He or she has now chosen to become a legalist and guardian of the law and experiences increased satisfaction with the judicial life.[19]

The Alpert et al., article concludes that "our model of socialization indicates the effect of organizational tenure upon both the individual judge and the individual-organization fit."[20] They have thus offered a theoretical schema of judicial socialization which can be applied to varying levels of courts.

The final article which offers an important contribution to the study of judicial socialization is a study of 30 federal district court judges. This is the work of Robert Carp and Russell Wheeler entitled *Sink or Swim: The Socialization of a Federal District Court Judge*.[21] Although the Carp and Wheeler study utilized a rather small sample of judges from a particular court system, their findings are generally considered to be the definitive work on most facets of judicial socialization. In contrast with both Feldman and Alpert et al.,[18] Carp and Wheeler moved away from simply categorizing the various stages of socialization, and instead focused upon the major problems facing judges during their early years on the bench. They found that socialization problems for the judges were either *legal, administrative,* or *psychological.*

Legal problems were substantive or procedural and were usually caused by the inexperience of the judge in handling criminal cases. The procedural problems ranged from a shaky understanding of the pretrial arraignment process through difficulty in drawing up proper charges to the jury. The *administrative* problems were presented as an unexpected difficulty. Most beginning judges had little appreciation for the complexities of managing a budget, staff, or docket. The *psychological* problems facing the judge were summarized by the authors as being mainly "the loneliness of the office, sentencing defendants, forgetting the adversary role, local pressure and maintaining a judicial bearing both on and off the bench."[22]

With so many problems facing the beginning judges, where can he or she turn for help? It was previously noted that there is almost no formal educative or training process currently available. The judge must, therefore, turn to a group of "socializing agents" who can informally educate him or her as to the legal and social prescriptions of the newly-acquired position. Carp and Wheeler, as well as others, have usually rated the judge's colleagues as the foremost training agents. They accomplish this task both through formalized professional meetings and seminars as well as informal exchanges during the workday. A second source of information is the lawyers who appear in their courtrooms. Blumberg believes that, based on his observations in the Kings County (Brooklyn) New York Criminal Courthouse, the judge's staff—law clerks, secretary, stenographer, and bailiff commonly provide him with critical advice on administrative and procedural matters.[23] Despite all of this possible help, Professor Neubauer is probably correct in concluding that "In the end, the judges must rely on themselves. Through reading in the law library and seeking out knowledgeable persons, judges engage in self-education."[24]

Law reformers, legal scholars, and other students of our nation's judicial system have long been aware of the absence of meaningful education programs for the beginning judge as a substitute for this "self-education" process. Although most judges still receive at best only a cursory orientation and continue to be dependent upon an informal socializing process, the past 20 years have witnessed many new bold programs and the prognosis for the future appears positive. The concept of judicial education was first translated into actual training seminars in 1961. Fifty sessions were conducted between 1961 and 1963 for state trial judges. The program was financed by both the American Bar Association and the W. K. Kellogg Foundation. Prior to these initial efforts, the idea that a judge needed to go back to school was not widely accepted, and viewed by many as an insult to the judiciary, inferring that they did not know how to do their jobs.[25]

By the late 1960s, the necessity for judicial education was accepted by bench and bar. By the end of the decade, the Federal Judiciary had opened its own academy in Washington, The American Academy of Judicial Education had begun conducting its National Trial Judges Academy, and the National College of State Judiciary had initiated its extensive training programs in Reno at the University of Nevada. In addition to the commencement of these specific programs, a national consensus of professional opinion had agreed upon the necessity for creating and implementing a widespread program of education for all levels of judicial officials. Standard 7.5 of the National Advisory Commission on Criminal Justice Standard and Goals exemplifies this national commitment. This Standard urges each state to "create and maintain a comprehensive program of continuing judicial education" and recommended that these programs have the following features:

1. All new trial judges within three years of assuming judicial office should attend both local and national orientation programs, as well as one of the national judicial educational programs. The local orientation program should come immediately before or after the judge first takes office. It should include visits to all institutions and facilities to which criminal offenders may be sentenced.
2. Each state should develop its own judicial college which should be responsible for the orientation program for new judges and which should make available to all state judges the graduate and refresher programs of the national judicial educational organization. Each state also should have specialized subject matter programs as well as two or three-day annual state seminars for trial and appellate judges.[26]

Despite the growing awareness of these programs, and encouragement from national commissions and organizations, there continues to be a lack of total commitment by all state and local court systems to institutionalize training and orientation programs. As of 1980, five states have no training programs at all (Maine, Montana, Vermont, West Virginia, and Wyoming), and of states with programs, only half are mandatory.[27] The National College of the State Judiciary in Reno, Nevada and the American Academy of Judicial Education of Washington, D.C., however, are two organizations that are aggressively attempting to improve the quality of judicial education. The American Academy, for example, states in their organizational material that they are currently able to "design and operate a state judicial academy, provide organizational support to the state educational officer, function under the supervision of a state education committee as the training arm of the state supreme court or develop whatever kind of special program is useful or necessary.[28] The work of the National Judicial College, has been summed up by its former Dean, Laurance M. Hyde, who stated: "The most important thing we offer is the chance to exchange viewpoints and experiences and to give them a sense of a national picture."[29]

Before moving on to the discussion of the socialization experiences of Philadelphia criminal court judges, it would be instructive to briefly reconstruct the major theories of judicial socialization. The major theoretical premise for the necessary existence of such a process is that following entry into the judiciary, with no prior training, the new judge must undergo a rather severe socialization process in which his or her views of proper role conduct will be significantly shaped. Since we have so few formal socializing processes, a variety of socializing agents, dominated by his colleagues on the bench, engage in an informal, yet effective, socialization/education process. Additionally, professional organizations have recently responded to the absence of these formalized educative structures and are rapidly beginning to develop a wide range of orientation and continuing education programs.

Since all of these new programs and recent research projects have been based upon what might be a questionable premise—that all new judges know almost nothing about their jobs and are in drastic need of educative programs—this study was performed to investigate a group of criminal court judges in Philadelphia, Pennsylvania's Court of Common Pleas to learn if their early years on the bench do, in fact, fit these premises.

THE PHILADELPHIA EXPERIENCE

As a result of spending four weeks during the summer of 1980 observing and interviewing judges in the Philadelphia Court of Common Pleas, the process of judicial socialization as described in the preceding section of this chapter did not occur. Because of either inherent self-confidence, easy adaptability or prior experience and training, these judges did not believe, or act as though they had undergone any evident socialization process. Although they admitted they received virtually no orientation or training, they generally thought they were able to do a competent job, often independent of aid from any socializing agents such as colleagues or law clerks.

The second section of this discussion of judicial socialization will examine the socialization experiences of the Common Pleas judges. Topics for analysis will be their prior backgrounds, how they were selected, first days on the job, possible socializing agents, and initial adjustments. In the final section, two important variables will be presented to explain the Philadelphia phenomenon, and an assessment of whether their socializing experiences were actually so unique.

In the review of earlier studies of judicial socialization, it is significant to note that nearly all of the major works have focused upon judges from either the state appellate or federal systems.[30] This emphasis upon appellate and federal courts has permeated not only studies of judicial socialization but the entire study of public law.

The judges interviewed for this study comprise nearly 45 percent of the active judges hearing criminal cases in the Philadelphia Court of Common Pleas. This court has jurisdiction over the disposition of all felony cases and has a total of 35 judges involved in various programs: homicide (8), calendar (14), and criminal list (13).

THEIR BACKGROUNDS

The underlying premise in justifying the existence of judicial socialization is primarily the belief that most judges lack the necessary courtroom experience to adequately prepare them for their forthcoming judicial responsibilities. This seems especially true in the federal courts where appointments are frequently made of high quality corporate lawyers who rarely have litigation experience, and are even less likely to be prepared to handle the inevitable criminal cases soon to appear on their calendars.[31]

It was interesting to note that even though Philadelphia's Court of Common Pleas handles both civil and criminal matters, nearly all judges, through a self-selection process generally related to their intellectual interests and previous legal experiences, have stayed either within the criminal or civil side without the expected rotation. This contrasts sharply with the Federal District Courts where judges will be faced with all types of cases and have no control over which category of dispute they will be deciding.

The explanation for the Philadelphia judges' self-confidence upon taking office, is most likely related to their prior work experiences. In contrast to the generally accepted belief that most judges come ill-equipped for the job with little litigation experience, 80 percent of the Philadelphia sample stated that they had had trial experience with nearly half having served in the prosecutor's office. One of the judges had been a law clerk for 20 years. Other types of legal experiences related to trial work were negligence (40 percent) and general business litigation (25 percent). Besides 50 percent of the sample being former prosecutors, several others had had experience with the criminal justice system, as 15 percent were formerly employed in the city's prestigious public defender office and 25 percent had had experience as private criminal lawyers. Nearly all of the judges interviewed, with only two exceptions, started out on the criminal side and have spent their entire judicial tenure on that type of case.

Another trend within the Philadelphia judiciary was similarity in educational background. This combined with the decidedly inbred nature— born and raised within the city limits—gave the court a homogeneous grouping rarely found at the appellate or federal level. It is also a finding consistent with my earlier work on criminal lawyers in which 22 of the 23 Philadelphia sample were raised or educated locally.[32]

The Selection Process: The Political Path

Despite the surprising amount of trial experience, particularly in the practice of criminal law, it clearly was the presence of political connections and activities which seemed to propel nearly all of the judges through the selection process. Common Pleas judges are elected to 10-year terms in Philadelphia and must be able to gain the support of the dominant leaders of the Democratic party, although a select number of "acceptable" Republicans are allowed to gain favorable backing. All judges interviewed attested to the extreme politicization of the judicial selection process. Previous studies of Philadelphia have also noted the significant impact that politics plays upon the entire criminal justice system.[33]

Immediately prior to running for judicial office, nearly half of the judges had held public office or were actively involved in politics (according to their own self-evaluation). Several of the judges had run (usually successfully) for Congressional and mayoral positions. Nearly all had at sometime in the recent past (within 10 years of receiving their judgeships) maintained a moderate level of political involvement. This manifested itself in a variety of tasks and responsibilities within the party organization. Their activities ranged from near full-time preoccupation with politics and elections at the ward, state and national levels, to a highly selective and limited participation in a few carefully chosen campaigns. Politics, for most of the judges, was a fascinating and important diversion which had played a significant role in their professional lives.

Despite the obvious interest in political affairs prior to becoming a judge, approximately 50 percent of the judges interviewed forcefully indicated that they did not seek out the judgeship as a political goal, but rather had it offered to them by friends who were influential party officials. The reasons for such good fortune was thought by the judges to be derived from long friendships with the city's political leaders, their distinguished professional reputations, and moderate visibility on the Philadelphia political and social scene—the last two criteria being logically related to the vote-getting potential of the candidate.

The political career of one of the city's judges, Thomas A. White, was highlighted in a recent *Time* magazine cover story entitled *Judging the Judges*, and offers a critical examination of the linkage between politics and judicial office in Philadelphia. According to the article, White was picked to fill a vacancy in 1977. Why? 'I'm Irish,' he says. 'Of course, I'm qualified,' he hastily adds. But he matter-of-factly explains that the Democratic Party needed an Irish judge to balance the ethnic makeup of the judicial slate. One of 16 children of an Irish Republican Army member who fled Ireland, he is also a life-long Democrat who managed to be elected to the state legislature in the Eisenhower landslide. Redistricted out of his seat in 1954, he decided to go to law school and became a criminal defense lawyer. All the while, he stayed active in Democratic ward politics and his loyalty was rewarded when he was backed for a judgeship by Congressman Raymond F. Lederer whom White describes as a "close personal freind."[34] Although the career of Judge Thomas White is an extreme example of the possible political involvement of Philadelphia's judges prior to their election, it is nevertheless a difference in degree rather than kind.

First Days on the Job and Additional Training

Traditional descriptions of the new judge's first days on the job are usually pictured as traumatic events in which the novice judge suffers from a sense of inferiority and uncertainty. The Philadelphia judges, however, recounted this memorable period as one of excitement and challenge. They generally were confident that they could handle the new job. There was little that was unexpected, and most felt that on-the-job training would shortly dispose of the few problems and uncertainties. The absence of a viable orientation program was noted, but most judges felt that for themselves, any extended type of training was not necessary (although many thought that some of their colleagues might have been brought along too rapidly and were in need of a lengthier indoctrination).

These sentiments should not be construed to imply a blasé attitude on the part of these novice judges. They were both flattered and sometimes puzzled by their new perquisites and respect. Even the idea of wearing a robe was foreign to them as they strolled from their chambers to the court-room. The bowing and scraping of City Hall functionaries is still an annoyance and embarrassment for several. A disappointment for the newer judges was their less-than-impressive offices (chambers) located in an undistinguished office building across the street from the City Hall Courthouse. Most of the judges implied that their offices were a noticeable step down in terms of size and elegance from their previous private law offices.

In Philadelphia, new judges are given a two-day orientation period which focuses primarily upon administrative concerns. They are also urged to attend state-wide judicial conferences held twice yearly and are designed to provide an educative component for the beginning judge as well as refresher seminars for the more experienced. These conferences were described as more social than educational. The only judge interviewed who did seem to require extensive preparation because of his lack of legal experiences was given a three-month stint on the Municipal Court which handles misdemeanors and less serious cases. None of the judges interviewed had been to the National Judicial College at the University of Nevada. Most were skeptical of such programs, describing them as being social affairs with little long-range value.

The Philadelphia judges interviewed generally exuded self-confidence in their capacity to master the art of judging in criminal cases without formalized training sessions. Any problems which did arise would be readily disposed of through informal conversations with trusted colleagues. No new plans appear to be projected in the near future to significantly alter the current limited and unstructured training process. So long as the judges continue to reach the court with respectable litigation backgrounds, the necessity for such educative programs may not be relevant for the Court of Common Pleas.

Socializing Agents

Being consistent with the rest of this study's findings, the Philadelphia judges did not feel any urgency for consulting with or relying upon the help of socializing agents. As noted in the introductory section, these socializing agents are generally a group of public officials within the criminal justice system who provide advice and information for the beginning judge. They include the judge's colleagues, his court staff (law clerk, bailiff, secretary, and stenographer), lawyers, and public officials such as prosecutors, public defenders, and court administrators.

Should a problem arise, most of the judges stated they would first turn to one of their more experienced colleagues whom they respected. The entire Court of Common Pleas meets two or three time per year, and then only to discuss pressing administrative matters. For the eight to ten judges assigned to the waiver unit which conducts non-jury felony trials, their intragroup monthly meetings were viewed by most of the interviewed judges as informative and useful. Most acknowledged that these lunch hour meetings offered the major interaction among the judges. Outside of these meetings, the beginning judge might select another judge or two whom he personally respected and contact him privately in chambers for advice. Typical difficulties for the novice judge were proper drafting of charges to the jury, judicious handling of obnoxious defense attorneys, and aiding incompetent prosecutors.

Nearly all judges interviewed were surprised by the lack of collegiality among their fellow members of the court. There was almost no socializing outside of a few official functions. Each judge seemed to have two or three close friends among his colleagues, but was rather disdainful toward most of the other members of the court. It was surprising to have every judge interviewed comment so negatively upon the ability of his colleagues. The most typical descriptions invoked the terms "lazy, slow-witted, inadequate, and mediocre."

The second group of socializing agents used by judges is the court staff. The Philadelphia judges did not emphasize the roles of their staff during their initial socialization, although they were appreciative of the many useful services that they did provide during their judicial tenure. The law clerk, typically a half-time employee with a law degree and an interest in criminal law, is the most critical member of the court staff. Although the amount and type of work delegated to the law clerk varied greatly among the judges, most seemed to rely upon them for tedious legal research. Some judges offered clerk positions to outstanding law school graduates and treated it as an honorific year-long position similar to a clerkship at the appellate level. Many judges, however, simply viewed the clerk as a professional aide who would remain with the judge for as long as both of them could tolerate each other. These clerks occasionally worked with the judge prior to his reaching the bench. One judge credited his law clerk of many years experience with personally reducing the number of possible appellate reversals.

Other possible socializing agents beyond the law clerks and their colleagues were either not mentioned or noted as being ineffective. This is not to imply that judges in Philadelphia are not friendly and open with members of the courthouse community. One is immediately struck by the convivial atmosphere in both the chambers and the courthouse, but this surface cordiality has not affected the independent decision-making of each judge.[35]

Adjustments

Although most Philadelphia judges indicated that their assuming judicial office did not necessitate any meaningful adjustments in their lives, each judge did note some slight alteration in his life which he had not fully anticipated. Almost without exception, the judges stated that their social lives and circle of friends did not change. If they were friendly with lawyers, both parties made a conscious effort to avoid topics which might prove uncomfortable, and studiously avoided talking about pending litigation.

A few of the judges were surprised by their difficulty in abandoning their previously held adversarial role. Especially during the first months on the bench, several judges stated that they had to restrain themselves from jumping into the fray to aid an incompetent attorney. One judge had trouble initially stifling himself from objecting to an attorney's arguments which were drifting off the subject. Too many years as a defense attorney or prosecutor leave a mark on courtroom behavior which often takes several months to erase. One judge candidly admitted that he would close his eyes in the beginning as the only way to refrain from showing emotion. The most unusual adjustment was by one judge who stated that as a top trial lawyer, he was working himself toward a nervous breakdown, and he found that the pace of court life was sufficiently slow to reduce stress and lower his blood pressure.

The Future and a Miscellany of Related Comments

It was interesting to note that outside of three exceptions, the judges expressed a strong desire to continue working in the criminal law area despite the fact that by being in a unified court system, they could easily choose to be rotated to the civil side. The administrative judge, realizing the preference of most civil judges to remain with their more familiar environs, was happy to keep things static and not coerce the judges into unpopular shifts. A possible explanation for this development may be related to the legal backgrounds of each group of judges. The civil judges, in particular, have been described as being quite unfamiliar with the criminal law and rarely litigated criminal matters prior to their assuming office. As previously noted, the criminal judges frequently came with experience in the prosecutor's office or an occasional criminal case, as part of their general litigation practice. Several of the criminal court judges stated that they resisted a switch to the civil side because they would not know the law as well, and they would be continually having to call their colleagues for advice. They found themselves finally becoming comfortable handling criminal cases and did not want to complicate their lives by having to re-tool and learn the myriad of civil law complexities. Other judges found the civil law boring and dry and preferred the excitement and drama of criminal cases. It was frequently described as being more significant since it dealt with people's lives and not merely the exchange of monies and property. Only one judge stated a strong preference for leaving the criminal law; he believed that the civil side held the greater intellectual challenge which he felt had been waning after his first few years on the bench.

Approximately one-quarter of the judges interviewed were looking forward to leaving the bench at the completion of their present terms of office. Another quarter were undecided about the future, while the remaining 50 percent had positive feelings about continuing on the bench indefinitely—either at the Court of Common Pleas or a higher court, such as the state appellate branch. For those contemplating leaving the court, monetary reasons were by far the most common explanation. Depressing working conditions, declining respect, and impossible caseloads were additional reasons. It was felt by nearly all of the judges interviewed that they were losing 50–75 percent of their potential income by remaining on the bench. One frustrated judge added that the longer he remained on the bench, the more difficult it would be for him to return to private practice where the continually changing laws would have him hopelessly out of date. He concluded that, despite financial hardships, he had to remain on the bench.

CONCLUSIONS

It appears from the findings of this study that the criminal court judges sitting on the Philadelphia Court of Common Pleas have not undergone the type of judicial socializaton process which was described in the initial section of this chapter. The overwhelming majority of judges interviewed in Philadelphia possessed the self-confidence and/or prior experience to assume their judgeships with almost no reliance upon socializing agents or training programs.

The Philadelphia experience as described in this chapter raises several important questions concerning the city's court system and the political environment which encapsulates and affects its operation. Is this city's criminal court system and political culture a unique situation? Is it such an anomaly that it may be discounted as merely an extreme, and therefore isolated phenomenon?

Although this question can only be definitively answered after future research investigates judicial socialization experiences in a wide variety of jurisdictions with diverse political cultures, my past decade of travels have replicated the Philadelphia experience.[36] What makes these conclusions even more credible is that my most recent observations of felony court judges during the past three summers verified the Philadelphia findings.

Because the study of the Philadelphia Court of Common Pleas represents a different type of judicial and political milieu from the federal district and state appellate court systems which have formed the primary database for most of the previous studies of judicial socialization, it may be hypothesized that the divergent environments are the critical explanatory variables. Thus, the Philadelphia socialization process may be typical for urban felony courts operating within a highly politicized setting, while the Carp and Wheeler study accurately describes federal and state appellate courts within their relatively less political settings.

Recent studies by Schmidhauser,[37] Richardson and Vines[38] and Abraham[39] have carefully documented the fact that most judges are selected from prestigious law firms which are heavily dominated by upper middle class, white, Anglo-Saxon Protestants. Although politics obviously plays some role in their selection, it is a minor factor when compared with the Philadelphia process. The very nature of the federal court system with its lifetime appointments and newly implemented merit panels attempt to remove the judge from political pressure. The judges are also frequently forced to relocate in a new city, forced to deal with criminal (as well as civil) cases for the first time in their lives, after professional seclusion within a large corporate firm. It is little wonder that these federal judges would be likely (and willing) candidates for judicial socialization.

Beyond the influence of the type of court system, is the equally significant factor of the type of political culture which surrounds that court system. This point was convincingly demonstrated in Martin Levin's important book, *Urban Politics and the Criminal Courts.*[40] Levin's study compared the criminal trial judges in a traditional city, Pittsburgh, where judicial selections reflected a highly politicized environment, with a reform city, Minneapolis, which had a weak political machine. In Pittsburgh, Levin found that the Democratic party machine selected judges from its own ranks and "have minority ethnic and lower income backgrounds and prejudicial careers in political parties and government rather than in private practice."[41] In Minneapolis, however, the selection of judges had been taken out of politics and controlled more by the bar association and large, business-oriented law firms. The judges selected also were most likely to come from both of these institutions.

As a concluding note, it is urged that in order to better understand judicial socialization, one should take into account two critical variables which appear to influence the process. The first is the *type* and *level* of the court. For too long, studies of judicial socialization have focused almost exclusively upon the federal or state appellate courts. The Philadelphia judges deciding felony cases within the Court of Common Pleas have experienced a far different socialization process than is found at the state appellate and federal judiciary. It appears that additionally, the professional backgrounds and style of judicial recruitment and selection also differ markedly from their federal and appellate counterparts. Obviously, this is not a call to terminate the study of the federal and appellate systems, but rather a recommendation to follow the leads of Eisenstein, Jacob, Levin, Neubauer, and others who have initiated serious investigations into the operation of our local trial courts.[42]

The second variable, closely related to the first, is to take into consideration the *degree* and *type of politicization* surrounding the local court system. This variable, as Levin has pointed out, can exert significant influence upon the operation of the court system from its selection and recruitment process all the way through critical sentencing decisions. The startling similarity between the Philadelphia political environment studied here and that of Pittsburgh studied by Levin appears to offer further evidence of the possible linkage between these sets of variables.

NOTES

1. John Paul Ryan et al. *American Trial Judges*. New York, Free Press, 1980.

   Institute of Judicial Administration, *Judicial Education in the United States: A Survey*. New York, 1965, p. 276 (mimeographed).
2. Preliminary Report of the Minority Judiciary, *Howard Law Journal* 18 (1975), p. 495.
3. Pasqual DeVito. An Experiment in the Use of Court Statistics, *Judicature* 56 (August/September 1972), p. 57.
4. "Preliminary Report of the Minority Judiciary," op. cit., p. 501.
5. This quote was attributed to Eugene Ehrlich by Bernard Shientag in his treatise *The Personality of the Judge*, New York, Association of the Bar of New York, 1944.
6. Dorothy Nelson. *Judicial Administration and the Administration of Justice*. Minneapolis, West Publishing Co., 1977 p. 683.
7. Bernard Shientag. *The Personality of the Judge*. New York, Association of the Bar of New York, 1944.
8. Alexander Smith and Abraham Blumberg. The Problem of Objectivity in Judicial Decision-Making, *Social Forces* 46 (1967) 1, pp. 96–105.
9. Ryan, op. cit., p. 124.
10. How to Break the Logjam in the Courts: An Exclusive Interview With Chief Justice Burger, *U.S. News and World Report* 85 (December, 1977), pp. 21–24; and Warren Burger. What's Wrong with Our Courts, *Journal of Insurance* 37 (September/October 1976), p. 2.
11. Larry Berkson. Judicial Selection Today, *Judicature* 64 (October, 1980), p. 176.
12. Henry Glick, *Courts, Politics, and Justice*. New York, McGraw-Hill, 1983.

    Richard Watson and Rondal Downing. *The Politics of Bench and Bar*. New York, John Wiley, 1973.

    James Eisenstein. *Politics and the Legal Process*. New York, Harper & Row, 1973.
13. National Advisory Commission on Criminal Justice Standards and Goals. *Courts*. Washington, D.C.: Government Printing Office, 1973, p. 158.
14. Berkson, op. cit., p. 177.
15. Delmar Karlen. Judicial Education, *American Bar Association Journal* 52 (1966), p. 1049.
16. David Neubauer. *America's Courts and the Criminal Justice System*. N. Scituate, Mass.: Duxbury Press, 1979, p. 168.
17. Daniel C. Feldman. A Contingency Theory of Socialization, *Administrative Science Quarterly* 21 (1976), p. 433.

18. Lenore Alpert, Burton Atkins, and Robert C. Ziller. Becoming a Judge: The Transition from Advocate to Arbiter, *Judicature* 62 (February, 1979), 325.
19. Ibid. p. 328.
20. Ibid. p. 335.
21. Robert Carp and Russell Wheeler. Sink or Swim—Socialization of a Federal District Judge, *Journal of Public Law* 21 (1972) 359.
22. Ibid. p. 373.
23. Abraham Blumberg. *Criminal Justice*. Chicago, Quadrangle Books, 1967, p. 124.
24. Neubauer, op. cit., p. 169.
25. Neubauer, op. cit., p. 169.
26. National Advisory Commission on Criminal Justice Standard and Goals, op. cit., p. 157.
27. Neubauer, op. cit., p. 170.
28. American Academy of Judicial Education. *Publicity Handout*. Washington, D.C., 1980.
29. Donald Dale Jackson. *Judges*. New York, Atheneum, 1974 p. 19.
30. Alpert, op. cit., and Carp, op. cit.
31. Both Joseph Goulden (*The Benchwarmers*, New York: Weybright and Talley, 1974) and John Schmidhauser (*Judges and Justices: The Federal Appellate Judiciary*, Boston: Little Brown, 1979) address this issue and draw similar conclusions.
32. Paul Wice. *Criminal Lawyers: An Endangered Species*. Beverly Hills, Sage Publications, 1978, p. 39.
33. *Freedom for Sale*. (Lexington, Mass.: Lexington Books, 1974); *Criminal Lawyers: An Endangered Species* (Beverly Hills, Sage Publications, 1978); and with Peter Suwak. Current Realities of Public Defender Programs, *Criminal Law Bulletin*, 1973.
34. Judging the Judges, *Time* (Magazine). August 20, 1979, p. 52.
35. Possibly the fact that these judges operate in so political an environment in which nearly all the actors are inbred, and have known each other for so long, accounts for the "small town" atmosphere of the courthouse.
36. The most recent studies in this field have been initiated by Arthur Rosett for the Twentieth Century Fund and John Paul Ryan for the American Judicature Society.
37. John Schmidhauser. *Judges and Justices*. Boston: Little Brown, 1979.
38. Richard Richardson and Kenneth Vines. *The Politics of the Federal Courts*. Boston, Little, Brown, and Co., 1970.
39. Henry Abraham. *The Judicial Process*. New York: Oxford University Press, 1980.
40. Martin Levin. *Urban Politics and the Criminal Courts*. Chicago, University of Chicago Press, 1977.
41. Ibid, p. 5.
42. James Eisenstein and Herbert Jacob. *Felony Justice*. Boston, Little, Brown, and Co., 1977; Martin Levin. *Urban Politics and the Criminal Courts*. Chicago, University of Chicago Press, 1977; David Neubauer. *America's Courts and the Criminal Justice System*. N. Scituate, Mass: Duxbury Press, 1979; and George Cole. *The American System of Criminal Justice*. N. Scituate, Mass.: Duxbury Press, 1975.

5

THE ART OF JUDGING

Because our nation has chosen to follow the English adversarial system of justice rather than the inquisitorial system, we have placed judges in an extremely difficult position. This delicate position may require even greater sensitivity and sophistication from our judges than is needed in the aggressive posture required for the inquisitorial system. During the conduct of the trial, (as well as critical pretrial decisions), United States judges must guarantee that the defendant receives a fair trial, that rules of evidence are properly enforced, that jurors are aided in reaching an enlightened verdict, and that society will be protected by a proper disposition. It is in the balancing of these seemingly irreconcilable demands that the criminal court judge must engage in the "art of judging." This chapter will offer an analysis of how the criminal court judges in our major cities attempt to balance these demands as they practice their craft.

As in other chapters within this volume, I have shied away from issues which appear overly legalistic. Instead, I will view the art of judging through an examination of those concerns which appear to be of most interest to the general public and are not overly technical. This chapter will, therefore, focus upon the following topics: maintaining neutrality, searching for the truth, keeping track of the proceedings, the limits of judicial intervention, managing the caseload, and maintaining compassion and interest over the years.

The job of the criminal court judge is complicated by the failue of the United States to educate and train public officials in the profession of judging. Instead, as was discussed in the preceding chapter, our nation has opted for amateur judges who are either elected or appointed to this challenging position. (Our national penchant for the untrained jurist contrasts sharply with most European national practices as well as that of Japan, where judges begin their training at the university. After graduation, each

Japanese judge must progress through a well-structured professional hierarchy.)

Upon joining the bench, the judge must unlearn the role of advocate which has underlined all of his or her prior professional life since law school. He or she must quell the adversarial instincts which may have been a key element in his or her earlier courtroom achievements. For several judges interviewed, this transition was a difficult task and involved a persistent, and conscious effort. One eastern judge confessed that the process took several years. He remembered that during his early years on the bench he felt himself rising unconsciously from his chair with the intention of making an objection to one of the attorney's remarks. Fortunately, he always regained his composure before actually embarrassing himself, but his court clerk asked him several times why he stretched and stood up so many times during the course of a trial.

Let us now consider the art of judging in terms of the judge's required objectivity.

MAINTAINING OBJECTIVITY

The criminal court judge, because of his or her respected position at the center of the proceedings, has a great responsibility not only to be fair in his or her dealings with all parties, but also to give the *appearance* of fairness. Respected defense attorney Henry Rothblatt has described this responsibility in the following terms: "The judge must not only be totally indifferent between the parties, but he must also give the impression of being so. He must scrupulously avoid any conduct on his part which may give the appearance or impression that he is not totally unbiased."[1]

An additional pressure upon the judge is the awareness that the slightest gesture or change of expression can draw the attention of the jury, witnesses, attorneys, and viewing public. During the conduct of the trial, all eyes are on the judge to see how he reacts to critical testimony, attorney behavior, or any other occurrence in the courtroom. Subtle, and frequently innocent actions, such as a slight frown or the closing of one's eyes can serve as unintended clues to the judge's thoughts. A recent article in the *Virginia Law Review* concluded that such nonverbal behavior poses a serious threat to judicial impartiality. The authors discovered that

> . . . psychological research seems to show that experimenters, through their nonverbal and paralinguistic behaviors, unconsciously convey to their subjects information which is received by them and influential in their behavior. Where the judge/juror relationship is analogous, there may exist a subtle threat to judicial impartiality that is far more serious than that imposed by the more obvious and more controllable verbal communications which are the subject of so much concern.[2]

The judge's quest for impartially and objectivity faces many personal and institutional obstacles. The very basis of our nation's legal system—its adversary system—is just one of the more obvious of these impediments. We have also noted that the United States refuses to adequately train or educate our judges before they don their black robes and sit on the bench. Have we created an impossible situation in which the judge can never provide the desired impartiality and wisdom? Although many members of the bar would answer this question in the affirmative, approximately one-third of the judges and lawyers interviewed seemed to be much more optimistic about the ability of our judiciary to remain impartial. The members of the *Virginia Law Review* who conducted the most recent and most comprehensive analysis of this issue, especially with regard to prejudicial nonverbal behavior, believe that several things can be done to diminish the problem.

Their first recommendation is for videotaped trials in order to control both the quality and frequency of nonverbal interaction. Another possibility is to redesign courtrooms so that the frequency of interaction will be lessened. Several cities, such as Washington, D.C. have tried to minimize judge-juror eye contact through courtroom design. The city's new courthouse has its carefully planned courtrooms organized so that the judge's chair faces away from the jury box at an angle which would make it impossible for the jury to observe his facial expressions, although it would still be able to hear his verbal instructions. Finally, the authors of the article argue that judges can be trained to control their nonverbal behavior and paralinguistic interaction, and that the communications are not completely beyond conscious control.[3] Actually, little has been done thus far to modify the judge's nonverbal behavior, the viability of such reform efforts is unclear, and most judges object to any interference in their professional prerogatives. It appears highly unlikely that any reforms will take place in the near future.

In addition to the Washington, D.C. experiment in courtroom design, the handful of cities that have attempted to confront this problem have limited themselves to the use of videotaping as an aid in dealing with communication problems. Despite these sparse and obtuse efforts at reforming errant judges, all of the cities visited seemed to avoid a direct solution to the problem which would involve behavior modification programs for the judges themselves. Not only were the judges unwilling to take part in such programs, but most were adamant in denying that a problem existed.

The ability of a judge to consciously, or unconsciously, shape the outcome of a trial is not a startling discovery. Nearly 50 years ago, Learned Hand wrote: "A judge is more than a moderator. . . . Justice does not depend upon legal dialectic as much as upon the atmosphere of the courtroom and that in the end depends primarily upon the judge."[4]

Several judges acknowledged their difficulty in maintaining the desired level of impartiality. One former public defender viewed his quest for neutrality as an intellectual challenge, and believed optimistically that despite his short time on the bench, he was making significant strides in overcoming his prior professional lifetime as an advocate. For a few judges, this adjustment sometimes required physical constraint. One New York City judge said his biggest problem was staying seated. As an attorney, he paced the court-room when arguing a case, and now felt oppressively restrained by his new position on the bench. A few judges also commented that they believed their position prohibited them from making public statements which could place them in a compromised position with regard to future cases. If a judge makes his position clear on a subject, how open-minded will he be considered when a subsequent case comes before him and raises that same issue? One Philadelphia judge felt frustrated in having to turn down a television appearance for fear of future implications; however, one of his colleagues who had written several books concerning the criminal courts, has appeared on several radio and television shows plugging her latest literary efforts. Obviously she does not share the same concern.

A few of the judges interviewed thought that given the nature of the adversarial proceedings over which they must moderate, and the frailties of human nature, the standards set for their judicial impartiality was unrealistic and unattainable for the average jurist. Does this mean that the standards should be lowered to more closely approximate reality? The judges in all cities were nearly unanimous in their opposition to such a move. The majority of judges believed that the best response to this problem was to attempt to select lawyers of high quality to the bench. This could be done most easily by mak-ing the job more attractive. In effect, this would mean raising salaries and eliminating, or at least reducing, the role of partisan politics in the selection process. Thus, potential judges of high quality would not have to make the financial and philosophical sacrifices now necessary in order to join the bench.

JUDICIAL INTUITION AND THE SEARCH FOR THE TRUTH

The major premise underlying the utilization of the adversary system is that it is the most effective means of obtaining a fair and just disposition. By having two opposing attorneys battling each other, while the judge sits to ensure that the proper procedures are followed, it is assumed that the truth will emerge. Although it is not the purpose of this chapter to assess the capability of the adversary process to achieve its laudatory goals, it is also important to understand how the judge handles the difficult responsibility of searching for the truth while maintaining neutrality. If judges are re-quired to maintain an impartial stance between the opposing attorneys, how can they also actively contribute to the discovery of the truth? Marvin Frankel, an eminent jurist and critic of the adversary system, does not believe that "this system permits much room for effective or just intervention

by the trial judge in the adversary fight for the facts. The ignorance and un-
preparedness of the judge are axioms of the system making him a kind of intruder once the trial begins."[5]

Frankel goes on to raise the critical question of whether the trial judge
should simply adopt the role of a relatively passive moderator. This would
mean a preference for the "virginally ignorant judge" to the inquisitive, active jurist. He clearly prefers the latter and justifies his choice by writing
that:

> . . . the struggle to win, with its powerful pressures to subordinate the
> love of truth is often only incidentally, or coincidentally, if at all, a ser-
> vice of the public interest. The rules of professional responsibility
> should compel disclosures of material facts and forbid omissions rather
> than merely proscribe positive frauds.[6]

Most of the judges interviewed agreed with Justice Frankel's conclusions and adopted "activist" postures of varying degrees. A minority of
judges, however, perhaps one-quarter of the sample, opted for the passive
position, choosing to remain outside of the protracted conflict as much as
possible. Many judges in this group stated that giving the appearance of
open-mindedness, especially in their relations with the jury and witnesses,
was of paramount importance. A handful of judges, who were representative of this position, were observed to convey an attitude in the courtroom appoaching disinterest in what was transpiring before them. One west
coast judge's behavior seemed to indicate almost a disdain for the brutish
trial over which he was presiding. During a three-day trial, his only reactions were to objections by the attorneys, and the delivery of an ab-
breviated and officious set of instructions to the jury at the trial's completion. When questioned about the impact of his passive stance, the judge
simply stated that this was the style in which he felt most comfortable. His
top priority was to remain neutral, and he had full confidence that the
adversary process would produce the desired result without his interference.

The majority of judges observed and interviewed, however, thought
that there should be a genuine search for the truth and only by having a
judge actively moderating the conduct of the advocates, and interacting
with jurors and witnesses, could this end be achieved. The degree of activism varied widely, and seemed to expand with the judge's desire to uncover the truth. Although even the most active judges were unwilling to
verbally criticize the adversary system as a means of reliable fact-finding,
their pattern of behavior clearly indicated a mistrust of the process. When
questioned on this point, the activist judges spoke of their strong commitment to a fair trial and just disposition, refusing to lay blame on the broader

theoretical construct of the system. The activist judges as a group, when compared to their more passive colleagues, appeared to have a more zealous enjoyment of their responsibilities and took firm control over all facets of their courtrooms.

One rather puzzling aspect of this search for the truth is the role of judicial intuition, or the "hunch" as it was commonly denoted. Since the judge may occasionally have to administer a trial without a jury, how does the trained jurist resolve difficult questions of fact, persuasively debated by opposing counsel? It is in response to this question that one most frequently hears reference to the use of *judicial intuition*. This was defined by judges as a form of learned hunch, developed through experience on the bench. It is bred of cautious cynicism, observation of previous incidents, and a clear comprehension of legal standards.

Judges are confident that in their conduct of a trial, they could suspend their personal feelings on the case and hold the prosecutor to the burden of proof, which in a criminal case means the judge must be convinced beyond a reasonable doubt. One of the most difficult complications which can easily undermine the judge's ability to remain neutral is knowledge of information obtained through pretrial hearings, such as suppressed evidence or confessions. If this highly incriminating evidence were accidentally made available to a jury, a mistrial would be inevitable. Nevertheless, our legal system has sufficient confidence in the professional behavior of our judiciary to allow them to gain access to this information and still continue to try the case. Judges were nearly unanimous in their belief that they, as individual judges, could still conduct a fair trial, despite the awareness of this prejudicial evidence.

These criminal court judges believed that as a result of their experience and ability, they could continue to remain effective, and ultimately reach a proper verdict based upon only the legally admitted testimony before them. Are these judges being naive as to their capacity to remain neutral? Have we created a system which confers an unwarranted degree of discretion upon criminal court judges? The judges interviewed felt confident of their *own* ability to handle these difficult issues, but were critical of their colleague's capacity to perform at the same high level of professional competence and integrity. Are the judges merely scapegoating by offering their more inept brethren as a sacrificial explanation for the criminal court's inadequate performance? Is there really much variation in judicial quality existing on our criminal court bench? Although my own intuitive response, based on my 12 years of experience, would be affirmative to both questions, I am hard-pressed to provide empirical proof for such conclusions.

KEEPING TRACK OF THE PROCEEDINGS

After observing a lengthy (3½ weeks) and complex murder trial, I was struck by the extremely difficult task facing the judge in keeping track of the protracted proceedings. Although such a thought may seem a rather mundane concern, the judge's ability to monitor and remember the proceedings before him is of critical importance. It has a direct relationship to the earlier issues associated with the judge's search for the truth, as well as his responsibilities in aiding the jury reach a proper decision. Nearly every judge interviewed devised some type of system for keeping track of his caseload as well as a more detailed note system for the actual trial. The judges usually relied upon their own notes rather than continually bothering the court reporter. Several judges confided that they were compulsive note-takers and would accummulate copious records of the proceedings. Many judges admitted that the note-taking served more purposes then merely tracking the critical junctures of a trial. One judge found it was an excellent ploy for keeping himself looking busy and thereby, not influencing the jurors or witnesses with unconscious actions. Another judge used his extensive note-taking as a guise to sustain his interest in the proceedings, which can become extremely tedious and repetitious. He remembered from law school that he could stay awake and pay closer attention in class by trying to take down as much as possible, and he easily transferred such conduct to the courtroom as an antidote for judicial fatigue.

A current topic of interest for judges concerned with keeping an accurate record of the proceedings is the use of videotapes to replace or complement the court stenographer's notes. Most judges favored the present stenographic system, fearing that videotaping would inhibit the jurors, and interfere in some way with the sanctity of the courtroom and the fair administration of justice. A vocal minority of judges interviewed were in favor of videotaping, and pointed to its successful adoption in several jurisdictions (with Florida and Alaska being mentioned the most often as examples of successful videotaping programs). These judges thought that too many significant features of the trial were not being captured on stenographer's notes. Inflections of voice, body language, and other physical gestures could only be preserved on videotapes.

Despite its seeming importance, few legal commentators have addressed the topic of judicial note-taking. Bernard Botein in his important work, *The Trial Judge*, briefly describes the variety of note-taking techniques—"some develop their own shorthand, others laboriously outline everything, some synthesize it down to a few sentences, remembered informally."[7] Botein recalls that his own notes became briefer as the years passed—a trend paralleled in all of the judges interviewed. The other important commentator on the subject of trial judge's notes is the respected former Federal Judge Harold Medina. He believes that "the number one menace is the judge who thinks his memory is so good that notes are a mere waste of time."[8] He urges each judge to develop a proficiency in note-taking so as to be able to succinctly capture the important points, and exclude the irrelevant minutiae. He believes the notes are critical if a judge is to offer a worthwhile charge to the jury. This charge should be a fair and accurate summary of the conflicting versions of the facts as given by the witnesses and a full and comprehensive statement of the rules of law governing the case. Medina's note-taking style was to keep notes for a single day on a page or two in a looseleaf binder. Occasionally he would signal the court stenographer to make a page of the stenographic record available so that when a recess was taken, he could write out the exact words used by a witness.

JUDICIAL INTERVENTION

Despite a judge's reluctance to become directly involved in the proceedings, occasionally the most passive judge must intervene. These interventions most frequently involve one of the attorneys, but judges must also be prepared to deal with jurors, witnesses, and the courtroom audience. As was noted earlier, judges fall somewhere between the extremes of activism and passivity in terms of their willingness to interfere with the progress of a trial.

The activist judge feels compelled to control nearly all aspects of the proceedings transpiring before him. He usually is contemptuous of both attorneys. He will intervene on behalf of the prosecutor when he feels he or she is losing the state's case, and a guilty defendant might be turned loose on society. He will also step in to aid the defense when he believes that the attorney's performance is denying the defendant his or her guaranteed rights to a competent counsel. The active judge also appears to have little confidence in the jury's ability to comprehend what is occurring before them. He is, therefore, compelled to clarify and explain a continuous series of legal points which he believes will otherwise escape their comprehension. One New York City judge typified the attitude of most activist judges by rationalizing that his extensive experience on the bench, as well as his innate sense of fairness, allowed him to intervene only at the proper times. Activist judges seemed to be aggressively self-confident in their abilities to get the job done and handle the most difficult situations with fairness and sensitivity.

At the other extreme, is the restrained or passive judge who avoids intervention at all costs. These judges will bend over backward to permit the widest range of attorney behavior before interfering. Although critics of the restrained position characterize these judges as lazy and shirking their sworn responsibility, the judges who have adopted this passive mode believe they are simply maintaining the strict neutrality that their oath of office requires. Their passive role is most consistent with their strongly held belief in assiduously avoiding even the remotest possibility of partiality in favor of either of the contestants. Several of the judges who favored the restrained position were former trial attorneys who were extremely conscious (as a result of past professional experiences on the other side of the bench), of a judge's potential power to influence the outcome of a trial. In order to avoid these feared pitfalls, they may have over-compensated in their unwillingness to moderate the proceedings before them.

Most judges interviewed were clustered around a centrist position which realistically recognized that there were going to be situations where they had to intervene, but consciously avoided extending their interaction very much beyond the required instances. In terms of dealing with attorneys, most of the judges were generally more willing to help a defense counsel and admonish a prosecutor than the reverse. They reasoned that their judicial responsibilities required them to guarantee a fair trial to each defendant and only by supervising the quality of his defense, and controlling the aggressions of the prosecutor, could this constitutional obligation be satisfied. This slightly biased position in favor of the defense seems to be a relatively recent development following the political trials of the 1960s and early 1970s in which many judges, (such as the recently deceased Julius Hoffman, who presided over the Federal District Court proceeding in which the Chicago Seven performed their histrionics), clearly favored the prosecution and played an active role in convicting anti-war demonstrators. This position is described in an oft-quoted article in 1971 by Professor Herman Schwartz which is entitled *Judges as Tyrants*. He wrote of the antics of Judge Hoffman during the Chicago Seven trial as an example of a dictatorial judge who had lost control of the courtroom and his professional demeanor. He found these judges to be strongly biased against unpopular defendants and often envisioned themselves as the judicial arm of the law enforcement process. What disturbed Professor Schwartz even more was that so much of a judge's power verges on the absolute because of much of what he does is unreviewable by an appellate court. Schwartz noted that "their (the judge's) gestures, inflections, even comments, which are sometimes deliberately omitted by the court reporters who work closely with them, cannot be readily reviewed by an appellate court."[9]

There are many judges, particularly those who have been on the bench more than 15 years, who are biased in favor of the prosecution, and were observed actively aiding the district attorney's efforts to obtain a conviction. Nevertheless, it appeared that for those judges reaching office within the past 10 years, there was a conscious effort toward neutrality, and if either counsel were to be favored, it was more likely to be the defense.

Although most judges are somewhat fearful of appellate court reversals based upon unwarranted or prejudicial intervention during a trial, the instances of such actions are very rare. Appellate courts have consistently been very lax in their supervisory responsibilities and have intimated that they will always look only at the total context in which a judge's conduct occurred. Appellate courts have generally permitted a trial judge to intervene during a trial in order to comment on the evidence, examine witnesses when they find it is necessary in order to elicit the truth, and clarify facts for the jury, and issue admonitions to the counsel in response to their actions or statements that may unfairly and adversely affect the rights of the opposing party.[10]

The potential for judicial tyranny is always present. It seemed to be most easily aroused when an aggressive defense attorney strained the patience of the trial court judge. This usually occurred when it was felt that the attorney was offering frivolous and excessive pretrial motions or was overly pugnacious and disrespectful in asserting his client's rights. When defense tactics include challenging the jury selection process, and may cause undesirable delay and postponements, the judge's anger can be provoked still further. One judge astutely commented that those judges most easily upset by these defense tactics were most likely to lack personal trial experience. This background in litigation meant the judge was experienced in such tactics himself, and realized that the attorney was merely advocating his client's best interests to the full extent of the law, and meant nothing personal toward the judge.

Judges who do overreact, and are accused of behaving tyrannically are rarely reprimanded or reversed by a higher court, unless their behavior was extremely egregious and had captured the media's attention. The judiciary, like most institutions, does not like to "wash its dirty linen" in public. Subtle coercion, a shift of responsibilities, even being "kicked upstairs" are the most typical forms of reprimanding a judge. Despite their apparent lack of collegiality, judges join together to protect the institution and share a fear of outside criticism. Thus, unpopular members of the court are rarely disciplined in a public fashion. As one judge stated: "Tomorrow it could be you, so no one wants to hurl the first stone."[11]

Although it is fairly unusual, a few of the judges commented that they had, on special occasions, called a witness when neither of the attorneys had done so. This power is grounded in the obligation of a trial judge to assist in the fact-finding process of the adversary system, ensuring a fair trial and preventing any miscarriage of justice. The rule against impeaching one's own witness remains the major reason for an attorney to ask for the trial judge's assistance in producing witnesses. When the court calls the witness, the party who requested the witness to be called (and in this case it will not be one of the attorneys), is the only one who can impeach the witness on direct examination.[12]

DEALING WITH INCOMPETENT ATTORNEYS

Nearly all of the judges interviewed stated that one of the most difficult aspects of their job occurred when they felt compelled to deal with an incompetent attorney. Most judges felt that they were much more likely to intervene with an incompetent defense counsel than with a prosecutor. They justified this preference by noting their constitutional obligation to see that the defendant received a fair trial, and this included assistance of a competent counsel. A plethora of recent law suits, both civil and criminal, challenging the competence of an attorney's performance, has prompted the trial judge to be more vigilant.

When will a judge intervene on behalf of a floundering defense attorney, and what form will the assistance take? The judges varied in how badly a defense attorney's performance had to falter before they would take action. This was related to each judge's personal definition of "incompetence" and associated Sixth Amendment guarantees. Other factors affecting his decision to intrude were the seriousness of the charge, and the inexperience of the attorney. As both of these factors rose, so did the likelihood of intervention. Inexperience, of course, was related to familiarity with criminal procedures and not merely the number of years in practice. I observed a midwestern judge repeatedly urge an older attorney to resign from a criminal matter (burglary charges), involving the son of a friend. The attorney had never tried a criminal case, this being the first time he had ever entered the criminal courts building during his entire professional career. The attorney finally agreed to step down from the case when the concerned judge offered to help him find an acceptable experienced attorney to defend his client.

Judges appeared to develop a series of strategies for coming to the aid of an inept attorney, short of asking him to resign from the case. The most common method was simply to call the attorney up to the bench for a "side-bar" conference and inform him that he needed to upgrade his performance. These conferences occurred in hushed tones along the bench, or sometimes behind it. If a jury was in session, they might be ordered to leave the courtroom in order to eliminate the possibility of the judge's comments being overheard. If the judge believed a more protracted discussion was necessary, he declared a brief recess and adjourned to his chambers with the attorney.

In order to expedite proceedings, the new criminal courthouse for the District of Columbia has a noise machine over the jury box. This permits the judge to have a side-bar conference, while the sound box imitates a pounding coastal surf. The jury can, thereby, remain in the courtroom without hearing the whispered conversations only a few feet away. Despite the charges of being an overpriced and frivolous gimmick, court administrators in Washington credit the device with saving appreciable amounts of time and inconvenience.

The judges were found to vary significantly as to the quality of help and advice they were willing to offer an erring attorney. Half of the judges would merely issue a vague warning that the attorney was straying off the point, omitting some vital elements, or simply failing to convince the judge (and in all likelihood the jury as well), of whatever point he was striving to make. Several judges, however, would be more specific, and offer clues as to what must be done in order to get the case back on track and at least preserve a slight chance for victory. A few judges were observed offering concrete suggestions as to avenues to explore and issues to raise, although it was always as a recommendation and never an order. Most typically this aid was couched in the phrase "I suppose you are going to ask this or that" and the densest attorney would usually take the hint. Occasionally, a judge who wished to avoid the delay of a side-bar conference and who had confidence in his ability to control the courtroom, would beckon an attorney close to his chair, and in hushed tone offer his advice directly without a formalized break in the proceedings.

In only the rarest instances would a judge insist that a lawyer resign from a case. This was most likely to occur with inexperienced public defenders handling very difficult cases. One judge, following what I believe was an accepted pattern, called a recess early in the proceedings after several side-bar conferences had failed to improve the quality of defense, and notified the lawyer's superiors that he *must* be replaced. These requests were always honored. Similar procedures were utilized when a prosecutor was thought to be incompetent or engaging in what the judge thought was unprofessional behavior. (Judges stated that they were compelled to take such strong measures because they were under pressure to dispose of the case without resorting to an additional trial.)

Most judges commented that the frequency of having to help attorneys was on the rise. They felt that the overall competence of attorneys was slipping. They reasoned that the caseload pressures had forced both the newer public defenders and prosecutors into the courtroom too quickly without adequate preparation. Several were critical of law school educations, terming them irrelevant to the pragmatic issues facing practicing attorneys following graduation, especially those working within the criminal justice system.

As noted earlier, most judges preferred to aid the defense rather than prosecution, yet nearly all admitted that in extreme cases of unacceptable performances, the prosecutor would also receive the advice of the judge. This "advice," however, was often a vague warning for the prosecutor to upgrade his efforts. If the prosecutor failed to improve his level of performance, most judges would notify his superiors, who either delivered their own tongue-lashing, or in extreme cases, replaced him with a new prosecutor.

In addition to offering advice to attorneys, several judges would intervene in the questioning of witnesses. This was usually done without thought to benefitting either prosecution or defense, but rather to aid the judge in better understanding the case before him. Judges also rationalized such interferences as being necessary to clarify points for the jury as well as helping to extract critical information from a nervous or recalcitrant witness. On occasion, attorneys would object to such activities when their opposition witnesses were being interrogated, although they were most likely to remain silent when their own witnesses were being questioned. This presents a ticklish situation for attorneys who realize that their objections can anger the judge and further strain their relations. Nevertheless, most attorneys thought that this risk must be taken in order to place the judge's interferences into the court record. It could be a possible source of reversible error and grounds for appeal.

The interrelations between judges and attorneys seemed most strained not by their behavior in the courtroom, but by the attorney's inability to appear in court on time, and be prepared to go to trial. This failure seemed to apply equally to both prosecution and defense. The attorneys simply tried to keep too many cases active at the same time, causing persistent scheduling conflicts and harried sprints between courtrooms.

The most firmly etched memory from my 12 years of court watching, is the frustrated judge, barking at his bailiffs to try to find attorney "X" who was "just there a minute ago." This attorney, who had slipped out of court 10 minutes earlier while the judge was trying to locate a missing witness, was quickly scurrying to another courtroom, three flights up, in order to check on a pre-sentencing hearing already scheduled for the same afternoon. After 30 minutes, the attorney sheepishly wandered back into the courtroom. Now the arresting officer, a crucial witness, had disappeared. With the defense attorney and the police officer out of the courtroom, the prosecutor decided it would be a golden opportunity to get a cup of coffee in his office two floors below, and catch up on the morning gossip. Fifteen minutes later, when the police officer and the defense attorney had reappeared, the prosecutor was chatting with his colleagues several courtrooms away. After an hour, when everyone was assembled before the judge, the court clerk noticed that critical paperwork, such as a prior arrest sheet on the defendant, was missing from the case file and another postponement was necessary.

These scenes, reminiscent of a Marx Brothers comedy routine with disappearing and reappearing actors, were observed repeatedly in every courthouse visited. The inability to gather all the requisite participants in a courtroom at the appointed time, and have them prepared to initiate proceedings, was one of the most frustrating events in the judge's nerve-wracking day. Despite the frequency of its occurrence, all judges were continually upset by these delays whenever they occurred in their courtrooms.

JUDGES AND JURORS

Another group of courtroom actors with whom the judge must interact during a trial are the jurors (usually collectively, but occasionally individually).

As the neutral arbiter standing between prosecution and defense, one of the judge's primary concerns is that the jury be "afforded a full and fair presentation of the facts and an understandable and uncomplicated exposition of the law."[13] Judge Botein, who has written a classic treatise on the trial judge, describes his role as a type of traffic cop, giving stop and go signals between opposing attorneys and the jury.[14]

Each judge has several opportunities to speak with the members of the jury and is obligated to instruct them at the following stages: (a) upon selection to the jury panel for the week, (b) before the voir dire is to begin (and in several states during the voir dire if he is primarily responsible for the questioning), (c) after the jury is sworn in for a case, and they are about to hear the opening argument, (d) when the case is submitted to the jury for its decision (this is commonly referred to as "charging the jury") and (e) just prior to their discharge.

During the course of a trial, there are also many permissible instances when the judge must communicate with jurors. Instructions, which are usually of an admonitory or cautionary nature are in most instances left to the judge's discretion and include some of the following topics: (a) urging objectivity, (b) prohibiting any outside communication, (c) warning against speculation or bringing in personal knowledge not offered in evidence, (d) forbidding the reaching of an early verdict (or by lot or chance) and (e) warning against deciding whom you believe *should* win.[15]

The opportunities for interaction between judge and jury just reviewed are all acceptable and often obligatory. Some judges, however, exceed these limits and communicate with the jury throughout the trial. By his gestures, facial expressions and other paralinguistic forms of communication, popularly referred to as "body language," the judge can subtly and often unintentionally "speak" to the jury and influence their behavior. The jury looks to the judge as their instructor and guide. Even beyond the formal instructions offerred by the judge at certain required stages of the proceedings, the members of the jury can be observed looking toward the judge for clues as to the proper interpretation of events transpiring before them. The most common example of this type of communication occurs when a witness is being examined by one of the attorneys. The jury continually looks to the judge to see how he or she is reacting to the testimony. So slight a movement as the judge shutting his eyes can convince some jurors that the witness should not be believed. One judge candidly admitted that jurors are "putty in our hands," and he thought he could influence their decision by a wide range of barely detectable behaviors which would never be reflected in the stenographer's official court record. Expressing disbelief at certain testimony or sagely nodding one's head as if in agreement, can exert a powerful influence on a jury which is virtually impossible for an opposing attorney to overcome. "It is because of this immense power," commented one judge, "that we have an especially high burden to preserve the image of impartiality."[16]

A large percentage of the judges self-consciously tried to prohibit the jury from having insights into their inner feelings. Some described themselves as maintaining a "stony silence" or a listless demeanor. Only one judge interviewed felt that his capacity for influencing jurors was overrated and modestly stated that "jurors don't seem particularly interested in my reactions and seemed to go their own way regardless of my desires."[17] He added that he was further convinced of his limited efficacy by chatting with jurors (after a case had ended), to learn why they reached a particular decision. Although a firm believer in the ability of juries to reach the proper decision, the judge also felt that the group dynamics occurring within the jury room were much more significant than their perceptions of the judge's desires.

Most judges agreed that juries usually do a good job of decision-making, although they may reach the proper conclusion for the wrong reason. Several judges commented that working with juries, and watching them during the progress of a trial was one of the most rewarding aspects of their job. These judges frequently like to thank each juror personally after a trial had been completed. Several of the judges also viewed juror relations as an excellent opportunity to educate the local citizenry as to the operation of the United States legal system. These judges would frequently clarify, summarize, and paraphrase everything that was occurring during the trial. This also included telling the jury who everyone in the courtroom was so they (the jurors) would not be distracted during the course of the trial. The entire experience in the criminal court systems was viewed as a priceless chance to enlighten the jurors and, hopefully, leave the courthouse as more intelligent and aware citizens.

I share with the judges a fascination with the social-psychological dynamics of jury behavior. As any visitor to a criminal courtroom soon realizes, watching a trial can be an extremely boring experience. Listening to tedious comparisons of a witness's testimony at the preliminary hearing, as contrasted with his statements before a grand jury or at the actual trial, is a very unexciting task. Jurors can be seen daydreaming, dozing, flirting, and engaging in a range of other activities which divert their attention away from the testimony. Nevertheless, the judge seems able to muster their energies at the critical points of the trial when they must be attentive. This appears to be one of the critical capabilities that a good judge must possess. He can bring them back from the far reaches of their daydreams and fantasies without influencing the direction of their decision. A chemistry can be developed in which a jury relies upon the judge for those subtle signals that will alert them, like school children being called in from recess—that it is time to begin getting serious. The jury almost always seems to respond.

Once the prosecution and defense have presented their final summations to the jury, the judge is then called upon to perform what most judges believe to be their most important task—providing final instructions to the jury just prior to their deliberations. The judge's charges to the jury are designed to clarify points of law which the jury must consider, as well as a reminder of the burden of proof which must be satisfied before certain critical conclusions are reached. Even while the jurors are deliberating, the judge must remain nearby in order to provide additional instructions or clarifications if requested. A final problem of the judge to ponder is how long must he wait for a jury to reach a conclusion, or if no conclusion is forthcoming, deciding that a mistrial must be declared because of the "hung jury." No judge could provide a universal rule, but given the expense and inconvenience of a retrial, nearly all judges thought that jurors were given more than enough time to reach a decision. All judges seemed strongly committed to erring on the side of caution and giving the jurors every chance to decide the case. Most judges would not dismiss a jury until he had carefully questioned all of its members as to their inability to reach a consensus.

PLEA BARGAINING AND MANAGING THE CASELOAD

Although a large portion of this chapter has been devoted to a discussion of the trial judge's responsibilities, most of the criminal cases are settled without trial through a process termed "plea bargaining," in which the defendant offers a guilty plea in exchange for a more lenient sentence. This process, by which approximately 80 percent of all cases are disposed, is an important tool for the judge as he attempts to deal with his ever-increasing caseload. As an example of the magnitude of plea negotiations, and the infrequency of trials, a recent report on sentencing in New York State found that 93 percent of all convictions were obtained by plea bargains, and only 4 percent of the cases went to trial.[18]

In most of the cities visited, the chief administrative judges recognized that some judges were better at disposing of cases in an efficient manner, while others were better suited to the slower, more tedious task of trying cases. Judges in the first category handled preliminary hearings, arraignments, and pretrial motions. All of these types of pretrial courts processed large numbers of cases on a daily basis. The judges assigned to trial court would usually be responsible for one or two trials per week depending on the complexity of the case. Judges usually remained within either the pretrial or trial divisions for most of the time on the bench. Occasionally, judges from the beleaguered pretrial division would be given an annual one-or two-month vacation to the slower-paced trial courts as a break from the action.

In Philadelphia, this specialization became even more detailed as trial judges were divided into jury and non-jury divisions. The non-jury judges engaged in what has been referred to as a "slow" plea negotiation and were assessed as the more lenient judges who would reward those defendants who were willing to forsake their rights to a longer, more expensive, jury trial with lighter sentences.

Those judges who proved themselves capable of handling large numbers of cases in a fair and efficient manner were "rewarded" for their efforts by having an increasing number of cases diverted into their courtrooms. What soon developed was a select group of judges who appeared to be carrying the entire system. At the opposite extreme was a large number of judges who were evaluated negatively (by their superiors and colleagues), either because of their laziness, inexperience, or lack of intelligence, and were "punished" by being given diminished responsibilities. This meant they were usually selected as trial judges and handled approximately 50–100 cases per year. The court administrators rationalize this procedure by stating a necessity for placing the best people at the critical junctures of the system and hiding the less competent ones in the slower-paced recesses of the trial division. There are several exceptions to this general trend. Certain competent judges are utilized in the more complex, and sometimes well-publicized trials which seem to require superior judicial ability.

Unfortunately, this system, despite its logical approach to dealing with the backlog of cases, has created a tension within most criminal court systems that is counter-productive. I was continually surprised in nearly every city visited, at how little respect each judge had for his fellow members of the bench. When asked about the quality of his colleagues, a judge would name two or three other judges whom he respected, but would invariably add that he was unimpressed with the majority of the members of the bench. This attitude also seemed to affect the social relations between judges, which as was noted earlier, was minimal. Contact was typically limited to a monthly or bi-monthly business luncheon. Most judges clearly preferred the company of old friends and family.

Despite the negative connotations associated with the term "plea bargaining," most judges indicated little displeasure with its utilization. It was viewed principally as a form of negotiation necessary to dispose of the many guilty defendants who glut the system. In most cities, the criminal justice system acts as a sieve in which the holes become smaller as a defendant moves through the system. Thus, those cases in which the defendant is probably innocent, or the prosecution will have a difficult time proving his guilt, are dismissed early in the process. Another reason many cases do not reach the felony courts is that the prosecutor often finds that a policeman's initial selection of a felony charge was unrealistic and has re-charged the defendant with a lesser, more appropriate crime. It has been estimated in the cities visited, that approximately 40–50 percent of the cases which began as felony arrests were either dismissed, or tried as misdemeanors.[19] These statistics indicate that of the remaining cases which reach the felony courts following a preliminary hearing, nearly all of the weak cases and innocent defendants have been screened out, leaving approximately 50 percent to be plea-bargained, and less than five percent to reach the trial stage.

What function does the felony court judge perform in plea bargaining negotiations? A recent national study by James Alfini and John Paul Ryan for the American Judicature Society concluded that ". . . the trial judge is often an important or crucial actor in the construction of plea arguments."[20] They qualify their conclusion, however, by adding that there is wide variation in the judge's plea bargaining role and point out that such factors as the judge's self-perceived skill at negotiating, and whether the state has a court rule or case law prohibiting or discouraging judicial participation, will affect their level of involvement.

Many officials believe that the judge should not lower himself to participate in the negotiations, but rather let the prosecutor and defense attorneys work out the arrangements. The American Bar Association has consistently objected to an active role for judges in plea bargaining sessions. The ABA position seems to have influenced the attitude of several appellate courts who are also negatively disposed. No empirical studies have been completed to validate this position by illustrating some ill effects upon judicial behavior or the administration of justice as the result of such judicial participation.

What percentage of judges do actually participate in these negotiations? Returning to the research of Alfini and Ryan, they discovered that the majority of judges do not participate in plea discussions, and "fully two-thirds restrict their role to ratifying in-court bargains struck between prosecutor and defense counsel."[21] The judges whom I interviewed seemed much more willing to participate in plea bargaining negotiations than the judges surveyed by Alfini and Ryan in their larger national study, which included judges from communities of widely varying size. It is possible, therefore, that our findings may not be as contradictory as first imagined. When Alfini and Ryan visited a select group of larger cities, they discovered that these judges were more willing to be active participants. This is fairly consistent with my research which focused solely upon urban jurisdictions.

In Professor Albert Alschuler's comprehensive research on plea bargaining during which he visited many of the same cities as myself, he developed an excellent typology for viewing the variety of forms the judicial role in plea bargaining may take:

1. Systems in which judges do not engage in plea bargaining, leaving it exclusively to the prosecutors.
2. Systems wherein neither judges nor prosecutors bargain explicitly with defense attorneys, but judges encourage pleas by consistently sentencing defendants more severely after a trial.

3. Systems in which judges participate actively in pretrial negotiations and offer specific benefits in exchange for guilty pleas.
4. Systems in which judges participate in the negotiating process but avoid specific pretrial promises.[22]

Of the 15 cities which I visited, the judges in nearly half of the cities favored Alschuler's fourth system of negotiation. The remaining cities were divided between actively participating with specific promises (Category 3) and those where judges merely encouraged pleas by consistent patterns of lenient sentences (Category 2). The variation in judicial style was more marked between cities than individual judges within the same court system. It appeared that, as a result of local rules, precedents, and customs, the judges in a particular city would generally adopt similar patterns of plea bargaining.

One trend in plea bargaining styles which has occurred within the last decade is the shift from Alschuler's Category 3, where judges were willing to offer specific benefits, to his Category 4, where the judges were active negotiators but avoid promising specific sentences. The trend is an inevitable by-product of recent legislation in several states, aimed at reducing the discretion of the judiciary, especially with regard to the breadth of sentencing alternatives. Many public officials, concerned with rising crime, and frustrated by their inability to control the problem, have attempted to make the criminal courts at least partial scapegoats. They accuse the courts of being overly lenient in their sentencing, fostering a type of permissiveness that not only fails to deter criminal behavior but also seems to encourage it. The plea bargaining process is viewed as a primary culprit. The solution offered by state and local officials is to enact statutes restricting the discretionary power of the judges, raising the penalties for various crimes, and guaranteeing that the penalty for a specific crime will be set within narrowly prescribed limits.

In New York City, for example, after a defendant has been found guilty of a specific charge, the judge must then consult his prior record to see what category of sentence he must impose. Depending upon whether the defendant has been previously convicted of a felony, and whether this was a violent felony, can significantly affect the severity of the sentence. The judge has very little discretion, simply identifying a category of defendant before him. This trend has meant that the emphasis today is on "charge bargaining" rather than specific sentences. Obviously, the more serious charges result in more serious penalties, but nevertheless, the earlier ability of the judge to have wide discretion within a particular charge has been lessened.

The reliance on prior record, and its impact on sentencing can create administrative confusion. One judge who agreed to a plea bargain with the understanding that the defendant's prior record sheets were current, had to withdraw his plea offer after more up-to-date information indicated additional convictions, including the use of a firearm. The judge was embarrased, but compelled to start all over again, offering the defendant an opportunity for a jury trial if he was still interested.

Most judges carefully avoided pressuring the defendant into agreeing to the plea. Typically, the judge, prosecutor, and defense attorney would conduct a side-bar conference where the various possibilities would be dicussed. The defendant would be left at a nearby table, a few yards to the rear. With lengthier discussions, the defendant would be temporarily returned to the lock-up. After the discussion was concluded, the defense attorney would go back and present the options to the defendant. This included the prosecutor's position, and the judge's attitude toward what the prosecutor was offering. The defense counsel would soon return with the client's decision. After the defendant accepted the plea bargain, all of the parties would gather before the bench for the formal arraignment. Most of the judges disliked this charade, during which the judge asks the defendant to reassure the court that no promises have been made in exchange for the plea, and he was not coerced into this decision by his attorney. Despite the objectionable nature of this oft-repeated scenario, judges and attorneys realize it is a necessary procedure in order to avoid future charges by the defendant that he was unwittingly duped into pleading guilty.

Although the working out of a plea bargain as just described is a calm exercise in negotiation, rarely reaching the level of adversarial confrontation envisioned in the idealized criminal court process, a few cities did allow for more lively negotiations. These usually occurred in the judge's chambers and developed into hotly contested arguments. In Chicago, for example, where plea bargaining appeared both forthright and formalized, the judge played an active role in hammering out an agreement. As one of the Windy City's criminal court judges said in a recent interview in which he was justifying his plea bargaining practices: "He (the defendant) takes some of my time—I take some of his. That's the way it works."[23]

MAINTAINING COMPASSION OVER THE YEARS

The serious difficulties inherent in the criminal court judge's job as described within this chapter, seem to indicate that most individuals could only maintain a high level of performance for a short period of years. Noting the distasteful working conditions, persistent, and oftentimes, conflicting pressures, and most importantly, the frustrating inability to see any visible improvements, one wonders how judges can maintain their sense of compassion and concern over the years. Given the lengthy terms of office which most judges serve (typically 8–10 years), how does a criminal court judge sustain himself and his professional integrity? Of all the difficult problems faced by the criminal court judge as he attempts to practice the "art of judging," this ability to maintain compassion over the years appears to be the most challenging.

Most judges admitted that despite conscious attempts to remain alert and compassionate, they were significantly affected by their years on the bench. The most common trait was growing skepticism. As one judge stated, "You just hear the same stories year after year. I cannot help being jaded, although I still think I am not a total cynic. . . ."[24] The repetitious nature of the job also caused several judges to comment on the persistent battle against boredom. The most demoralizing aspect of their position, however, was seeing the same faces reappear year after year. The judge is privy to a never-ending parade of broken promises and weakened wills which have plummeted their clientele deeper and deeper into the depths of human despair and misfortune. To be a participant, witnessing this depressing downward spiral of society's failures, is an experience few can be expected to endure for very long. In fact, at least half of the judges interviewed, were either seriously contemplating resigning at the end of the current term, or had already made a commitment to step down.

Despite the dismal picture just presented, every city had a handful of judges who were able not only to endure these frustrations, but also to continue to sustain a high level of excitment and energy toward their work. They stated that they could not imagine doing anything else. These judges were not martyrs, but appeared to genuinely enjoy their work and looked forward to each new day on the bench. The rewards for this small group of judges lay in the confrontation with the challenges facing them in their courtrooms. They relished the chance to use their judicial power to try to unravel the legal, social, and personal complexities which were laid before them.

In the next chapter, we will continue our exploration into the responsibilities of the felony court judge, focusing in greater detail upon the strains and hardships which complicate his professional life.

NOTES

1. Henry Rothblatt. Prejudicial Conduct of the Trial Judge in Criminal Cases, *Criminal Law Bulletin* 2 (September, 1966), 3.
2. Judges Non-Verbal Behavior in Jury Trials: A Threat to Judicial Impartiality, *Virginia Law Review* 61 (October, 1975), 1295.
3. Ibid. p. 1296.
4. Leslie L. Conner. The Trial Judge: His Facial Expressions, Gestures and General Demeanor: Their Effects on the Administration of Justice, *Criminal Law Quarterly* 6 (Summer, 1975), 175.
5. Marvin Frankel. The Search for the Truth: An Umpirical View, *University of Pennsylvania Law Review* 123 (May, 1975), 1031.
6. Ibid.
7. Bernard Botein. *Trial Judge*. New York, Simon and Schuster, 1952, p. 52.

8. Harold Medina. Trial Judge Notes: A Study in Judicial Administration, *Cornell Law Quarterly* 49 (Fall, 1963), p. 1.
9. Herman Schwartz, Judges as Tyrants, *Criminal Law Bulletin* 7 (March, 1971), p. 129.
10. Judicial Intervention of Trial, *Washington University Law Quarterly* (Fall, 1973), 843.
11. Confidential interview with Philadelphia Court of Common Pleas Judge, July, 1980.
12. Power of a Trial Judge to Call a Witness, *South Carolina Law Review* 21 (1969), p. 224.
13. Botein, op. cit.
14. Ibid
15. Jack Pope. The Judge-Jury Relationship, *Southwestern Law Journal* 18 (March, 1964), 46.
16. Confidential interview with Philadelphia Court of Common Pleas Judge, July 1980.
17. Confidential interview with New York City Acting Supreme Court Judge, July 1981.
18. Crime and Punishment in New York, *Report of Governor Carey by the Executive Advisory Committee on Sentencing,* 1979, p. 22.
19. Donald M. McIntyre and David Lippman. Prosecutors and Early Disposition of Felony Cases, *American Bar Association Journal* 56 (1970), 1156.
20. James Alfini and John Paul Ryan. Trial Judge Participation in Plea Bargaining, *Law and Society Review* 13 (1979), p. 479.
21. Ibid.
22. Albert Alschulen. The Trial Judge's Role in Plea Bargaining—Part I, *Columbia Law Review* 76 (November, 1976), p. 1059.
23. Ibid., p. 1089.
24. Confidential interview with New York City Supreme Court Judge, July 1981.

6

STRAINS AND HARDSHIPS
OF THE JOB

From the perspective of the layman, the life of a judge appears to be one of elevated status and privilege. It is viewed as a highly respected profession which offers the opportunity to pursue altruistic aims—the attempt to reach fair and just judicial decisions—while enjoying a comfortable salary and pleasant working conditions. The public imagines the judge arriving at his specially designated parking space a few feet from the courthouse entrance in time for the leisurely commencement of courtroom business at ten o'clock. Upon entering the courthouse, doors are held and deference is extended, as the judge moves toward his chambers, exchanging morning salutations with a seemingly endless line of well-wishers. The royal treatment extends into his spacious, elegant offices as his secretary brings him his previously sorted correspondence along with a cup of coffee. The law clerk also is ready for the judge's morning appearance as legal memos, schedules, and other bits of critical information are deferentially presented. Following a perusal of the morning paper, and a brief ordering of the day's business, the judge is helped with the donning of his robe and strides purposefully into the courtroom where the bailiff announces his arrival and demands immediate subservience.

Once in the courtroom, wearing the impressive robes and sitting above all other participants, the judge's power and status appear to reach greater heights. Lawyers, defendants, witnesses, the courtroom audience, all stand in awe. After a two or three-hour morning session, the judge breaks for lunch, which his office staff has obtained for him prior to his return to chambers. By two o'clock the judge has returned to the courtroom where he will eloquently orchestrate the proceedings before him for the next two hours. Following a conclusion of the day's business, the judge will return briefly to his chambers to catch up on the latest mail and gossip, and by five o'clock he has returned to his chauffeur-driven car and heads back to his palatial residence to dine, socialize and entertain prominent personalities. The summers mean two-month vacations and shorter working days. The winters are interrupted by professional meetings in the Caribbean and long weekends in Vermont.

For the criminal court judges observed during the past decade, very few experienced the pleasant and productive existence described in the preceding paragraphs. Their working environment, as described in Chapter Two, contained few of the amenities just mentioned. Instead, they found themselves in chaotic working conditions where the mounting caseloads, public pressures, and dismal surroundings forced many of them to contemplate early retirement.

Although this chapter will focus upon an extended examination of the strains and hardships facing the criminal court judge, it might be useful to briefly discuss first some of the positive attributes of their job. Given the abundance of negative factors undermining their professional existence, what are the satisfactions that this beleaguered group receives from their position? Most judges apologized for the altruistic nature of their response to this question, but nevertheless stated a sincere belief in their ability to serve the community. Within the context of a criminal proceeding, this is usually translated into the judge's belief in his capacity to reach a just and fair decision; a decision which will be in the best interests of both society and the defendant. Judges seemed confident that they could protect the defendant's constitutional guarantees from the most aggressive prosecutor, while also being sufficiently aware of the necessity for a community to protect itself from a criminal element.

In fleeting moments of candor, several judges did admit that they enjoyed the status and deferential treatment occasionally associated with their lofty position. It was nice to have doors opened, and crowded hallways suddenly made passable, as they moved through their judicial domain. The loyalty of the staff, extending from bailiffs, through secretaries and law clerks, is another factor permitting a judge to have a clear sense of his power and prestige. Although sociologists inform us that the status of judges, particularly at the local level, has declined over the past few decades, most of the judges believed that their professional status was still elevated and most of the legal community remained both envious and respectful.

Several judges found that the intellectual challenge of their job was its most attractive element. These judges were excited by the constantly changing nature of the legal conundrums confronting them each day. How could they effectively balance the needs of society with those of the defendant's personal tragedy? How were they to interpret the subtle and changing rhythms of the Burger Court as it attempted to erode the decisions of the earlier Warren Court? The caseload explosion, in both the state and federal courts, has driven judges, defense attorneys, and prosecutors into law libraries in order to keep up with the most recent decisions. As one Denver lawyer recounted to me in 1977, "You must subscribe to everything and go to all the seminars and collect all the advance sheets. It is crucial to pay attention to your clients, but you must also pay attention to the intellectual side of the criminal law."[1] Time after time, the senior lawyers harked back to the pleasures of the old days when one could practice criminal law "out of your hat," but then noted that those time were long past.

Despite the positive feelings many criminal court judges held toward their positions, they were also upset by what they perceived to be several major liabilities in their professional lives. Although this chapter will examine a wide range of problems and hardships troubling criminal court judges, the three following factors were repeatedly emphasized by most judges as being the most unpleasant aspects of their jobs: inadequate compensation, forced involvement in politics, i.e., the necessity of winning nominations and elections, and dismal working conditions.

Felony court judges in the cities visited earned from $40,000–$75,000 per year. To the general public, this figure may seem to be an impressive salary for a public official. For the judges interviewed, however, they were nearly unanimous in their belief that their wages were inadequate. Most judges explained their dissatisfaction on the basis of the significantly higher salary they thought they could be earning if they had remained in private practice. The judges felt that on the average they had suffered a 50 percent reduction in wages by joining the bench, and that the differential between their judicial salary and earning capacity as a private practitioner was growing wider with each passing year. Exacerbating the financial pressures was the fact that most judges were in their late forties and early fifties, and they were the parents of children about to enter college. The reality of having to finance this extremely expensive investment in higher education made nearly all of the judges keenly aware of their financial limitations. Several judges stated that because of these monetary pressures they could only afford to serve one term on the bench, and would then return to private practice. Judges also pointed to the difficulty of readjusting their lifestyles as a result of taking this 50 percent reduction. They and their families had become used to certain amenities which were difficult to give up, having once been experienced. Additionally, there were previous financial commitments such as the mortgage payments on a home which had to be paid despite the reduced salary.

A few judges interviewed in each city were cynical about the great financial losses suffered by their colleagues as a result of joining the bench. These judges thought that a large number of their brethren had not been financially well off prior to becoming judges, and had actually received an increase in salary as a result of their new positions. These judges were frequently products of a highly politicized system of judicial selection and received their appointment as a result of many years of loyal party service. They had frequently held bureaucratic positions within city government which paid less than their present salary. If they did have an association with a law firm, it was usually in name only. Their legal work was more likely business-related, typically in the area of real estate or insurance, and rarely amounted to incomes approaching that which they currently earned on the bench.

How many judges have actually suffered significantly as a result of joining the bench? How many have profited from this move? These questions are almost impossible to answer. What we can conclude, however, is that a large proportion of our criminal court judges perceive themselves as being underpaid. When judges do believe that they are not being sufficiently compensated, and are thereby relatively deprived, their attitudes can have negative repercussions upon their job performance. It seems quite plausible that judges who complain most about their salaries are least likely to devote themselves unselfishly to their professional responsibilities.

A second major liability for most judges is the necessity for becoming involved in local politics. Although judges serve lengthier elective terms than legislative and executive officials, they resent having to enter the political arena at all. This was especially true for judges who had been primarily successful private practitioners before reaching the bench, and who had only a passing exposure with local politics. They had allowed themselves to be considered for judicial office out of a sense of civic duty, and felt that it was unnecessary and even degrading to have to "dirty" themselves in the political process. The political rallies, fund raisers, and closed-door strategy sessions were all despised diversions from their primary goal which was simply to decide cases and serve their cities. Whether the selection process was by election or appointment, followed by retention elections, the judges were still required to participate in the political process and interact with the local party leadership. Lawyers interviewed in several cities, cited their unwillingness to enter the local political scene as the primary reason for their reluctance to become judges, despite being considered likely candidates for a judicial nomination.

The third major problem which upset and depressed a high percentage of judges revolved around the unpleasant working conditions. Even in cities such as Washington, D.C., and Los Angeles, California, where the courthouse facilities are of recent vintage and impressively furnished, judges complained about their working conditions. Crowded calendars, inadequate staffing, and ineffective security are the most common manifestations of these undesirable conditions. In the majority of ciminal courthouses, their physical deterioration has also contributed to the depressing setting. These older facilities, with paint peeling from their institutional green walls, clogged toilets, overflowing trashcans, and inoperative telephones, serve as visible reminders of the low status accorded to all members of the criminal justice system, including their most prestigious members—the criminal court judges.

Since some judges came to the bench from lucrative private practices, they were frequently used to luxurious working conditions, including opulent and spacious offices. They were typically served by competent legal secretaries, a bevy of eager law clerks, and young associates who were anxious to please. The judges who reached the bench from these impressive law firms were usually the most upset over their new working conditions. They could not fathom the paradoxical nature of this situation in which they would have to suffer a degrading reduction in the quality of their work environment as a "reward" for achieving their newly elevated professional status.

More troublesome to most judges than the depressing physical setting, was their vulnerability to physical attack as a result of the absence of reliable security measures. Nearly every judge interviewed, recounted some incident which occurred to him or one of his colleagues. These incidents varied in their seriousness from verbal abuse to aggressive assaults, but all were of a terrifying nature. Currently, any judge who works after dark can request an armed escort to his car. So many courts, however, are understaffed in terms of bailiffs, that the hallways and chambers are unprotected after four o'clock, and the judges are fairly easy prey for any vengeful defendant who is at liberty. The judges are acutely aware of this problem, and like the general citizenry, live in fear of criminal attack.

Thus far, this chapter has discussed the major liabilities and assets associated with the position of criminal court judge. The remainder of this chapter will discuss those specific strains and hardships which the judge experiences as he attempts to carry out his professional responsibilities. The first problem area—sentencing—was agreed upon by all the judges as being the most difficult as well as the most frustrating aspect of their job.

SENTENCING

The most difficult job for a felony court judge was the sentencing decision. Although the judges stated a variety of reasons, there was general agreement that this was the most frustrating and perplexing part of their job. Many judges were uncomfortable with the responsibility placed upon them for making a decision so heavily laden with serious consequences. Nearly all of the judges were cognizant of the horrible conditions awaiting a defendant sentenced to serve time in a penal institution. Not only would the defendant lose his freedom for a long period of time, and be separated from his friends and family, but the judges were aware that there would be a great likelihood that the defendant would be beaten, robbed and possibly raped by his fellow inmates. The judge also knew that in nearly every case the defendant would eventually re-emerge into society unchanged except for being more bitter and more inclined toward a life of crime.

Complicating the emotional strain under which judges must reach sentencing decisions, is the increasing public outcry against the supposed leniency of their decisions. The mass media, concerned citizen groups, local politicians, and members of the law enforcement establishment such as police and prosecutors, have all been united in their criticism of judicial sentencing. The police and prosecutors, in particular, have been most vocal in their disparaging remarks. The judges realize that the police and prosecutors may be partially motivated in their negative comments, by a desire to shift the spotlight away from their own crime-fighting inadequacies. However, the public appears convinced that the judges and their ineffective sentencing decisions are a primary reason for the breakdown in society's ability to control crime and keep their local neighborhoods safe.

In addition to the pressure and heavy responsibility attached to the sentencing decision, the judge is also frustrated in this endeavor by a lack of reliable background information on the defendant which could aid him in reaching an intelligent decision. For example, there was a recent controversy in the New York County criminal courts (Manhattan) between judges and probation department officers who exchanged charges as to respective blame for the pre-sentence reports being both seriously delayed, as well as fraught with errors and omissions.[2] The judges charged that the quality of pre-sentence reports has deteriorated to the point where they are of very little use in sentencing decisions. The probation department countered by stating that the judges have placed unreasonable time and workload pressures on their depleted staffs, and are using the probation department as scapegoats.

A final problem for judges attempting to conscientiously balance the needs of the defendant and society during the dispositional process, is the absence of viable alternative forms of treatment for the defendant. The judge can either send the defendant to prison for a period of years, or return him to the community by placing him on probation. The selection of prison seems to offer only a temporary solution, since the defendant will eventually be released, angrier, and possibly more adroit in his criminal activities. Given the unrealistically large caseloads for probation officers, the defendant placed on probation receives almost no supervision or guidance, and is also likely to soon be arrested for another crime. For the defendant with special psychological or physical problems, his chances of receiving viable help is also negligible. Halfway houses, and other shelter alternatives in the community have not been established in sufficient numbers to provide a meaningful alternative, except in a few isolated instances. Federal, state, and local budget reductions have also undermined these rehabilitative and reform efforts.

The present criticism of judicial sentencing has grown from the public's belief that the courts have been both too lenient and too inconsistent. The result has been a perceived pattern of irrational and undesirable sentencing decisions in which both the defendants and the general public are being mistreated. Defendants arrested for the same crime receive divergent sentences. The judges defend such variation on the basis of their obligation to individualize each sentencing decision, considering unique factors which relate to the specific defendant.

Within the past decade, the majority of state legislatures have responded favorably to the public clamor and have increased the severity of its sentences while reducing the discretionary power of the judge by creating determinant rather than indeterminant sentences. With determinant sentences, if a defendant is found guilty of a particular crime, the judge *must* sentence him to a narrow range of minimum and maximum years or months. Additional restraints on the judge's sentencing choices may be determined by whether the defendant has prior felony convictions, whether these convictions involved violence, whether a gun was used in the current offense, whether the victim was a senior citizen, or whether heroin or some other dangerous drug was used or sold in large quantities. If any, or a combination of these factors are present in the defendant's case, then the judge is directed to alter his sentence as dictated by each of these special circumstances.

Most of the judges interviewed were not pleased with the shift from indeterminant to determinant sentences. Many judges were also upset by what they felt was an unnecessary increased severity of sentences, believing that the current lengths were sufficiently severe. The leniency issue, however, was not nearly as important to the judges as the lessening of their discretionary powers.

Judges object to the reduction of their sentencing power because of its inhibiting effect upon their abilty to reach what they believe to be a just disposition. Confident of his expertise, educated by his experience, the judge believes that he can only reach an intelligent sentencing disposition by being allowed to consider a wide range of mitigating factors concerning the defendant's background and any unusual aspects surrounding this particular crime. It is by being able to ponder the wide range of factors and being able to utilize a variety of sentencing alternatives, that the judge can effectively fit the disposition to the crime *and* the defendant. This particularistic style of sentencing was an outgrowth of penal reforms dating back to the 1920s,[3] and reflected a need to treat each defendant as an individual. Thus, the presence of disparities between individuals charged with the same crime was not a problem to be lamented, but rather a reflection of the judge's recognition of the unique circumstances in each case, and a testimony to the judge's perspicacity and care.

What are the factors a judge considers in the sentencing decision? Many judges try to inquire into the defendant's background in order to determine whether the present criminal activity has followed a discernible trend of anti-social behavior, or is clearly an aberration in an otherwise law-abiding lifetime. Unfortunately, many defendants do not easily fall completely within either category. If they did exhibit such clearcut patterns, the judge would have a fairly easy time with the sentencing decision. Those defendants with consistent patterns of criminal behavior would be sent to jail, and those who have committed an isolated act would receive probation. Many defendants, however, are more likely to have had an earlier criminal record, but only involving less serious property crimes. Others may have a conviction for a felony, but it could have occurred many years earlier, perhaps when he was a juvenile. During the intervening years, he may not have committed any crimes.

Judges also consider a defendant's previous opportunities for rehabilitation. If the defendant seemed to be making a sincere effort toward putting his life back in order, a second or third chance may be offered. On the other hand, if a defendant has failed to avail himself of opportunities which the court has offered in the past, such as a drug program, vocational training, or psychiatric counseling, the court is more likely to give up on the defendant and sentence him to prison. The attitude and motivation of the defendant as manifested through his track record in these rehabilitative programs is of crucial significance to the judge. These factors were considered in most instances where defendants were to receive prison sentences (when they were not clearly mandated by statute due to the serious nature of the crime), to be the most persuasive factor in the judge's decision. The defendant was thought to have insulted the court by his refusal to take advantage of this earlier, generous opportunity for a second chance.

Judges are willing to read character references on behalf of the defendant as submitted by defense attorneys, but the facts of the pre-sentence report concerning the seriousness of the present offense, the defendant's past criminal record, and his willingness to participate in previous rehabilitative programs, combine to provide the most critical information influencing the judge's sentencing decision. The prosecutor usually attempts to counter the defense attorney's plea for leniency with an equally unrealistic recommendation, stressing the necessity for protecting society from sociopaths such as the defendant. Most judges, particularly those sentencing large numbers of defendants after accepting guilty pleas, are unmoved by the posturing of both prosecution and defense, and generally adopt a reasonable compromise position.

As more and more jurisdictions grow upset over supposed judicial leniency and sentencing disparities, determinate sentencing statutes are being enacted, usually in combination with lengthier sentences. This means that not only are the judges given a narrower range of alternatives (i.e., 5–7 year term instead of a 2–10 year), but certain categories of crimes and defendants *must* receive specific sentences. These states have frequently classified crimes, according to severity, into a number of categories. Any defendant who falls within a category must receive a particular sentence depending upon the number and type of previous convictions. New York State terms defendants with previous felony convictions "predicate felons," and if a weapon was used in the earlier crimes, the defendant falls into the most serious grouping termed "violent predicate felon." In addition to determinate sentencing statutes, states have attempted to utilize several other alternatives reforms. One of the most popular is *presumptive sentencing,* which is utilized in New Jersey. *Presumptive sentencing* means a judge is bound by a recommended sentence from the legislature for a specific charge, and if the judge chooses to go beyond the narrow limits of this recommendation, the judge must write an explanation to justify such action. Information relating to possible mitigating circumstances or unique personal situations must be presented to authorize any sentencing deviation.

For several decades judges themselves have attempted to reform their sentencing practices. They were clearly aware of the public antipathy. Their reform efforts have involved both educative and institutional changes which have been geared primarily toward resolving the disparity question. The educative reforms are typified by the development of sentencing institutes such as the popular National College of Judges in Reno, Nevada. These programs are usually one or two weeks in duration and attempt to teach judges that differing personal perspectives can influence sentencing decisions. Hypothetical case histories of defendants are distributed to the judges in attendance, and each must impose his or her own sentence, and then explain it to their colleagues. The judges quickly comprehend how their personal backgrounds and individual personalities influence their ability to impose a particular sentence. The Institute believes that by educating judges as to the divergent opinions held by their colleagues, they will be more careful in the future to control personal prejudices affecting their professional behavior. Whether these courses can have long-range effects upon a judge's sentencing proclivities has never been conclusively established. Critics of these programs believe they are more of a busman's holiday, and the many diversions of Reno serve to undercut the capability of formal instruction to significantly alter judicial behavior.

Other reforms such as sentencing councils, and appellate review of sentences have also attempted to reduce unwarranted disparities by developing procedures designed to enroll larger numbers of judges in supervising each other's sentences, and in some instances requiring written justifications.[4] The sentencing council is a device which permits several judges of a multi-judge court to meet periodically to consider what sentences should be imposed in pending cases. It is a procedure used primarily by federal district courts. Its primary advantage is that it shows the participating judges their

differing sentencing practices, and then offers a forum in which these differences can be debated and a consensus formed. The most bothersome
aspect of the councils is the permitting of judges to meet prior to the sentencing hearing. This means that the sentencing judge, who has final
responsibility for the sentencing, may have had his objectivity impaired by
the council's earlier discussions.

Although nationally we have always allowed appellate review for sentences which failed to conform to statutory limits, nearly one-third of the
states do not permit appellate review on the merits of the sentence. Additionally, a growing number of states have interpreted their general review
statutes to grant such authority for appellate review. Usually this review is
conducted by the regular appellate division, although several states have
created special courts staffed with experienced judges solely for the purpose
of reviewing sentences.[5] Several judges interviewed were upset by appellate
review and sentencing councils, viewing these reforms as an indication of
the lack of faith by their colleagues in their ability to reach an appropriate
disposition. It was believed to be another example of the trial court judge
losing power as a result of public frustration over the rising crime rate. It
was especially upsetting because it was fellow members of the bench who
wilted under public pressure. It was expected to cause even greater tensions
between trial and appellate judges. Since these reforms are still in the em-
bryonic stages and affect only a minority of jurisdictions, it is premature for
both judges and critics to offer conclusions as to the long run consequences
of these reforms.

The large majority of criminal court judges, maybe because they
realized the importance of their sentencing responsibilities, spent a great
deal of time agonizing over such decisions. An equally weighty factor causing the judges anguish over sentencing decisions was their increasing
awareness of the horrible conditions presently existing in our various state
penitentiaries. A sentence meant not only loss of freedom but could most
likely mean subjecting the defendant to rape, robbery and other forms of
violence, rampant within prison walls. A final influence upon the judge is
the serious over-crowding in nearly all state prisons. Sentenced defendants
commonly must wait months in county detention centers until a vacancy
opens up in a state facility. All of these factors combine to convince a
judge that only the most heinous criminals deserve to be sent to prison.
Thus, many defendants who previously might have been sentenced to
prison are receiving probation. Judges are aware that only the toughest
criminal will be able to survive in these institutions. It was also interesting
to note that several judges made it their practice to follow-up on defendants after sentencing, and recognized a long-term responsibility for
guiding someone toward the perils of incarceration and toward a possible
return to respectability.

OUTSIDE PRESSURE

In Chapter One, the various external pressures affecting judicial behavior and the overall performance of the local criminal justice system were briefly introduced. These included the media, local politicians, community groups, and the appellate courts in addition to several broader sociocultural variables. Given the specific theme of the present chapter, we will briefly examine the effects of criticism from several of these groups, and discuss why this verbal abuse constitutes one of the most unpleasant aspects of the criminal court judge's job.

Judges desire the independence and insulation from these outside groups because they believe it is a critical ingredient in preserving the proper climate for them to perform their job with optimal objectivity and effectiveness. When this isolation is destroyed or compromised by the intrusion of external influences, judges rarely offer public comments or reactions to charges, but rather seethe internally and grow increasingly aloof from the public they are sworn to serve. Nevertheless, during the years spent observing and interviewing judges, I found they usually reserved their most acerbic private comments for those media and local political figures who have maligned their professional efforts.

Most judges are successful in their efforts to avoid the media's spotlight. They are careful to abstain from pretrial decisions, plea bargains or sentences which can be expected to upset and possibly outrage the public. Judges acknowledge that the media in the words of one Philadelphia judge, "can really do a number on you if they want to." This awareness has a chilling effect on judicial behavior because the defendants lack a countervailing group of advocates within the media to argue their viewpoint. This imbalance is not lost upon judges who comprehend that pro-prosecution decisions will rarely raise public concern or media attention.

Approximately one-third of the judges interviewed, however, did not seem to be intimidated by the possible repercussions from public exposure of their courtroom actions. These judges, who were most typically less prosecution-oriented than their more reticent (rabbit-eared) brethren, appear to almost relish the media's attention, and delight in flashing their judicial opinions dramatically before the public. Their more reserved colleagues are often the harshest critics of these outspoken judges. Mutterings of grandstanding, overly active egos, and political careerism are typically directed toward those judges basking in the public limelight.

There does seem to be a slight trend toward growing numbers of judges willing to move into the limelight and abandon the protected isolation of the courtroom. They justify their newfound courage and loquacity on the basis of an urgent need to correct the public image of the criminal courts being a major cause of their city's crime problems. Unwilling to remain scapegoats for the failings of society in general, and the criminal justice system in particular, these judges felt a grave need and professional responsibility to educate the public about realities and complexities of their city's crime problems and the failings of the criminal justice system. One eastern judge went so far as to urge his colleagues to bring citizens from the community into their courtrooms, especially high school students, in order to teach them how the system actually operates. He had been performing such quasi-educational courtroom sessions himself for many years, and felt it was probably his most worthwhile achievement.[6]

ADMINISTRATIVE TEDIUM

Nearly every judge interviewed stated that one of the most annoying aspects of their job was the administrative tedium. They complained not only of the ever-increasing demands for paperwork from their superiors, but of the frustrating lack of cooperation from other public agencies upon whom they are dependent for critical information. One retired judge from a southern city commented that he was so busy with administrative details that he had no time to think. He felt that he was becoming more of a clerk and less of a judge.[7] The bureaucratic spirit of the state and federal government has clearly permeated the local criminal courts. Judges in several cities were required to keep a time sheet in which they had to record how they spent each hour of the working day, including the length of their lunches.

The Washington, D.C. court system seemed extreme in its fetish for judicial accountability. The more typical administrative frustrations are the expected by-product of our overworked and understaffed court system in which many diverse parties and agencies, including those in agressive competition with one another, must be convinced or cajoled into cooperating. The chaotic scenes depicted in earlier chapters of this volume, illustrate the wide range of individuals who must be coordinated and in possession of the requisite information and documentation before the judge can begin to process a case. This complex process begins as early as the preliminary hearing, and is repeated at every subsequent appearance. The public defender or defense counsel must be present with his client and in possession of the proper case file. The prosecutor must also be prepared with the defendant's prior record, a copy of the police department's arrest report, as well as statements from witnesses, and any other relevant information. If the defendant failed to make bail and was detained in the local jail, the sheriff's department must transport him to the courtroom. The judge may also wish to see any preliminary reports from the probation department relevant to the defendant's background. The arresting police officer is also often required to be present, and he may have some necessary evidentiary material. The situation is further complicated where additional state or federal law enforcement agencies possess important information relevant to the case (i.e., FBI, State Police, Military Police, Drug Enforcement Agency, Immigration Bureau, etc.). The judge, finally, must also turn to his clerk to make sure he has before him the proper case folder which lists all previous court action taken with regard to the case.

The odds are highly in favor of one or more of these previously mentioned individuals or documents not being in the proper place at the proper time. Additionally, when one realizes that in the average case, approximately six court appearances will be required, it is even more likely that each case represents an ongoing bureaucratic nightmare for the criminal judge. During the many years of courtroom observation, especially at pretrial proceedings, where a large number of cases must be processed, it seems fair to estimate that every other case, and frequently two out of three, are missing a critical individual or document. This necessitates a postponement until a future date when everyone can try again. At this subsequent proceeding, the odds improve only slightly that all required elements will be present, allowing the case to be processed.

Judges do appear to be able to exercise a limited degree of influence in reducing the number of postponements. This may be accomplished either by gaining a reputation as a no-nonsense judge who will consistently penalize anyone failing to appear in his courtroom at the required time, or he becomes a judge who is willing to drive both himself and his staff unmercifully in a never-ending struggle to control the docket and ensure the prompt appearance of all parties. Judges who adopt either of these styles, and especially the latter, run a strong risk of antagonizing their personal staffs as well as the courtroom workgroup. These tensions can cause the other actors to become uncooperative or recalcitrant, and eventually be counter-productive to the judge's laudatory goals. Thus, the abrasive judge, striving for courtroom efficiency may be less successful in his search than a more complacent judge who slogs throught his pile of cases in a relaxed and friendly manner.

The Court Administrator is the public official whose position was created in order to assist the judge in completing these burdensome tasks. The power of this administrative judge and those of his administrative assistants varies significantly from city to city, but generally one expects this official to be held accountable for controlling the behavior of his management specialists. It is ironic, that despite the fact that these administrative officials were developed for the purpose of aiding the judges with their managerial responsibilities, they have, at least in the eyes of most judges, made their professional lives more miserable by appreciably increasing the amount of tedious paperwork which must be completed.

The Administrative Judges and their staffs are likely targets for the frustrated judges who are overwhelmed by files, records, and miscellaneous documents. Also, because the court administrators are technically responsible for the working conditions, including maintenance of the physical plant, and provision of professional amenities, they are blamed for all of the problems that upset the judges. As the minor irritations continue to mount, and begin to multiply in both frequency and severity, the hostility of the criminal court judge also begins to escalate. When the air conditioning system malfunctions during the same day that the Xerox machine breaks down, and a law clerk is mugged in the lavatory, the judge is likely to designate the Office of Court Administrator as the primary cause of all such woes.

Sereral administrative judges are able to survive in the nerve-wracking environment by utilizing a "stick and carrot" method of dealing with the sitting judges. He makes the judges cognizant of his autocratic potential for making their lives pleasant or miserable. His power to control which chambers a judge may be assigned, which courtroom he will have, who will be assigned as his bailiffs—all are critical factors affecting the quality of the judge's professional existence. It may therefore, behoove the judge to cooperate with his Presiding or Administrative Judge as much as possible, for the alternative may lead to a very unpleasant tenure on the bench. Since all judges receive nearly the same salary in a particular jurisdiction, the only way of indicating their relative superiority would be in the possession of a better office, or more stylish courtroom. The Administrators hold the keys to both status and comfort in the criminal courthouse!

As a closing note, the judges themselves do seem to contribute to this administistative chaos and are not entirely blameless. Their prior experience as attorneys, assisted by a handful of loyal clerks and secretaries, has not prepared them for the massive and detailed administrative responsibilities presently facing them. Scheduling cases, dealing with various public bureaucracies, shuffling an endless flow of records and documents, are all tasks which most judges have never had to confront. An insensitive public, inadequate staff, and budget-cutting legislators all contribute to exacerbating this already serious dilemma. The fragmented efforts to deal with these administrative problems through increased use of computers as well as additional training for the staff, does not seem an adequate response to so deep-rooted a problem.

MAINTAINING ORDER IN THE COURTROOM

Nearly all judges are concerned with disorder in their courtrooms. They fear outbursts from both attorneys, and defendants, as well as courtroom spectators. Nevertheless, in terms of actual incidents observed during my 12 years of investigations, as well as those recounted from almost 100 judges interviewed, revealed the extreme rarity of such occurrences. In the most definitive study of courtroom disorder by Norman Dorsen and Associates of the Bar Association of the City of New York, it was discovered that after sending out questionnaires to 4600 trial judges throughout the United States, 107 judges reported a total of 112 cases of disorder in their courtrooms.[8] These incidents occurred most frequently during serious felony cases, although a surprising number (8) during divorce proceedings were noted. Seventy-four of the cases involved criminal defendants (13 of whom were later found to be mentally disturbed), while 17 were spectators and 8 were attorneys. The court dealt with these disturbances by issuing contempt citations (32), warnings (24), binding and gagging of defendants (17), removal from the courtroom (13), declaring a mistrial (1), and clearing the courtroom (1).[9]

Despite the serious nature of most of these courtroom incidents, the empirical evidence from the Dorsen report clearly indicates their rarity. Only 2 percent of the large national sample of trial judges questioned were able to report even a single incident taking place in their courtrooms.[10] Nevertheless, because the number of incidents does seem to be on the rise, and even more importantly, because the judges and members of the local bar associations are so concerned with the problem, it has assumed a prominence justifying a brief discussion within this chapter.

The types of behavior problems facing a judge and his level of concern depend a great deal upon whether it is the defendant, or one of the opposing attorneys causing the problem. Defendants have been found to commit the following categories of misbehavior: passive disrespect, isolated emotional outbursts, noncooperation and repeated interruptions. Presented in ascending order of severity, the list is also in descending order of frequency. The overwhelming number of incidents which I observed involved passive disrespect. When combined with the second category of "single outbursts," it appears that at least 90 percent of the total number of incidents have been explained.

The frequency of the disrespect was so high in several courtrooms that it appeared that the judges were barely cognizant of the contemptuous attitude of the defendant. It is always difficult and quite perplexing for a middle-class person such as myself, to observe defendants in situations such as arraignments, and sentencing hearings where common sense would seem to dictate that one would dress and behave in a way which would be least likely to antagonize the judge. Despite the seriousness of these proceedings, in which the defendant's future freedom is at stake, defendant after defendant (especially those between the ages of 18 and 24) was unwilling to alter his insulting manner and appearance. This obvious lack of respect toward the judge and the court was manifested through slouching postures, grunting responses, and sullen stares.

Research by Jaros and Mendelsohn in Detroit's Records Court[11] clearly supports the premise that judges will penalize defendants who appear disrespectful in their courtroom (and conversely, reward those defendants who have the sense to try to placate the judge by exhibiting remorse and respect). Thus, it is truly puzzling as to why these defendants persist in their masochistic ritual. One can only imagine that there must be some strong belief in the necessity for maintaining a "macho image" before friends and spectators in the courtroom. Deference to the court may be equated with weakness in their distorted social education, and no sign of weakness is to be shown, even if it is certain to cause serious personal hardship. Some defendants may also believe, along with the general public, in the leniency of the courts, and in a "revolving door" system of justice; the courts never seem willing to treat their cases seriously. These defendants fail to realize that as they become older, and their crimes grow more serious, the court's patience will run out and they will face a lengthy prison term rather than the expected probationary sentence received in the past. Their previous guilty pleas have lulled them into a false sense of the court's impotence; a myth which will explode before they realize that they have finally gone too far.

The other forms of defendant misconduct—isolated outbursts, non-cooperation, and repeated interruptions—all occur during that procedural rarity, the trial. The defendant as a virtual non-participant for most of this proceeding, may be driven to these emotional outbursts out of frustration with the slow-paced, and at times, incomprehensible legal maneuvering. Many defendants also sense the higher stakes involved in a trial which is usually reserved for the most serious cases. By refusing to plead guilty, the defendant understands that he is risking a lengthy sentence if convicted. Pretrial court appearances are frequently of so short a duration and of such narrow scope, that the defendant lacks both the time and purpose for misbehavior.

When a defendant does misbehave, the judge has a wide range of available sanctions. These extend from the more commonly utilized preventive strategies such as issuing a warning or negotiating a solution, to the more repressive tactics of holding the defendant in contempt, removing him from the courtroom or binding and gagging. Defendants who turn out to be suffering from emotional distress, or are mentally ill are most likely to receive these rarely dispensed sanctions. In my 12 years, I witnessed only one incident in which a defendant was removed from the courtroom.

Attorneys may also be disciplined by the judge because of their misbehavior. These infractions include making disrespectful remarks, refusing to obey proper court procedures, using purposefully obstructionist or dilatory tactics, and engaging in repetitive or excessive argumentation. These forms of misbehavior may take on blatant or subtle manifestations, especially the use of questionable delay tactics, or overly aggressive cross-examinations of witnesses. When a judge believes that a lawyer has intentionally (and repeatedly), engaged in some form of misbehavior, he may sanction the attorney through any of the following methods: civil or criminal contempt citations, discipline by local bar association, suspension of right to practice, and removal of out-of-state lawyer's permission to practice. The Dorsen report, as well as my own observations have concluded that formal sanctions are extremely rare. Of the 100 judges interviewed, only one reported sanctioning an attorney—a criminal contempt citation, jailing the lawyer overnight.

In conclusion, although there seems to be a slight trend toward increasing disrespect for the judiciary, the number of actual incidents remains minuscule. If problems arose in the courtroom with attorney misbehavior, the judge would invariably utilize any of his formidable informal powers to sanction the erring lawyer. Judges interviewed disdained use of sanctions except in the most serious cases. They believed that any judge who was willing to use his contempt power with any degree of frequency indicated a critical weakness in both his judicial temperament and his abililty to control his courtroom.

JUDICIAL MISCONDUCT

The judges themselves are not immune from occasional transgressions. Even though these instances of judicial misbehavior may be rare, they are still an issue of great public concern.

As was seen in the forms of attorney and defendant misbehavior, judicial misconduct can range along a very broad continuum from the very serious to the relatively minor. Also, as was discovered with regard to attorneys and defendants, the preponderance of incidents cluster at the least serious end of the spectrum. Examples of these less serious types of judicial misconduct are acts of rudeness or bias, and forms of undignified behavior. These acts commonly occur when judges are overly aggressive in their questioning of witnesses or comment too frequently on the evidence. Both of these behaviors can give the impression of partisanship to the jury and spectators. This problem can also be seen in the perceived abuse of attorneys which implies an unprofessional preference or hostility toward one of the adversaries. This last topic was discussed at great length in Chapter Five and although it may only be categorized as a "less serious" form of judicial misconduct, it is the most common type, and can have a significant impact upon the ultimate outcome of the trial.

Given the chaotic conditions found in the courtroom, and the various pressures exerted upon the criminal court judges, it is to be expected that they may not be able to continually maintain a calm and dispassionate temperament. The frustrations of needless delays, incomplete records, insolent defendants, and incompetent attorneys, all contribute to a debilitating and enervating judicial experience. Occasionally, one does find a judge who lacks the necessary character traits, and his anger quickly rises to the surface. Frustration may cause judges to become rude or abusive toward attorneys, defendants or an officer of the court in close proximity when their tempers reach the boiling point.

The more serious categories of judicial misconduct are the result of either the incompetence or venality of the judge. Although these transgressions are extremely isolated, they are always important media events. With the post-Watergate period of heightened citizen scrutiny of public officials and their moral behavior, the media devotes a great deal of attention to any breach of the public faith, especially by a judge. One student of the subject, Charles Ashman, believes the problem is so widespread that he wrote a book on the subject entitled *The Finest Judges Money Can Buy*, and has toured the nation expounding the topic of judicial corruption.[12]

Ashman has collected the case studies of nearly 200 corrupt judges. His book contains chapters on the relationship between organized crime and the judiciary, judicial avarice, moral decadence, court jesters, and political manipulators and grafters. His compilation offers a frightening portrait, but one must realize that he is covering *all* federal and state judges during a 40-year period.

Without minimizing the problem, nearly all research on this topic has found judicial malfeasance to a be very rare occurrence. There can be observed on a daily basis, judges losing their tempers, raising their voices, and permitting their emotions to be observed by everyone in the courtroom. This, however, seems to be much more a product of courtroom pressures than an abundance of unsuited, ill-tempered judges who should be relieved of their duties. In addition to devising a much needed system for spotting and removing those judges who cannot stand the strains and tensions of the criminal courtroom, it seems to make even greater sense to focus our reforming energies upon the sources of the courtroom confusion and implement policies geared toward its reduction.

When a judge does begin to exhibit a pattern of behavior which threatens his legitimacy as a neutral arbiter and compassionate dispenser of justice, it is critical that action be taken. Even if these instances of misconduct are rare, they serve to undermine the credibility and efficacy of the entire judicial structure. The public expects, and demands its judges not only to be fair, but to give the appearance of such behavior. Anything less will seriously weaken the public's confidence in the criminal courts.

Why should judges, given their lofty position, be tempted to commit an act of malfeasance? Many judges, especially those who have served in office for a long period of time, may believe that they sometimes become so frustrated with the law, and seeing incompetent attorneys and guilty defendants passing through their courtrooms, that they believe themselves justified in bending the law so as to bring about a more socially desirable end (at least in their own personal opinions). After sitting on the bench, some judges may begin to think they *are* the law, and believe that they must actively pursue those ends which they *know* to be right, despite the fact that this may cause them to utilize questionable, and at times unlawful, means. They are encouraged in this pursuit because of their knowledge that most of what they do is unreviewable by appellate courts and that other sanctions are almost never used.

What types of sanctions are available to discipline a judge? The oldest, and most cumbersome, is impeachment which is occasionally threatened, but rarely used. Appellate review and investigation by local bar associations have been attempted in several jurisdictions. However, in the past decade, the most popular innovative method has been investigations conducted by Commissions or Boards of Inquiry. These institutions seem to be modeled after either the California or New York systems. In New York, the State Commission on Judicial Conduct has no investigative arm, no screening mechanism, and appears to be dominated by the state legislature and governor. Their most recent action (March 1, 1983) in censuring a judge for addressing a female lawyer derisively as "little girl," has not helped the credibility of the Commission. The *New York Times* reported:

> Six of the nine members of the Commission made up of judges, lawyers, and private citizens, felt that Justice Jordan should be publicly admonished. Two thought he had behaved improperly, but voted to admonish him privately. One said the Justice has done nothing wrong, that the lawyer was too sensitive, and the Commission was overreaching.[13]

The California Commission on Judicial Qualifications is composed of five judges appointed by the State Supreme Court, two lawyers appointed by the state bar association and two laymen appointed by the governor. The Commission has a permanent staff with the use of outside investigators. It can act on its own initiative in a wide range of cases. Professor Albert Alschuler in his study of courtroom misconduct discovered that in 1972, it received approximately 100 complaints from angry litigants. Two-thirds of the complaints were settled by the staff. The Commission has been fairly successful in resolving disciplinary matters quietly and informally. Only three cases were referred to the State Supreme Court, and 50 judges resigned while their cases were under investigation. Alschuler concluded that

> the California experience has demonstrated that a commission system can be effective in disciplining judges for abusive courtroom behavior. Nevertheless, one may have an uneasy feeling about a regime that emphasizes confidentiality, accomplishes its results primarily through backroom settlements, and that is dominated by members of the elite professional group that it is designed to control.[14]

One additional jurisdiction which I visisted appeared to be operating a viable disciplinary institution. In Washington, D.C. the city utilizes a Commission of Judicial Disabilities and Tenure. The Commission is formulated and operates in a manner similar to the California system, but it has broader powers. Its responsibilites are extended to the area of approving reappointments in addition to dealing with discipline and involuntary retirements. In 1976–77, they handled 32 complaints regarding conduct and eventually conducted one disciplinary proceeding. Their main task seemed to focus upon reappointment proceedings for four members of the city's Superior Court whose terms were ending.[15]

The seemingly effective commissions in California and the District of Columbia appear to have a minimal impact upon curbing the problem of judicial misconduct. Judges, like most professional groups, do not wish to "wash their dirty linen in public." They would much prefer to deal with their erring colleagues through informal pressure. No one wants to be the first to point an accusing finger, since all the judges realize that they too could soon be on the wrong end of a commission inquiry. In addition to these rather expected complications, the cumbersome legal bureaucracy of the courts also emerges as a serious obstacle in the way of expeditious decision-making.

In concluding this section on judicial misconduct, one must remember that the number of venal or corrupt judges in our judicial system appears very small. There are many judges who lack the judicial temperament, abuse attorneys, or act prejudicially in favor of one of the parties, but thankfully, the actual number who intentionally commit acts of malfeasance while on the bench remains extremely small. The other problems of abusive and ill-tempered judges are not to be ignored, and must be addressed if we are to restore the public faith in our urban justice system. I believe, however, that this can best be accomplished by improving the judge's working conditions and allowing for criminal court decisions to be made in a safe and sane atmosphere, free from the turbulence, and confusion which presently exists.

NOTES

1. Paul Wice. *Crinimal Lawyers: An Endangered Species.* Beverly Hills, Sage Publications, 1978, p. 102.
2. Barbara Basler. Justice Aides in Dispute Over Lag in Sentencing, *New York Times.* October 10, 1981, p. II, 1.
3. Ronald Goldfarb and Linda Singer. *After Conviction.* New York, Simon and Schuster, 1973, p. 39.
4. Twentieth Century Fund, *Fair and Certain Punishment,* New York, McGraw-Hill, 1976, p. 19.
5. President's Commission of Law Enforcement and Administration of Justice. *Task Force Report: The Courts.* Washington, D.C.: Government Printing Office, 1967, p. 26.
6. Observations and interviews gathered in Philadelphia, Pa. during the summer of 1980.

7. Interview with retired District of Columbia criminal court judge during July 1980.
8. Norman Dorsen and Leon Friedman. *Disorder in the Court.* New York, Pantheon Books, 1973, p. 6.
9. Ibid. p. 7.
10. Ibid. p. 6.
11. Dean Jaros and Robert I. Mendelsohn. The Judicial Role and Sentencing Behavior, *Midwest Journal of Political Science.* 11 (1967), 471.
12. Charles Ashman. *The Finest Judges Money Can Buy.* Los Angeles Nash Publishing, 1973.
13. E.R. Shipp. Judge Censured for Addressing Lawyer as Girl, *New York Times.* March 1, 1983, p. II, 1.
14. Albert Alschuler. Courtroom Misconduct by Prosecutors and Trial Judges, *Texas Law Review* 50, (April 1972), p. 694.
15. Annual Report of District of Columbia Commission on Judicial Disabilities and Tenure. (October 1976-September 1977), Washington, D.C. 1977.

7

CONCLUSIONS AND
RECOMMENDATIONS

In all of the previous chapters of this volume, I have served as a conduit for the opinions and observations of judges and other critical actors within the criminal justice system. Occasional attempts were made to explain some of the causes of these opinions and observations, but as a general format, the interviewees were allowed to speak for themselves. My job was to set the scene and organize their responses in a meaningful fashion. In this concluding chapter, I have stepped from behind my mask of neutrality to offer my personal conclusions and recommendations concerning the urban felony court system.

One final justification for the personalized nature of this last chapter relates to my position as an outsider. Because I have never had a vested interest in the results of my research, I hopefully offer a somewhat more objective analysis of the system's strengths and weaknesses, especially in comparison with the many public officials that I interviewed. Many of the comments and opinions offered by judges, prosecutors, and defense counsel were affected by their limited vision. Their myopia may have been brought on by institutional patriotism or self-aggrandizement, but in either case, the truth suffered. As a hopefully neutral social scientist, my final observations may escape the trap of personal self-interest, and present the reader with a useful collection of conclusions and reforms.

This chapter is divided into two major divisions—personal convictions and suggested reforms. The conclusions have been subdivided into three categories: (1) conclusions which indicate that the criminal courts may not be as bad as the public perceives them to be; (2) conclusions which are troubling, but are more the product of the chaotic conditions in the criminal courthouse, rather than any purposeful action by criminal justice officials, and (3) conclusions which are most upsetting because they represent intentional actions by court officials in order to avoid responsibility for the worsening conditions within the courthouse.

PERSONAL CONCLUSIONS—MODIFYING MISCONCEPTIONS

Narrow Purpose of the Criminal Justice System

The most important thing to remember about the criminal courts is that they have a very narrow purpose—to adjudicate cases and determine if the prosecution can prove that a defendant is guilty, beyond a reasonable doubt.

The judges are only neutral arbiters whose professional oath of office requires them to uphold the laws of their jurisdiction. If the electorate is sincerely upset over the way laws appear to allow defendants to have the "upper hand" in our adversary system of justice, then their recourse is to elect legislators and executives who will change the current laws. This is, in fact, happening in several states with the passage of laws designed to eliminate plea bargaining, remove the judge's sentencing discretion, and re-institute the death penalty.[1]

It should be remembered that the courts are only a receptacle for the criminal justice process caseflow. They are limited to only those instances where the police have made an arrest, and the prosecutor has chosen to press charges. They cannot initiate actions to fight crime, but can only adjudicate and dispose of those cases dumped into courts by the local police and prosecutors. Their restricted area of responsibility is immediately terminated once they have completed their sentencing responsibilities. Problems in the prisons and inadequacies in our probation and parole systems are, therefore, outside the direct control of the criminal court judge.

Unfortunately, the judge is the most visible member of the criminal court system. The public makes the erroneous assumption that since he is at the pinnacle of the criminal justice system, and its symbolic leader, he must also possess the necessary far-reaching powers to affect the crime problem. And thus, when the crime problem is not resolved, but actually becomes more serious, the judge becomes the focal point for the citizen's frustration and anger. Other actors in the system, such as the police, prosecutors, probation officers, and prison officials, could do the judge a great favor by coming before the ill-informed public and correcting their distorted image of the judge's responsibilities. But since the outcry focuses primarily upon the judge, this allows the other actors to be spared the public's scorn, and they are willing to allow the criminal court judge to wriggle uncomfortably within the blinding, and misdirected, spotlight.

The criminal courts have always been a dumping ground for society's misfits and losers. People who, because of mental, physical, educational, or socioeconomic deficiencies, cannot succeed in the legitimate world, become the clientele of the criminal courts. This book has not attempted to discuss the etiology of crime, but after spending 12 years in hundreds of courtrooms, watching thousands of defendants pass by, I cannot help but conclude that the overwhelming majority of defendants are poor, confused, and emotionally immature. They are a sad group, probably outsiders, unable or unwilling to comply with the dictates of the law. The criminal courts have no direct impact upon those societal and psychological forces thought to be responsible for contributing to the development of this criminal class.

Obviously, judges cannot be totally absolved from having some affect upon the crime problem. Their sentencing practices and case dispositions can have a deterrent effect upon the defendants appearing before them, with an even less direct influence upon the behavior of potential criminals. The issue of deterrence and its relation to the certainty and severity of sentences is presently being debated and re-shaped by legislators even more than by judges.

After interviewing numerous defendants and examining the problem of deterrence in social science research, I remain unconvinced that individuals contemplating a criminal act are either dissuaded or persuaded to follow through on their anti-social inclinations because of a rational analysis of the sentencing proclivities of the local judiciary. The carefully planned jewel thefts, and precision bank robberies depicted on television and in the movies constitute an infinitesimally small percentage of our criminal activity. The bulk of crimes is committed in a random, almost spontaneous, and even unthinking manner, dependent primarily upon situational opportunities which propel the criminal into action. It is amazing to discover how large a percentage of defendants are drunk or "high" on drugs at the time they choose to commit a crime. Many others are in emotional states which inhibit rational thinking, or careful prior analysis. Such crimes as assaults, rapes, and homicides usually occur when an individual is in a state of great tension or excitation, although a wide variety of other crimes may also occur during these periods of intense, and sometimes uncontrolled emotionality.[2]

Acceptable Dispositions

Closely related to the necessity for realizing the narrow and specific responsibilities of the criminal courts, is the critical question of how well the courts are carrying out their prescribed duties. Are guilty defendants being acquitted, and even more importantly, are innocent persons being found guilty? As a general answer to this question, it appears on the basis of my experiences and reading, that the criminal courts are convicting the guilty (although it may not be for the crime originally charged), and are only in the rarest of instances convicting the innocent (despite recent Phil Donahue shows to the contrary). In a few isolated cases in which innocent persons are found guilty, it is usually because an eyewitness, or the victim, has either purposefully, out of some intense dislike, or simply out of carelessness, identified the wrong person. There is little a judge can do to unravel the personal motivations behind such egregious errors, nor can he ignore the significance of this evidence.

Critics of the criminal justice system point out that although the judges are finding large numbers of defendants guilty, the plea bargaining process and the high percentage of pretrial dismissals indicate that the judges are imposing too many light sentences on criminals, or none at all. Since plea bargaining will be discussed in the next section, let us concentrate upon the high percentage of defendants who have their cases dismissed. It should first be noted that the dismissal decision is usually that of the prosecutor, rather than the judge. In most cities, it was discovered that between 25–40 percent of all defendants arrested for felonies had their cases dismissed. Of these dismissals, at least three-fourths were based upon decisions by the prosecutor. In several cities, such as New Orleans and Milwaukee, the prosecutor's office would carefully review all felony arrests *prior* to the preliminary hearing which was to go before a judge in approximately one week following the arrest, and initial court appearance. At the preliminary hearing, a judge will have his first opportunity to weigh the evidence and possibly dismiss the case if probable cause is lacking. At a subsequent court appearance before the judge and/or a grand jury, a few weeks later, another judge will have a second opportunity to review the case and dismiss or indict, depending upon whether the prosecutor satisfies the probable cause burden.

Thus, the typical judge is active in the dismissal decision in only one-fourth of the instances where such a decision is reached. The large majority of dismissal decisions are made primarily by the prosecutor's office, *prior* to any judicial review of the evidence. The prosecutor and his staff have concluded as early as possible in the proceedings, that they do not have sufficient evidence to convict the defendant. Most prosecutors do not utilize the "probable cause" standard, but rather look ahead to the ultimate dispositional standard of "beyond a reasonable doubt." If the prosecutor believes he has less than a 50/50 chance of satisfying the latter standard, he will usually dismiss the case. Prosecutors, like the rest of the criminal justice establishment, have limited and usually insufficient resources, so they must choose only those cases which are sure victories and do not require unusual expenditures of time and manpower. A very few cases which possess notoriety, or seriousness as a result of media exposure, may force a district attorney into keeping a case in which he has a slight chance of winning, but as a general rule, he will only prosecute the certain winners.

Merely by concluding that judges are doing an acceptable job of convicting the guilty and acquitting the innocent, does not automatically mean that all is rosy with the dispositional process. Complicating the evaluation of a judge's performance is the final stage of the dispositional process—what do we do with the guilty defendant? Unfortunately, the judges are severely handicapped in reaching intelligent, compassionate decisions by the absence of available alternatives beyond simply sending the defendant to prison. Judges realize that prisons are horrible places where only the toughest survive. Most individuals can expect to be beaten, raped, and robbed during their confinement. The other dispositional alternatives, if statutorally available, involve some form of probation. Given the serious understaffing of most probation departments, the defendant will receive insufficient supervision, or counselling during his probational period. Between the two extremes of prison and probation, the judge has almost nothing else available to him. This lack of choice forces some very bad decisions for both the defendant and society. Currently, a few states are trying to develop alternative community treatment facilities as a compromise measure, but most cities cannot afford these new institutions.[3] The development of such alternatives is not the responsibility of the judge, nor is the improvement of the inhuman prison conditions, or the ineffective and overworked probation department, but all three problems have serious repercussions for the judge as he attempts to dispose of his cases.

Plea Bargaining

In addition to being criticized for dismissing too many cases, an even greater area of concern to students of the criminal justice system is the plea bargaining process. Although the judge rarely initiates such compromises, he is still held accountable because he will ultimately sentence the defendant for the agreed-upon charge. Judges have been accused of being overly eager in their efforts to reduce their caseloads, and too willing to accept plea bargains which may threaten the safety of society by being extremely beneficial to the defendant. Plea bargaining has, therefore, developed a negative connotation in terms of its purported leniency. The judges are depicted as "giving away the courthouse" in their ineffectual negotiations. Violent felons emerge from court with felony charges reduced to misdemeanors, and a probationary sentence of a few years.

Empirical studies, reinforced by my own observations, do not seem to bear out these charges. Through statutory changes, as well as the professional actions of most judges, defendants are receiving lengthier sentences than ever before. The average sentence of a defendant incarcerated in a New York prison has increased from one and one-half years to two and one-half years in a period of less than three years.[4] The state prisons are filled to capacity, and are overflowing. Also, judges have had their sentencing discretion significantly narrowed, so they really have little choice in their ability to manipulate legislative decisions.

Plea bargaining has become a symbolic concept, intended to depict the criminal court judges as a group of irresponsible public officials who are secretly negotiating with other criminal justice officials in an ineffectual manner. I believe that plea bargaining is essentially a "red herring" issue in which critics of the court use it to panic the public into thinking that it is a new device which has allowed an intimidated judiciary to surrender to the criminal forces. There are several common sense reasons for my attitude on this controversial topic. First, plea bargaining has been going on for a very long time. Historians have documented its presence in our court systems for more than 50 years.[5] It is simply a form of compromise, no different in fact, from the negotiations which dominate the civil courts, particularly in negligence cases, 90 percent of which are settled prior to going to trial.[6]

What the public must understand is that almost every defendant brought into criminal court is guilty of something. It may not be of the exact charge for which he is accused, but numerous studies have consistently verified that more than 90 percent of the felons indicted will eventually plead guilty.[7] As noted in an earlier section, a very small percentage of defendants (generally estimated to be less than 5 percent), may be innocent. Nearly all of these defendants were erroneously charged with a crime either by an unintentionally inaccurate identification or a purposefully vindictive action. There may also be a miniscale grouping of defendants who simply happened to be in the wrong place at the wrong time.

What, then, is the overworked and understaffed criminal justice system to do with all of these guilty defendants? As a practical solution, it expedites the disposition of cases by offering the defendant a reduced charge in exchange for his guilty plea which saves the court enormous time and expense. In addition, the prosecutor and judge also realize that nearly all defendants are guilty, and the plea ensures that the state will not have to run the risk of trial, and experience the possibility of an acquittal. Thus, all members of the courtroom workgroup, including the defense counsel who is aided in processing more cases more quickly, benefit when the defendant agrees to a plea bargain.

Research into plea bargaining has revealed that the public's fears concerning serious felons having their charges reduced to misdemeanors have generally been unfounded. Studies have shown that the plea bargain may serve as a compromise to reduce the policeman's traditionally inflated charges down to a more realistic level. Most police officers who fear that plea bargains will undermine the seriousness of their arrests, tend to initially "over-charge" the defendant. The police continually err on the side of retribution and severity in anticipation of the plea bargain in selecting the original charge. In my study of bail, many police officers admitted they purposefully over-charged in order to force the judge to set as high a bail as possible, causing maximum inconvenience to the defendant, i.e., financial hardship in raising the money, or preferably, loss of freedom during the pretrial period if the bond could not be raised. All of this over-charging may, therefore, mean that when the plea bargain is completed, his newly compromised charge may be much closer to the realistic charge which the defendant should have received initially.

I do not applaud plea bargaining as a perfect solution. It is a necessity in an imperfect judicial system. Sometimes, defendants are pressured into guilty pleas out of fear of receiving a more harsh sentence, if conviction followed a trial. It is deplorable to short-change anyone's constitutional due process guarantees for the sake of expedience. Some lawyers and prosecutors also abuse the system by bargaining with several cases at one negotiation session, exchanging a light sentence in one case for a harsh sentence in another. This clearly undermines the basic principle of each defendant having his case decided on its own individual merits. Group or bulk dispositions are a distasteful outgrowth of plea bargaining, and although they may be exceptional occurrences, they should never take place, even as an isolated incident. Thus, plea bargaining does have the potential for abusing the rights of the defendants, but so do many other tenuous practices of the criminal law. The answer is to reduce the caseload to more sensible levels, and eliminate the pressures which encourage such transgressions.

PERSONAL CONCLUSIONS—TROUBLING YET UNINTENTIONED

The many conclusions discussed in this section were thought to be rather troubling aspects of the criminal courts, although they were not the product of intentional actions by any criminal justice officials or institutions. Rather, they emerged from the chaotic conditions discovered in our criminal courthouses. These conditions seem to be the product of the wide-ranging economic, political, and social pressures outside of the control of the criminal courts.

The System

We have continually spoken of the felony courts as part of the criminal justice "system." The word *system* is a key concept if the courts are to undergo any type of viable reform. The other institutions in this system—the police, corrections, and probation—must also be remembered as being inextricably linked with, and affected by the behavior of the criminal courts. Too long have we observed well-intentioned efforts at improving the courts, providing only temporary relief to a problem by applying a band-aid where massive surgery was required. Courts, like so many public agencies, seem to be unable to deviate from their crisis-management mentality, which limits criminal justice officials to only short-term solutions. Inevitably the problem does not disappear, but rather festers and spreads, then resurfaces in a slightly altered form as an even more serious dilemma plaguing some other element of the system. The criminal justice system needs to maintain its homeostatic condition, and if it is tinkered with at some point in the organism, this can be expected to cause a reaction at some other point in the body.

One of the best examples illustrating this phenomenon occurred in New York City nearly a decade ago. It grew out of a well-intentioned effort to reduce the many idle hours wasted by the city's police as they waited to be called as witnesses in the criminal courts. Frequently, officers would be called three and four times for court appearances before they were able to present their evidence and return to duty. The resulting loss of available man-hours, as well as the expense of overtime pay, motivated the court system and trial court administrators to utilize a recently acquired computer system in order to solve the problem. The electronic brain was able to develop a method of scheduling which allowed a policeman to be notified a few hours prior to his required appearance. The system quickly proved itself capable of guaranteeing that police officers would be certain to have their cases heard on their initial appearance. By eliminating numerous unnecessary court appearances, and wasted man-hours sitting around courthouses, police and court management officials agreed that the officers were now able to return to the streets and devote more time to their crime-fighting responsibilities. They concluded, in fact, that approximately 18 percent more police officers were now on active duty than prior to the re-scheduling solution.

The corrected situation, however, was not without costs. Although the police department applauded the computer's accomplishments by allowing deployment of more officers on active duty, the courts soon realized that an unintended side effect would create new problems. With an 18 percent increase in the police department's daily work force, it was inevitable that more defendants would be arrested, and the overworked courts would be handed an even greater number of cases to process. This is, in fact, what happened as arrests in the ensuing months increased nearly 20 percent. With state law and budget constraints fixing the number of judges, the criminal courts were caught in a deluge of cases which nearly collapsed the system. The pretrial detention facilities, legal aid attorneys, prosecutors, and probation officers were all overwhelmed by the subsequent prisoner increase.

The point of recalling this incident is certainly not to argue against court reforms, such as the computerization of cases and scheduling of witnesses. However, whenever any reform is contemplated, the court, police, and correctional officials must work together. There must be a realization by all criminal justice practitioners that policy changes cannot be made unilaterally. They must be aware of the ramifications and consequences of some decisions upon other, inter-related institutions. Unless such system-wide repercussions are contemplated, the continued series of "band-aid" reforms will not only fail to reach the deeper problems but may likely be a contributing cause to the creation of new dilemmas.

The Clash of Two Worlds

A somewhat cynical private criminal lawyer whom I recently interviewed, offered the observation that the real adversary system which operates in our urban criminal courts is not between the prosecution and defense, but is actually between the victims and defendants against the judges, prosecutors, and defense attorneys (usually translated into public defenders). The unstated premise is that the courts are often the battleground for a struggle between the under-class and the upper-class. Because so many defendants in our cities are black or brown, this observation may appear to be one of racial implications. However, as I traveled around the country and observed courts in which few of the defendants were members of racial minorities, the lower-class membership/affiliation seemed a constant reality. Additionally, one rarely finds many upper- or even middle-class defendants from any racial or ethnic group. Thus, when race or ethnic background is controlled, the significance of socioeconomic status becomes even more obvious.

The lower-class backgrounds of the defendants (and incidentally, most of the victims as well), is even more apparent, when contrasted with the upper- and upper-middle-class backgrounds of the judges and attorneys. The court officials who are on the periphery of criminal court action (probation, correction, and custodial officers), seem to be at least aspiring toward upper-middle-class respectability. How does one deduce a lower-class background from merely observing the defendants in court? Clues are offered in the style of dress and lack of articulation, although the truly convincing evidence is the fact that approximately 80 percent of all defendants declared themselves indigent and depended upon the services of a court-appointed lawyer (either public defender or assigned counsel).

The consequences of being poor have continual and critical impact upon the defendant's chances for obtaining an acquittal or dismissal. Beginning with the initial bail decision, a defendant who cannot raise the required bond will be forced to remain in pretrial detention for several months until his case is settled. Defendants who have been unable to obtain their pretrial freedom are seriously handicapped in preparing their defense, as well as supporting their families through difficult times.

A second, and even more serious consequence of their economic status is their inability to obtain their own attorneys and, therefore, being forced to rely upon an assigned counsel or public defender. Although studies have shown insignificant differences between public or private legal defense, the perception of a major difference by both the defendants and the general public, makes this an issue of great symbolic importance.

A third effect of the defendant's social and economic status to influence his treatment is during the preparation and evaluation of the pre-sentencing report. In reviewing the defendant's lower-class background, the judge and probation officers seem to be rationalizing the minimal effect that incarceration may have upon this person's life. The almost inevitable history of prior experiences with the police of most urban lower-class defendants seems to seal their fate; the judge is reassured about his present decision because of knowledge of past transgressions.

Most defendants are not only poor but also of a racial minority, and some critics of the criminal justice system have brought charges of institutional racism. My 12 years of courtroom observations have convinced me that almost all members of the courtroom workgroup have conducted themselves in a non-prejudicial manner. A rare racial incident may occur to taint an entire city's court system. I have been continually impressed by the absence of racially-motivated decisions by criminal court personnel.

Communications Gap

Closely associated with the presence of so many lower-class defendants, is another serious problem which is less obvious and rarely discussed. I am referring to the abysmal system of communication between the court and its clientele. Although the lower-class origins, and frequently related inferior educational backgrounds of the defendants may contribute to this problem, the carelessness and callousness of responsible officers of the court to effectively communicate is the primary reason for this disturbing condition.

The proceedings in criminal court are extremely important to a defendant who may lose his freedom and be separated from his family for a lengthy period of time. Nevertheless, anyone observing the criminal courts soon realizes that the defendant is often the one person in the courtroom who is least aware of what is transpiring. The defendant is left standing behind the attorney's table while his lawyer, the prosecutor and the judge converse in hushed tones, deciding his fate. When an attempt is made to include the defendant in their conversations, legal jargon and confusing terminology is used which would baffle college graduates. Defendants who have spent considerable time in the criminal courts, pretend to understand the legal procedures affecting their lives; they do not really understand what is occurring.

The communications problems are exacerbated by the growing number of Spanish-speaking defendants who are being processed by the criminal courts. Every city visited had a critical shortage of interpreters. In New York, court proceedings had to be continually halted until one of the few available translators had finished his or her work in another courtroom.

Judges who are anxious to move their cases become willing to have defendants whom they clearly know to be barely literate in English, waive their rights to a translator. Politely acquiescing to the judge's request for the defendant's waiver, both the defense attorney and the defendant allow for the proceeding to continue without an interpreter. The judge will attempt patiently to explain to the defendant what is happening with his case, but the defendant's overly condescending behavior in his eager effort to please the judge indicates a language barrier that even the best intentioned judge cannot surmount.

The failure in communication is a personal tragedy for the defendant, and is only part of the confusion and frustration in the courtroom. The basic problem of having the defendant, witnesses, and other necessary officials appear in the proper courtroom at the required hour becomes a logistical impossibility. When one considers that each defendant must make six, seven or even more required appearances, one may better grasp the staggering magnitude of the problem.

Rarely is anything done to try to communicate to the defendant what is transpiring and what he must do to comply with the judge's orders. The faulty acoustics produced by the high ceilings of the courtrooms allows the court clerk's instructions to drift upward; the noisy, chaotic gallery behind the defendant causes a continual distraction; the confusion in front of him as impatient judges, agitated prosecutors, and beleaguered public defenders converse in a rapid perplexing language which is never clearly explained—all of these things combine to provide a setting in which the communication between court and defendant is impossible. The loss is everyone's.

Fiscal Crisis

Many of the problems facing the court have at least partial roots in the fiscal crisis confronting nearly all of our cities. Communication could be improved if there were more money to hire more Spanish translators. This would also help to speed up the flow of cases, since judges would not have to postpone proceedings until an interpreter could be found. With more public defenders, the individual caseloads could become more manageable. This would not only improve the quality of defense (since defenders could spend more time on fewer cases), but would help the court expedite cases. By increasing the size of probation departments, more reliable and comprehensive pre-sentence reports can be completed in shorter periods of time and the reduced number of defendants assigned to each officer will permit a viable supervisory and rehabilitative function to be accomplished.

Despite rising crime rates, court administrators are facing cutbacks in personnel and resources. The many positive results emanating from the creation of additional positions described above have not occurred, and as one considers the future, the prognosis is even bleaker. The social, economic, and educational problems which appear to be related to the perpetuation of a crime problem, are also negatively affected by the scarcity of public monies. This can only mean that the serious problems which face the courts today, will only continue their downward spiral given the unpromising economic forecast.

It seems amazing that the American public, with its great concern and fear over crime, is so obsessed by frugality and an unwillingness to spend public monies, that it would rather live in fear, behind closed doors, and allow the basic quality of its existence to deteriorate rather than permit the government an opportunity to remedy the situation by the expenditures of its tax dollars!

A Decade Without Change

My frustration over the public's unwillingness to fund possible reform programs has been intensified by the lengthy period of time in which no significant improvements have been made within the urban justice system. In the 12 years that I have been intensively studying the nation's criminal justice system, and crossing the country repeatedly in order to visit countless cities, I have not observed any significant improvement in either the effectiveness or efficiency of the urban criminal courts. Despite the creation by the federal government of the Law Enforcement Assistance Administration, which spent billions of dollars to fight crime as well as improve the quality of justice in our criminal courts, those institutions seem even worse off today than when I began my peregrinations in 1970.

As indicated in the previous discussion of the urban fiscal crisis, the cities and their criminal justice institutions have failed to receive adequate funding during the past decade, and the situation is worsening. The federal role in aiding local courts has also taken a radical turn downward as the LEAA went out of existence on April 1, 1982. Although the agency had experienced severe cutbacks in funding during its last five years in operation, its termination signaled a depressing decision by the government to discontinue its financial involvement in local criminal justice.

More significant than the continued shortage of funds and resources during this period has been the absence of meaningful reforms and innovations. The same "new" programs that were proposed in the early 1970s have either been abandoned, or exist in almost skeletal form. I am most aware of this phenomenon in the bail reform movement which I studied from 1969–72 for the United States Department of Justice.

New programs designed to ease the inherent economic discrimination existing within the traditional bail system were being developed and implemented in nearly every major city. Additionally, diversion programs for youth and first offenders were offering a second chance without the stigma of an arrest record. These programs often received federal funding in the early 1970s with the hope that state and local governments would be persuaded to pick up the tab eventually. Unfortunately, this did not occur, and most of those well-intentioned programs have either disappeared or have been drastically reduced. I believe that today's bleak economic outlook for our major cities is largely responsible for this loss of momentum, but the retributive attitude of the public toward persons accused of crimes may be an even more salient influence.

Inability to clarify the objectives of reform programs has clearly contributed to the initial confusion surrounding them and their ultimate demise. Were they designed to make our nation's criminal courts more efficient prosecutors, or were they created to help ensure a more just and humane criminal justice process? Could both objectives be pursued at the same time or were they mutually contradictory? The Law Enforcement Assistance Administration, itself, never adequately clarified its mission. During my two years as a Visiting Fellow at LEAA's National Institute for Law Enforcement and Criminal Justice in Washington, I was a participant observer as the agency struggled to define its goals during 1976–78. By the end of this two-year stay, I was convinced that they were no closer to a resolution of the basic issues than upon my arrival 24 months earlier. How could they spearhead a national effort toward improving the administration of justice when they were unable to agree upon what they wanted this system to accomplish? Their legacy in 1982 is a continued debate over the proper ends of the reform movement, but the sad conclusion seems to be that even if a resolution does occur, it will be too late. The means that were once available have evaporated, and are unlikely to return in the near future.

One final point about reform attempts: even if everyone was in agreement as to the desired ends, and a drastic increase in the level of funding occurred, the chances for meaningful improvement of the criminal justice system would still be quite slim. This pessimistic view is based on the observed flow of cases which force the courts into a perpetual crisis-management posture, moving from one trouble spot to the next. If only one could call a recess for six months or a year to obtain the cooperation of the criminal element to just hold off for a while until the authorities have time to clear the dockets, clean up the old mess, and start anew, we might have a chance of making the proper adjustments in the system. Unfortunately, such a whimsical notion as a "rest period" cannot be achieved, and the reforms and alterations are now attempted under impossible conditions which hardly permit the old machinery to creak along at its current pace, let alone allow for some meaningful tinkering and restructuring. Continuing the metaphor, the machinery is often too hot to touch, and one can only step back in awe and anticipation as it chugs and wheezes along a path that could lead to its eventual self-destruction.

PERSONAL CONCLUSIONS—TROUBLING AND INTENTIONAL

Institutional Parochialism

One of the greatest obstacles to improving the quality of justice dispensed by our urban criminal courts is the persistent attempts by the courts to insulate themselves from public scrutiny. This desire to follow an insular life, has created within the courts an aura of parochialism which severely inhibits its ability to deal openly with the public which it must serve. The urban criminal courts were previously described as a small isolated village, suspicious of outsiders and extremely protective of its inner workings. This description is consistent with the unwillingness of the courts to reach out and educate the public as to the realities of its operations and resulting problems.

It is true many urban felony courts have been harshly (and in many instances unfairly), criticized by politicians and the media. The retreat away from the heat and discomfort of such public exposure is a natural reaction. Nevertheless, the criminal courts have a serious responsibility to educate the public about the constitutional rights of the defendant, and the professional obligations of all officers of the court. The courts have been frequently depicted as being more concerned with the rights of the defendants than the safety of society. Their extensive use of plea bargaining is perceived as setting free dangerous criminals, even after they have admitted their guilt. The judges are offered as scapegoats for the rising crime rates. Criminals are often thought by the public to be brazenly unafraid of being apprehended and convicted. The courts are viewed as either incapable, or unwilling, to impose the type of severe sentences which might deter future criminal acts.

As this book, and most contemporary research in this field has shown, most of the negative perceptions of the court are unwarranted and inaccurate. It would appear important for the criminal courts to attempt to correct these erroneous conclusions by actively educating the public about their job and their limited accomplishments. Instead, the courts have backed into the shell of their encapsulated world. Increasingly, the general public and interested researchers are turned away from the courthouse. The court officers become more and more protective of the judge, and each other. Access to judges and the courtroom workgroup is prevented to preserve their mutual interests. All have been "burned" by past exposure to the outside world, and the reassurance of the secure, and trusted, inner sanctum is a welcome retreat.

Today, however, seems the wrong time for the court to back away from its educative responsibilities to reduce the public's ignorance. If the public is not made aware of the court's constitutional obligations, then current public attitudes will only become more intense. The elected public officials who do have the potential to enact legislation to improve the situation, will then be faced by an increasingly disturbed public, pressuring them into uninformed and emotional actions which will only serve to further intensify the plight of the urban criminal courts.

Low Quality Indigent Defense

With serious budgetary cuts affecting the quality of services offered by urban criminal justice programs, it is interesting to see where those reductions are being made. Those agencies hardest hit by the fiscal crisis are obviously at the bottom of the court's list of priorities. The court-related functions which have consistently had their budgets reduced by state and local authorities have been the agencies responsible for providing legal defense for indigents. This would include the public defender program, or an assigned counsel system with attorneys receiving an hourly wage on a per case basis.

Chapter Three has documented the widespread nature of this problem, as nearly one-third of the states in this country have been unable to pay defense attorneys to represent indigents accused of crimes. The Supreme Court of the United States has also contributed to the problem in its denial of *certiorari* in the case of *Wolff* v. *Ruddy* (617 SW 2nd. 64 [1981] Missouri) which permitted the State of Missouri to force attorneys to accept indigent criminal cases without fee, or face state disciplinary action.

The obvious message to the legal community, and the public at large, is that indigent defendants are not very important! Additionally, lawyers sense that the court is willing to tolerate a minimum level of effort, realizing that most defense attorneys cannot afford to put out the extra effort to hire an investigator, locate unwilling witnesses, or work in the law library on weekends. The loser in all of these fiscal cuts is the indigent defendant, who is faced with being represented by an attorney who lacks the motivation, resources, assistance, and compensation to provide a viable defense. Those courts and public agencies who have made these reductions in defense services are taking a clearly discernible step toward eroding the very foundations of the nation's Sixth Amendment guarantee of right to competent counsel. Even if such reductions were initiated at the state level, the local criminal courts would not acquiesce. To remain silent at this time is to endorse a policy which is robbing the poor of their constitutional protections, and ultimately weakens the system of justice for all citizens.

Individual Malfeasance

Judges and other members of the criminal court workgroup are similar to all other public officials in terms of their being occasionally motivated by factors other than the public good. Power, fame, and wealth are three of the major temptations which may alter the course of judicial behavior away from its loftier goals. Chapter Six noted how the strains and hardships of his position have sometimes driven a judge into unprofessional behavior. Usually, the deviations caused by these three temptations occur in a more subtle and imperceptible fashion. Judges have the same economic pressures as all upper-middle-class individuals, striving to pay their children's college educations, while also maintaining sizable monthly mortgage, car, and other expenses. Because many judges were wealthier as private practitioners prior to joining the bench, they frequently enjoyed a luxurious lifestyle, or incurred debts which are very difficult to pay off on their present judicial salaries. Judges also must co-exist with colleagues whose egos and sensitivities are continually clashing with each other.

Rather than cause radical shifts in judicial temperament and behavior, those judges who seem overly concerned with the pursuit of the three goals mentioned above may still be able to perform their professional tasks, but at a lesser degree of competence of which they are capable. Usually, only their colleagues on the bench and the courthouse regulars are aware of their diminished efforts. Sometimes, however, a judge becomes overwhelmed in his quest for one of the seductive goals. When this occurs, the judge's behavior may reach proportions that the public cannot ignore. A recent incident in New York involving a power struggle among the Chief Justice of the State Court System, the Administrative Judge for the Supreme Court of Manhattan, and the New York County (also Manhattan) District Attorney, illustrates one of the unique incidents where a judge is viewed publicly in a grasp for power.

The problem began in the Supreme Court of New York County, whose criminal division had been short of judges for several years. As a partial solution, Administrative Judge Milonas, with the advice of knowledgeable public officials, would promote the most competent Municipal Court Judges to Acting Supreme Court Judges. The increase in prestige and salary troubled those Municipal Court judges who were not promoted, and they complained to Chief Judge Cooke. Cooke appeared more than willing to flex his bureaucratic muscles over Judge Milonas, and to eliminate the squabbling among Municipal Court judges. The Chief Judge, therefore, agreed to rotate *all* Municipal Court judges up to the higher court for a set tour of duty. At this point, District Attorney Morgenthau, who was satisfied with the existing system, and was pleased with the performances of the current group of Acting Justices who were selected by Milonas on a merit basis, took legal action to prevent Chief Judge Cooke from initiating his rotational scheme. Judge Cooke's colleagues on the Appellate Court eventually heard the case, and agreed with Morganthau that the Chief Judge had exceeded his authority by failing to consult with his colleagues on the Appellate bench. It proved to be a rather short-lived victory for Morgenthau and Milonas, however, because the unabashed Judge Cooke returned to his colleagues to ask them for approval of his rotational plan, which they now sheepishly approved, and the Municipal Court rotation plan soon went into effect.

Chief Judge Cooke appeared intent on convincing Administrative Judge Milonas that he was clearly in charge of all aspects of the state system. It did not matter that nearly all informed members of the city's criminal justice community agreed that the merit selection procedures were working smoothly, and the new proposed system would be an obvious step backward in terms of the consistency and quality of felony court judges in New York County. The public, and those unfortunate defendants caught in the web of New York's Supreme Court were the losers in this unnecessary and deleterious clash of egos.

Institutional Malfeasance

Similar to the forces swaying individual actors away from the lofty goals of justice and fairness, the institutions may also move off target in search of other, less noble ends. Criminal justice institutions are no different from any other bureaucratic organization when it believes its power is being usurped, its territory is being invaded, or ultimately its very survival being threatened. Institutions, like individuals, can also move irrationally out of control in an insatiable grasp for increased power and prestige.

One of the clearest examples from my research experiences which illustrates disturbing institutional behavior occurred during my study of bail reform in the early 1970s. An eastern city was attempting to develop a workable bail reform program, but was having a difficult time raising the necessary funding. Only $60,000 could be raised for the local criminal court to administer and staff this agency, but at least it could be tightly controlled by the judges and their friends in the city's dominant political party. At this time, a group of private citizens, led by a black woman active in the city's church life, was able to obtain funding from the federal government for $250,000! Unfortunately, one of the conditions of the federal aid was that the local court had to agree to allow this woman's civic group to control the bail reform program. Rather than relinquish control over the staffing and supervision of the bail agency, the city rejected the $250,000 federal grant and decided to stick to their meager program whose sole virtue was that it would not have to share its control with any outside organizations. Again, it was the defendants of the city who would be denied a viable bail reform agency and who would ultimately suffer as a result of this institutional narrow-mindedness.

REFORMS

Although this examination of the urban felony courts has been primarily a descriptive and analytical discourse, it seems necessary to offer at least a select few reforms which I believe might contribute to developing the criminal courts into a more efficient and humane institution. These reforms are presented with the understanding that the preponderance of the most serious problems facing the courts are the result of forces outside of the control of the justice system. The complex social, economic, and psychological forces which contribute to our steadily increasing crime rate are factors which must be addressed by concerned citizens and their elected public officials. The courts can help to enlighten the public and their political representatives, and it has been frustrating to note that generally the criminal justice officials have opted to neglect this opportunity. Nevertheless, there are problems which exist within the province of the criminal courts' capabilities to solve, or at least ameliorate, and it is these areas of reform which will now be addressed.

Caseload Reduction

The major problem area which I believe the criminal courts must address, and which is also at the root of so many related problems, is its overwhelming caseload. Fortunately, it is a problem area in which the criminal court can have some impact.

I believe the best way to reduce the court's caseload is to remove victimless crimes from its jurisdiction. Victimless crimes are criminal acts in which the victim is a willing participant. Government has decided that the victim's choice of activity should be prohibited because of its immoral nature. In other words, the government is carrying on its *parens patriae* function to stop what it considers behavior that is especially damaging to the individual, and likely to be harmful to the moral fiber of the entire society. Victimless crimes include gambling, prostitution, alcoholism, and drug addiction as its major categories of prohibited offenses.

It is not necessary to enter into a discussion of whether these personal activities should be entirely outside the control of public agencies, but rather to simply state that the *wrong* agency is presently charged with responsibility. Victimless crimes can be much more competently and humanely treated by alternative social and medical facilities. It has been estimated in several reputable research studies that elimination of victimless crimes from the criminal court dockets could reduce caseloads by approximately 40 percent.[8] If one then also turns over family disputes to crisis intervention units as well as family arbitration panels, another 10 percent of the caseload would also be removed. Thus, these caseload reforms could have the potential to cut the court's business in *half*.

The present treatment of alcoholics is an excellent example of how the inclusion of victimless crimes within our criminal justice system is a wasteful and inhumane process, draining off the precious resources of the courts. It seems time for American society to recognize alcoholism as a medical problem. Therefore, it should be treated by medical and social agencies, and not the criminal courts. The same argument can be made for drug addiction which has already been declared by the Supreme Court of the United States in *California* v. *Robinson* (370 U.S. 660 1962) to be an illness, which if treated simply as a criminal act by the courts would violate the Eighth Amendment's prohibition against cruel and unusual punishments. Since so many drug addicts are arrested for selling drugs, rather than mere addiction, the impact of this reform would not be as far-reaching as the proposal to eliminate alcoholism, but for whomever the reform extricates from the hellish nightmare of criminal prosecution while undergoing withdrawal, it would offer a wonderfully humane alternative. Proof of addiction to both drugs and alcohol would necessitate required medical certification and a compulsory period of medical and rehabilitative detention, but at least the loss of freedom would be associated with a rational goal.

Many states have begun to move toward the legalization of gambling by establishing state lotteries and permitting off-track betting. Although these actions are usually motivated by economic necessity, they still have the very positive side-effect of removing a sizable number of cases from the criminal court docket. If all gambling were brought under state control, the revenue production would be greatly increased, but from the court's perspective, even more significantly, a very large number of cases would be removed from the court's caseload. The legalization of prostitution would also benefit state treasuries, but the control of social diseases associated with sexual intercourse would benefit both the client and the prostitute. The European experience in legalization of prostitution should provide a positive model for the United States to follow.

A final group of cases which crowd the dockets are the family disputes which could be better handled either through a community arbitration panel or a social service agency trained in crisis intervention. Presently, a neighborhood arbitration board sponsored by the Vera Institute of Justice is operating successfully in Brooklyn, NY. Its ability to divert cases out of the criminal justice system while constructing workable solutions to the family problems, has been applauded by judges, prosecutors, and community leaders. It is a model which can easily be replicated in other cities, and seemingly guarantee positive results.

The impact of a nearly 50 percent reduction in caseload as a result of adopting recommended reforms cannot be overestimated. It will allow the criminal courts to turn their attention (and limited resources), toward the real criminal element which is threatening the quality of life in most urban communities. It also permits a more rational and humane treatment of alcoholics and drug addicts, who should be treated as medical and social problems, rather than criminals.

Caseflow Management

Beyond reducing the caseload, the nation's urban felony courts are also in drastic need of more efficient management. The chaotic scenes depicted in earlier chapters illustrate the futile and frantic efforts to try to coordinate the punctual appearance of all requisite actors and paperwork in the proper courtroom at the proper time. Some strides can be taken to ameliorate, at least partially, the current chaos by utilization of better management techniques. The problem has long been recognized. In 1973, the Peterson Advisory Commission on Standards and Goals recommended in Section 9.4 of their report on caseflow management that:

> a central source of information concerning all participants in each case—including defense counsel and the prosecuting attorney assigned to the case—should be maintained. This should be used to identify as early as possible conflicts in the scheduling of the participants to minimize the need for later continuances because of schedule conflicts.[9]

If the courts are truly committed to a system of caseload management envisioned in the Peterson Commission report, and desires to eliminate the senseless confusion presently transpiring, they must realize that there are inevitable financial and bureaucratic costs. An example of one reform which I believe has the potential for providing substantial benefits at modest cost is the creation of a team of "caseflow managers." Each manager would be assigned a manageable number of cases and would be personally responsible for having the required personnel and paperwork in place at the appointed hour. His or her job would begin with the initial court appearance signaling a decision by the prosecutor to charge the defendant. These "caseflow managers" would be acting as ombudsmen for the *judge* at each stage of the proceeding, ensuring that when a specific case was called, it would be ready. No longer would multiple postponements and continuances dominate each day's proceedings. These pretrial case managers could be retrained or borrowed from the clerks of the trial division, who often experience free periods. A visit to the criminal courthouse corridors in the afternoon, on floors allocated to trials, reveals the underutilization of these facilities and assigned personnel.

Judicial Selection

The desire to uncover ways to select better individuals to the criminal bench has fostered a perpetual debate among judicial reformers. My experience has convinced me that the more we can de-politicize the selection process, the better chance we will have of selecting high quality judges. I would also recommend adoption of the European model of developing a professional judiciary as a separate branch of the legal profession. Employing the European model, training programs could be developed which would provide special education for a select group of qualified lawyers in the theoretical and practical aspects of judging. It would also be possible to move this group of specialists through a professional hierarchy in which they could progress up from law clerk to local magistrate, then on to the appelate bench, depending upon their levels of competence. This suggestion may sound startling, but American justice has too long remained ethnocentric, failing to realize that we are in the very small minority of civilized nations using a system of amateur judges.

Re-allocation of Resources

If the criminal courts cannot expect to receive increased financial aid to provide for additional resources, then it is imperative that they utilize the resources which they do possess in as intelligent a manner as possible. This, unfortunately, does not seem to be the case. While complaints of mismanagement and inefficiency are directed toward nearly every segment of the criminal justice process, the juvenile courts and adult misdemeanor courts appear to be hampered the most by a blatant misuse of personnel, resulting in drastic under-staffing. The felony trial division, on the other hand, seems to be the only branch of the system which has a surplus of resources.

Emphasis upon the felony courts can be easily justified because of the serious nature of their cases. Due to intensified media attention devoted to more serious crimes, the public is most aware of felony courts and seems to expect the justice system to devote a disproportionate amount of its resources in this direction. If, however, one is truly concerned with protecting society and improving the operations of our criminal court system, we need to realize that we might have a slight chance of reaching the youthful offender, or first-time criminal, when he initiates his antisocial behavior. If we wait until he makes his appearance in the felony court, it may already be too late. The 16- or 17-year-old felon will inevitably possess a previous criminal record which indicates an escalating pattern of criminal behavior. Typical patterns show the defendant as a 12-year-old shoplifter, a 13-year-old trespasser and truant, a 14-year-old burglar, a 16-year-old assaulter, and now a 17-year-old armed robber. Our court resources are only geared toward the armed robber when our best chance to turn this individual around was at the time of his shoplifting or petty larceny arrest.

The clearest indication of this unbalanced and irrational allocation of resources is in the probation department. This critical agency is charged with supervising defendants whom the judge has decided should not go to prison, but need to have their conduct monitored for a period of years. If, during this time, the probationer commits a new crime, or violates one of the more serious conditions imposed by the sentencing judge, he can be sent to prison for the time remaining on his probationary sentence. Probation is a concept that sounds good in theory, but seems to break down in practice. The breakdown occurs under the sheer weight of the caseload of each probation officer. Instead of having 20 or 30 defendants whom he could competently supervise, and possibly guide back to a law-abiding position in society, the adult probation officer is saddled with impossible caseloads of 80 or more defendants.

The statistics in the juvenile and misdemeanor courts are even more shocking as they climb to two and three times the number found in the felony courts. Thus, in those courts (juvenile and misdemeanor), where the probation officer may have a fighting chance to do some good and direct a first offender away from a life of crime, we inundate him with an impossible number of clients. His massive workload short-circuits the efforts of even the most highly motivated probation officers. They will inevitably suffer a "burn out" from the work conditions and resign following less than one year of service. In a study I conducted of Pennsylvania juvenile probation officers, the average job experience for the entire statewide workforce was 16 months.[10] This indicates that the system is not helping defendants who might be salvaged, and is creating a force of inexperienced and frustrated probation officers, at the same time.

Court administrators and responsible judges are probably the most heavily criticized for shifting resources from the headline-grabbing and fear-inducing crimes of the felony courts to the less threatening misdemeanor and juvenile institutions. However, it appears that the crime problems are so serious that enlightened judges and administrators as well as politicians, must courageously force changes in defiance of public opinion. These public officials must begin to assume a posture of leadership and aggressively advocate those reforms which are necessary, despite their unpopularity with the masses. The shifting of court resources to favor the juvenile and misdemeanor courts is clearly one of those issues.

Miscellaneous Reforms

The opportunity to suggest reforms in the criminal justice system can easily get out of hand and lead to excessive pontifications. Since the major thrust of this book has been in the descriptive and analytical area, I will conclude this short section with two brief recommendations that I believe could be easily implemented and extremely beneficial. First, on a very pragmatic level, it seems silly to continue to rely upon court stenographers, rather than electronic taping (recording) of court proceedings. Errors and inability to indicate tone and temperament of the remarks are just two of the persuasive reasons to scrap the stenographic system. The second reform is more important on the human scale, and relates to the bail system and its blatant, yet ignored, system of economic discrimination. It is now time to realize that a defendant's financial condition should not be the basis for obtaining pretrial freedom. If the defendant is shown to be a poor risk for reappearance, or can be shown to be a risk to specific witnesses or the community in general (due to his pattern of previous antisocial conduct), he should be preventively detained. If he does not present these risks (as nearly 90 percent of the defendants do not), he should be released on his own recognizance. The defendant's financial condition should have no effect upon the critical issue of pretrial freedom. If the defendant released on his own recognizance fails to appear, or violates a condition of his release, he could then be brought in and detained until his trial, charged with the additional crime of forfeiture of appearance.

After spending the past 12 years observing, describing, and analyzing the urban court system, I now conclude this volume which offers personal reactions and impressions, and cannot help but wonder if the conclusions drawn are unique or shared. Do I possess an unusual filtering and storage system which has inaccurately recorded my recollections of the past decade? I imagine every writer or researcher has had bouts of doubtfulness from time to time. One way to reduce the anguish caused by such periodic attacks of self-doubt is to seek out some trusted colleague, or respected author who has worked on similar topics and undergone similar experiences, and then compare reactions, hopefully to discover parallel conclusions. Although I do not know Howard Senzel personally, his experiences within the New York City criminal courts as a participant observer (he served as an administrative assistant for the District Attorney's office), were so close to mine that I found his book, *Cases*, a reminiscent account of my own experiences. His eloquent chronicle of the pathetic melodrama played out in the Arraignment Court at 100 Centre Street offered an insightful collection of musings. I would like to conclude my own book with the following quote from his volume which summarizes so well my own deepest feelings concerning the urban criminal courts:

> The narratives of popular culture bombard the collective conscience with accounts of perfect courts that hear cases of good triumphant and evil banished. In AT-1 (New York City's Arraignment Court), justice

and its perfect administration is the pursuit, but the fundamentals of social organization in the Western tradition appear to have slipped away. Anything can happen . . . Or as those who know it best (the defendants themselves) say, "You got those constitutional rights overhere, but when you'in trouble, you'in trouble."[11]

NOTES

1. To Die or Not to Die, *Newsweek* October 17, 1983, p. 44.
2. Stuart J. Miller, Simon Dinitz, and John P. Conrad. *Careers of the Violent*. Lexington, Mass.: Lexington Books, 1982.
3. For an excellent critical overview of this issue, see Robert Martinson. What Works?—Questions and Answers About Prison Reform, *Public Interest* 35 (Spring, 1974), p. 22.
4. Crime and Punishment in New York, Report prepared for Gov. Hugh Carey by the Executive Advisory Committee on Sentencing, Albany, March 1979.
5. Plea bargaining was noted in the Wickersham Commission report filed with President Hoover in 1931 as well as New York's Seabury Commission and Roscoe Pound's study of the Cleveland Criminal Justice System, all written around the time of the Wickersham report.
6. Marc Franklin, Robert Chanin, and Irving Mark. Accidents, Money and the Law: A Study of the Economics of Personal Injury Litigation, *Columbia Law Review* 61 (1961), pp. 1–39.
7. These figures are found in the Vera Institute of Justice's 1977 monograph—Felony Arrests: Their Prosecution and Disposition in New York City, and the 1973 NILE & CJ Summary Research Report—Prosecution of Adult Felony Defendants in Los Angeles County.
8. Edwin M. Schur. *Crimes Without Victims*. Englewood Cliffs, N.J.: Prentice-Hall Inc., 1965; and Norval Morris and Gordon Hawkins. *The Honest Politicians Guide to Crime Control*. Chicago, University of Chicago Press, 1970.
9. The National Advisory Commission on Criminal Justice Standards and Goals. *Courts*. (Washington, D.C.: Government Printing Office, 1973).
10. Joseph Szakos and Paul Wice. Juvenile Probation Officers: Their Professional Paradox, *Pennsylvania Association of Probation, Parole, and Correction* 34 (March, 1977), pp. 21–30.
11. Howard Senzel. *Cases*. New York, Viking, 1982, 3.

BIBLIOGRAPHY

Abuse of Attorneys by Judges, *Cleveland-Marshall Law Review* 14 (January 1965), 79.

Activist Judge, *Georgia Law Review* 7 (Winter, 1973), 202.

Albert Alschuler. Courtroom Misconduct by Prosecutors and Trial Judges, *Texas Law Review* 50 (April, 1972), 629.

Albert Alschuler. The Trial Judge's Role in Plea Bargaining, *Columbia Law Review* 76 (November, 1976), 1059.

American Bar Association. *The Function of the Trial Judge.* Chicago, 1972.

Charles Ashman. *The Finest Judges Money Can Buy.* Los Angeles, Nash Publishing, 1973.

J.L. Barkai. Lower Criminal Courts—The Perils of Procedure, *Journal of Criminal Law* 69 (Fall, 1978), 270.

Stephen Bing *et al* The Quality of Justice in the Lower Criminal Courts of Metropolitan Boston, Boston, 1970 (mineographed).

Abraham Blumberg. *Criminal Justice.* New York, Quadrangle, 1967.

E. Bear. Judges as Middlemen, *Justice System Journal* 2 (Spring, 1977), 210.

C. Bohmer. Judicial Attitudes Toward Rape Victims, *Judicature* 57 (February, 1974), 303.

Joseph Borkin. *The Corrupt Judge.* New York, C.H. Potter, 1962.

Bernard Botein. *Trial Judge.* New York, Simon and Schuster, 1952.

Andrew Bruce. *The American Judge.* New York, Macmillan, 1924.

L.I. Canner. Trial Judge and His Facial Expressions, *American Criminal Law Quarterly* 6 (Summer, 1968), 175.

Robert Carp. Sink or Swim—Socialization of Federal District Judge, *Journal of Public Law.* 21 (1972) 359.

Robert Crater and Leslie Wilkins. Some Factors in Sentencing Police, *Journal of Criminal Law* 58 (December, 1967), 503.

D.W. Craig. To Police the Judges, *Journal of Criminal Law* 57 (September, 1966), 305.

Stella Crater. *The Empty Robe.* Garden City, Doubleday, 1961.

Criminal Law Attorney's Dilemma—What Should the Lawyer Do When His Client Intends to Testify, *Journal of Criminal Law* 61 (March 1970), 1.

Criminal Law Judge Remarks to Defense Attorney, *Missouri Law Review* 39 (Spring, 1974), 252.

George Crockett. Black Judges, *Wayne Law Review* 19 (November, 1972) 61.

Disqualification of a Judge for Bias—In Re Murchison, *California Law Review* 44 (May, 1956), 425.

Disqualification of a Judge for Prejudice, *Oregon Law Review* 48 (June, 1969), 311.

Norman Dorsen and Leon Friedman. *Disorder in the Court.* New York, Pantheon, 1973.

Ronald Dworkin. Hard Cases, *Harvard Law Review* 88 (April, 1975), 1057.

James Eisenstein and Herbert Jacob. *Felony Justice.* Boston, Little Brown, 1977.

Marvin Frankel. Adversary Judge, *Texas Law Journal* 54 (March, 1976), 465.

Marvin Frankel. *Criminal Sentences.* New York, Hill and Wang, 1972.

E.C. Freisen. Judicial Seminar for Judicial Education, *Judicature* 46 (July, 1962), 22.

Lois Forer. Judicial Responsibility and Moral Values, *Hastings Law Journal,* 29 (July, 1978), 1641.

J.A. Gazell. Principal Facets of Judicial Management, *Criminology* 9 (August, 1971), 131.

Alvin Gershenson. *The Bench Is Warned.* Columbus, Book Company of America, 1964.

Herman Goldstein. Trial Judges and the Police, *Crime and Delinquency* 14 (1968), 14.

Edward Green. *Judicial Attitudes in Sentencing.* New York, Macmillan, 1971.

Mark Greenberg. Blake's Vortex of Criminality, *Villa Law Review* 22 (April, 1984), 304.

F. Greenberg. Task of Judging the Judges, *Judicature* 59 (May, 1976) 458.

D. Guttman. Program for Judicial Education, *Trial* 9 (May, 1971), 49.

John Hagan. Extra Legal Attributes and Criminal Sentencing, *Law and Society* 8 (Spring, 1974), 357.

Paul Hoffman. *Courthouse.* New York, Hawthorn Books, 1979.

D. Hogarth. *Sentencing as a Human Process.* Toronto, University of Toronto Press, 1971.

D.W. Jackson. Salient Interactions—State Trial Judges and the Legal Profession, *Justice System Journal* 1 (1976), 24.

Donald Jackson. *Judges.* New York, Atheneum, 1974.

Howard James. *Crisis in the Courts.* New York, McKay, 1967.

Judgment Intuitive—Function of the Hunch, *Alabama Lawyer.* 25 (1964), 83.

Judges Nonverbal Behavior in Jury Trials, *Virginia Law Review* 61 (October, 1975), 1266.

Judicial Intervention in Trials, *Washington Law Quarterly* (Fall, 1973), 843.

H.F. Keefe. Advocacy and the Criminal Trial Judge, *Trial* 13 (July, 1977), 43.

M.L. Kelley. Objectivity and Habeas Corpus, *University of Michigan Law Journal* 10 (Fall, 1976), 44.

J.E. Kennedy. Judge–Jury–Counsel Relations, *Kentucky Law Journal* 54 (Winter, 1965), 243.

B.D. Kenyon. Judicial Immunity, *New Hampshire Bar Journal* 19 (December, 1977), 93.

Carol Kilgore. *Judicial Tyranny.* New York, Nelson, 1977.

S.F. Lancaster. Disruption in the Courtroom, *Military Law Review* 75 (1977) 35.

William Landis. Legality and Reality—Some Evidence on Criminal Evidence, *Journal of Legal Studies* 3 (June, 1974), 1287.

Martin Levin. *Urban Politics and the Criminal Courts.* Chicago, University of Chicago Press, 1977.

Limits of Judicial Intervention in Criminal Trials, *Georgia Law Review* 11 (Winter, 1977), 371.

Henry Lummus. *The Trial Judge.* New York, Foundation Press, 1937.

Donald McIntyre. A Study of Judicial Dominance of the Charging Decision, *Journal of Criminal Law* 59 (December, 1968), 463.

D.G. McNeil. Judicial Bias and Prejudice, *San Francisco Brief Case* 8 (May, 1958), 14.

H.R. Medina. Trial Judge's Notes—A Study in Judicial Administration, *Cornell Law Quarterly* 49 (Fall, 1963), 1.

B.S. Meyer. Trial Judge's Guide to News Reporting, *Journal of Criminal Law* 60 (September, 1969), 287.

Maureen Mileski. Courtroom Encounters, *Law and Society* 5 (1971), 1.

Frederic Miller. Discipline of Judges, *Michigan Law Review* 50 (1952), 1.

Frank Milton. *The English Magistracy.* Oxford, Oxford University Press, 1967.

P. Mirfield. When Is a Judge Not a Judge, *Public Law* (Spring, 1978) 42.

Lawrence Mohr. Organization, Decisions, and Courts, *Law and Society* 10 (1976), 1.

Stuart Nagel. Comparing Elected and Appointed Judicial Systems, *Sage Professional Papers,* 1973.

Peter Nardulli. *The Courtroom Elite.* Cambridge, Mass., Ballinger, 1978.

Dorothy Nelson. *Judicial Administration and the Administration of Justice.* St. Paul, West Publishing, 1974.

David Neubauer. *America's Courts and the Criminal Justice System.* North Scituate, Mass., Duxbury, 1979.

J. Pope. Judge–Jury Relationship, *Southwestern Law Journal* 18 (March, 1964), 46.

Power of a Trial Judge to Call a Witness, *South Carolina Law Review* 21 (1969), 224.

Prejudicial Remarks in Louisiana Criminal Cases, *Louisiana Law Review* 16 (June, 1956), 780.

Preliminary Report of the Minority Judiciary, *Howard Law Journal* 18 (1975), 495.

Proceedings of the National Judicial Conference on Standards for the Administration of Criminal Justice, *Federal Rules Decisions* 57 F.R.D. 229 (1972).

William Rehnquist. Sense and Nonsense About Judicial Ethics, *Record* 28 (November, 1973), 694.

Simon Rifkind. Are We Asking Too Much of Our Courts? *FRD* 70 (June, 1976), 96.

G.D. Robin. Judicial Resistance to Sentencing Accountability, *Crime and Delinquency* 21 (July, 1975), 201.

Maurice Rosenberg. Judicial Discretion in the Trial Court, *Syracuse Law Review* 22 (1971), 636.

Henry Rothblatt. Prejudicial Conduct of the Trial Judge in Criminal Cases, *Criminal Law Bulletin* 2 (September, 1966), 3.

A. Samuels. Acquittal of the Guilty, *Dalhousie Law Journal* 3 (May, 1976), 243.

Austin Sarat. Judging in Trial Courts, *Journal of Politics* 39 (1977).

Search for Truth, *University of Pennsylvania Law Review* 123 (May, 1975), 1060.

Charles Sheldon. Searching for Judges in Oregon, *Judicature* 61 (March, 1978), 376.

Bernard Shientag. *The Personality of the Judge.* New York, New York Association of the Bar of New York, 1944.

Charles Silberman. *Criminal Justice, Criminal Violence.* New York, Random House, 1979.

James Simon. *The Judge.* New York, McKay, 1976.

Herman Schwartz. Judges as Tyrants, *Criminal Law Bulletin* 7 (March, 1971), 129.

Symposium—Nonjudicial Activities of Judges, *Chicago Bar Record* 51 (November, 1969), 92.

A. Tate. Judge as a Person, *Louisiana Law Review* 19 (February, 1959), 438.

Taylor v. Hayes, *Kentucky Law Journal* 63 (1974), 495.

Nina Totenberg. Will Judges Be Chosen Rationally, *Judicature* 60 (August, 1976), 92.

Toward a Disciplined Approach to Judicial Discipline, *Northwestern University Law Review* 73 (October, 1978), 503.

Twentieth Century Fund. *Fair and Certain Punishment.* New York, McGraw-Hill, 1976.

Arthur Vanderbilt. *Judges and Jurors.* Boston, Boston University Press, 1956.

M. Volcansk–Clark. Why Lawyers Become Judges, *Judicature* 62 (October, 1978), 166.

J.C. Wallace. Judicial Administration in a System of Independents, *Brigham Young Law Review* (1978), 39.

Glenn Winters. *Handbook for Judges.* Jacksonville, H. & W.B. Drew Co.

Bob Woodward and Scott Armstrong. *The Brethren.* New York, Simon and Schuster, 1979.

Bruce Wright. Black Judges in America—A Statistical Profile, *Judicature* 57 (1973), 18.

L.R. Yankwich. Art of Being a Judge, *University of Pennsylvania Law Review* 105 (1957), 374.

INDEX

195

San Francisco, Calif. 38; criminal courthouse 44–5
Schmidhauser, John 116
Schwartz, Herman 127
sentencing 145–50; absence of reliable information 146; alternative forms of treatment 146; appellate review 149–50; disparities 30, 147; factors considered 148; judicial discretion 41; particularistic approach 147; public dissatisfaction 145; restrictions on judicial discretion 147; trend toward longer sentences 148
sentencing councils 149
Senzel, Howard 184
Shientag, Howard 98
Simon, James 1
Sixth Amendment 78, 82
Skolnick, Jerome 12
Smigel, Erwin 10, 11
socializing agents colleagues 106; self-education 107
Spangenberg, Robert 87
Spector, Arlen 31, 58
Suffet, Fred 58
Suwak, Peter 6

Teiterbaum, William 60–1
Terkel, Studs 11
territorial imperative 178
Thomas, Wayne 4
Tigar, Michael 54
The Trial Judge 125

United States judicial socialization process 104
United States Attorney General 54
United States Congress 8, 36; District of Columbia Committee (House) 37
United States Department of Health and Human Services 8

United States Department of Justice 2, 9; criminal justice program development 173; LEAA 5, 29, 173; LEAA Visiting Fellow Program 2, 174
United States Federal District Court socialization process 106
United States Supreme Court 26
United States v. *DeCoster* 54, 82
United States v. *Havens* 81
United States v. *Mendenhall* 81
University of Illinois 5
urban fiscal crisis 172

venality 158
victimless crimes 180
victims 68; background 170
videotaping 121, 125, 184
Vietnam War 20
Vines, Kenneth 116
Virginia Law Review 120
voir dire 132

Wall Street Lawyers 10
Warren, Earl 142
Washington, D.C. 36–7, 144; Commission on Judicial Disabilities and Tenure 160; courtroom design 120; felony court judges 2; judicial record keeping 152; level of adversariness 32; mixed public defender system 63
Watergate 77
Weber, Max 41
West Virginia 85
Wheeler, Russ 106
White, Thomas 111
white collar crimes 59
Wice, Paul 58
Wolff, Donald 71
Wolff v. *Ruddy* 71, 85–6, 91, 176

Ziller, Robert 105